P9-DGR-209

Sexism and Language

Alleen Pace Nilsen
Haig Bosmajian
H. Lee Gershuny
Julia P. Stanley

Sexism and Language

Alleen Pace Nilsen
Haig Bosmajian
H. Lee Gershuny
Julia P. Stanley

Endorsed by the NCTE Committee on the Role and Image of Women in the Council and the Profession and the NCTE Committee on Public Doublespeak.

National Council of Teachers of English
1111 Kenyon Road, Urbana, Illinois 61801

NCTE EDITORIAL BOARD: Evelyn Copeland, Charles Cooper, Bernice Cullinan, Donald Stewart, Frank Zidonis, Robert F. Hogan, *ex officio*, Paul O'Dea, *ex officio*

Staff Editor: Diane Allen. Book Design: Tom Kovacs
NCTE Stock Number: 43733

Copyright © 1977 by the National Council of Teachers of English. All rights reserved. Printed in the United States of America.

Library of Congress Cataloging in Publication Data
Main entry under title:

Sexism and language.

   Bibliography: p.
   1. Sex discrimination against women—United States—Addresses, essays, lectures.   2.   English Language—Social aspects—United States—Addresses, essays, lectures.
3.   Sex role—Addresses, essays, lectures.   4.   Stereotypes (Psychology)—Addresses, essays, lectures.
I. Nilsen, Alleen Pace.   II.   National Council of Teachers of English.
HQ1426.S4   301.41'2   76-58260
ISBN 0-8141-4373-3

Acknowledgments

Grateful acknowledgment is made to the following authors and publishers for permission to quote from their works in this volume: Stanzas from "The Man-Moth" reprinted with the permission of Farrar, Straus & Giroux, Inc., from *The Complete Poems*, "The Man-Moth," by Elizabeth Bishop, copyright © 1969 by Elizabeth Bishop. / Two poems and a portion of a third by E. E. Cummings: "O sweet spontaneous," copyright, 1923, 1951, by E. E. Cummings. Reprinted from his volume, *Complete Poems 1913-1962*, by permission of Harcourt Brace Jovanovich, Inc. "she being Brand," copyright, 1926, by Horace Liveright; copyright, 1954, by E. E. Cummings. Reprinted from *Complete Poems 1913-1962* by E. E. Cummings by permission of Harcourt Brace Jovanovich, Inc. Lines from "my father moved through dooms of love" by E. E. Cummings, reprinted from *Complete Poems 1913-1962*, by permission of Harcourt Brace Jovanovich, Inc. / "On a Squirrel Crossing the Road in Autumn, in New England," from *Collected Poems 1930-1976* by Richard Eberhart. Copyright © 1960, 1976 by Richard Eberhart. Reprinted by permission of Oxford University Press, Inc., and Chatto & Windus. / Stanzas from "Another September" from *Poems & Translations* by Thomas Kinsella, included by permission of the poet, the Dolmen Press, Ltd., Dublin, and Atheneum Publishers; copyright 1953, 1954, © 1957, © 1958, © 1960, © 1961 by Thomas Kinsella. / "I Am A" reprinted from *Diving into the Wreck, Poems, 1971-1972* by Adrienne Rich. By permission of W. W. Norton & Company, Inc. Copyright © 1973 by W. W. Norton & Company, Inc. / "Myth," from *Breaking Open*, by Muriel Rukeyser, reprinted by permission of Monica McCall, ICM. Copyright © 1973 by Muriel Rukeyser.

174922

Contents

BRIDWELL LIBRARY
SOUTHERN METHODIST UNIVERSITY
DALLAS, TEXAS 75275

Introduction

"If you can bravely smile
when loved ones doubt you, ... "

"If you can trust yourself
when all men doubt you, ... "

Which lines were written for females? Which are now intended
for males? You guessed it. The first are from a poem entitled "If for
Girls" by J. P. McEvoy, while the second are from Rudyard
Kipling's "If" now retitled "If for Boys" by a well known but herein
nameless greeting card company. And how did we know how to
assign the lines to the appropriate sex? On the basis of female/male
stereotypes operating in our culture. Males have been assigned
certain characteristics such as strength, aggressiveness and power,
while females are assigned passivity and powerlessness.

This book is about these female and male stereotypes as they are
codified in language, more specifically in American English. The
various selections in this volume make strikingly clear just how
widespread in our language is the image of " ... the female ... as
the invisible other," as H. Lee Gershuny puts it, or the female as the
negative pole, since males occupy both the positive and neutral poles
(Simone de Beauvoir, *The Second Sex*).

As the NCTE Women's Committee has been, since its creation in
1971, deeply and directly concerned with both the role and image of
women, we felt it appropriate, if not imperative, to bring to English
teachers' attention an analysis of the image of females in the
language we speak, read, write and teach. And since such linguistic
treatment of both males and females clearly involves a distortion of

viii

actual behavior, it is also appropriate to be joined in the venture by the NCTE Committee on Public Doublespeak.

As with racism, so with sexism; we all lose when another is diminished and belittled. We all have much to gain from "fair and equal treatment under the language." Thus it is our hope that this volume will serve to clarify the dimensions of sexism in language and to help its readers deal with the distortions of human behavior—both male and female—encrusting our language.

Johanna S. DeStefano, Chair

From the NCTE Committee on Public Doublespeak

Some two years ago, I first sensed a need for a book which would expand teachers' awareness of sexist language. What little I personally had been able to discover about this topic—mainly from articles in journals and magazines, since few books even touched on it—confirmed my belief that sexist language is having a serious impact on the ways that all people think about themselves and others, and thus on the ways we act toward one another. But I did not know the breadth and depth of that impact, nor did I have a very clear idea of how to counter it in my dealings with others, both within and without the classroom.

Since sexist language can quite clearly be termed a form of semantic distortion, I invited the members of the NCTE Committee on Public Doublespeak to work with the NCTE Committee on the Role and Image of Women in the Council and the Profession in compiling a volume which might address the need for more information on the nature and scope of sexist language. *Sexism and Language* is the product of that collaboration.

While this book is not, and does not purport to be, the final scholarly treatment on the subject of sexist language, it provides a great deal of useful information on how and why sexist language is employed in our society. Having read the book, I feel that I am better prepared to identify and eliminate sexist language from my own discourse and to recognize and respond to the sexist language which I encounter from others. I hope that you will enjoy and benefit from reading the pages which follow. I did.

Dan Dieterich, Chair

Linguistic Sexism as a Social Issue

Alleen Pace Nilsen

The feminist movement probably had its beginnings when Eve sat down and confided in her oldest daughter that she had unfairly received the blame for the expulsion from the Garden of Eden. But rather than quibbling about such a long ago date, this history will begin with 1970, when the general public was beginning to notice the waves emanating from such books as Simone de Beauvoir's *The Second Sex* and Betty Friedan's *The Feminine Mystique*.

Several years after these books came out, people began to look specifically at language in relation to sexism. But in a way, language was a part of the modern American feminist movement from the very beginning. The title of Chapter One in Friedan's book is "The Problem That Has No Name." Her book provided the name and within a few years *feminine mystique* was a household phrase along with such other terms as *Ms.*, *sexism*, *consciousness raising*, *sexual politics*, *women's liberation*, *feminist*, *libber*, *chauvinist*, *MCP (male chauvinist pig)*, and more recently, *linguistic sexism*.

The latter term is the subject of this book. This chapter opens with a chronological sampling of related material from the print and broadcast media. Though incomplete, it creates a background of events and attitudes for the discussions that follow and shows the continuing interplay between academia and the mass media. The result of this interplay has been not only a public awareness of sexism in English, but also an increased interest in the study of language from many different viewpoints, i.e., the sociologist's, the psychologist's, the anthropologist's, the linguist's, the writer's, and the historian's.

1

Toward a New Awareness: A Chronology

Spring 1970. Benjamin Bradlee, executive editor of the *Washington Post*, sent a memo to his staff on the subject of the meaningful equality and dignity of women. He advised writers to avoid such terms as *divorcée, grandmother,* and *blonde* as synonymous for woman and to drop sexist adjectives such as *vivacious, pert, dimpled,* and *cute.*

August 7, 1970. In a two-page *Life* magazine article illustrated with seven posed photos, Ann Bayer used a fictionalized and somewhat apologetic style to write about one of her friends named Hyperia, who was "so conscious of the sexism rampant in our society that she finds it in the most outlandish places", i.e., the language. Hyperia didn't like "devious paternalistic devices" which men use in calling women *cookies, gumdrops, sugar, honey,* or *cheesecake.* Hyperia went on to complain, "Look how close their insults are to their compliments. If you're not a *bombshell,* what are you? A *battle-ax.* If we're not *chicks,* we're *dogs* or *cows* or—ugh—*bats.* And when we're not *fauna,* we're *flora; clinging vines, shrinking violets, wallflowers.*" Another thing Hyperia didn't like was that men not only see women as things, but they see things as women—mostly horrible things such as *hurricanes, black widow spiders,* and torture instruments like *the iron maiden* (p. 62A-63. Italics added).

October 16, 1970. *Life* magazine devoted parts of eleven pages to Clare Boothe Luce and her role as an "outspoken defender of Women's Lib before it became fashionable." It published her version of Henrik Ibsen's *A Doll's House,* "A classic play about a woman who wanted to be equal to a man, rewritten in the light of recent events." Nora's reply to Thaw's suggestion that all she needs is to get pregnant remains one of the best lines in the play:

> *Nora:* Thaw, I *am* pregnant. But not in a feminine way. In the way only men are supposed to get pregnant.
> *Thaw:* Men, pregnant?
> *Nora* (nodding): With ideas. Pregnancies there (taps his head) are masculine. And a very superior form of labor. Pregnancies here (taps her tummy) are feminine—a very inferior form of labor. That's an example of male linguistic chauvinism." (pp. 54-67).

November 12, 1970. A UPI news feature declared, "The status isn't quo any more and girl talk certainly is not what it used to be." Based on an interview with David Replogle, president of the G. & C. Merriam Company, the article was entitled "New Vocabulary for Liberationists." It gave the following words or phrases as either being new or having new meanings in informal oral language: *Rap Group, Sensitized, Sexist, Male Chauvinism, Sexegration, Feminist, Girlcott, Herstory, Femme Lib,* and *Sexual Politics.* Whether or not such items find their way into standard dictionaries depends on how long the lib movement maintains its drive and whether new groups will continue it, Replogle said. He added, "Today's groups produce a more exciting word climate than, say, in the days of the suffragettes, because of instant communications."

December 1970. At an American Dialect Society meeting held in conjunction with the Modern Language Association, Mary Ritchie Key presented a paper, "Linguistic Behavior of Male and Female," to only a sprinkling of an audience. But no sooner had she returned to the Irvine campus of the University of California, where she teaches linguistics, than requests began to come in for copies of her paper. It was accepted for publication in *Linguistics,* but it did not appear until almost two years later, and between the time of the ADS meeting and its publication, she mailed out hundreds of copies to people who sent requests because of a rapidly developing interest in a new field of dialectology (*Linguistics 88* [Aug. 15, 1972]: 15-31).

Winter 1970-71. Virginia Slims cigarettes launched an advertising campaign to go with their motto: "You've come a long way, baby." The bold face headline read, "Presenting some new clichés Virginia Slims would like to drop into the English language," followed by a listing:

> A woman's best friend is her dog.
> A woman's home is her castle.
> The bigger the woman, the harder she falls.
> No woman is an island.
> We hold these truths to be self evident: That all women are created
>   equal.
> Woman shall not live by bread alone.
> One small step for woman, one giant step for womankind.

The ad concluded with, "After all, when you have your own slim cigarette, you really deserve your own clichés, too."

Spring 1971. "Neuter title for women" was the subheading given an Associated Press story by Lynn Sherr which appeared in the *Ann Arbor News*. The main title was *"Miss, Mrs. or Ms.?"*

"United only in their conviction that a woman's marital status is nobody's business a growing number of American women have quietly begun to erase the terms *Miss* and *Mrs.* from natural usage. They are replacing both with the neuter title, *Ms.* (pronounced Miz)." The writer went on to say that the women are acting under no directives from any of the major women's organizations, and that the new, neutral monosyllable is slowly creeping into the vocabulary of the business world. "About one-fourth the mail I get is addressed *Ms.,*" reported a married Boston attorney. Carol Burris, an active member of NOW, said that the only time she has trouble with titles is with newspaper reporters. "They insist on *Miss* or *Mrs.* because their papers won't print *Ms.,*" she said. "There's a ridiculous social value on a wedding ring. Your stock goes up because you've caught a man."

(Editor's Note: It is interesting that the terms *neutral* and *neuter* are used interchangeably in the article and the headline. *Ms.* may be a neutral term in that it does not show whether a woman is married, but in the grammatical sense of the word it certainly isn't neuter, in that it is a carrier of feminine gender.)

January 25, 1971. "Women's Lib Adds Church to List" was the headline on a UPI story by Patricia McCormack. She cited the ending of a prayer at a Women's Strike for Equality, where those assembled didn't say "amen," but rather "Ah-women." They did this to make the point that discrimination against women by organized religion is one of the wrongs they want to right.

January 1971. The Association for Children with Retarded Mental Development, Inc., in New York received more publicity than usual for its annual awards banquet. For the first time in twenty years it was giving its "Man of the Year" Award to a woman, Mrs. Stephen (Ricki) Goodyear. Pre-dinner publicity said the association was taking a poll on what to call the award.

August 13, 1971. The cover story and the beginning of a three-part feature in *Life* magazine were devoted to the women's movement. The article began with a two-page spread superimposed on an artist's rendition of a dictionary definition of *woman*. In tones of grey the definition was given as "Typifies the negative or passive principle in nature; symbolizes adultery, body politic, chaos, church, city, disorder, disunity, earth, fecundity, idol-atry, kingdom, moon, mother- (fade out) (fade in) -trayal, lies, quarrels; if preg- (fade out).

Headlines on following pages read, "wiles and witchery of *'foul effeminacy'*" and "prehistory to *Playboy*, a woman's place is in the body." The latter page showed an ad for a GT Tiger "Hi-Performance muffler," which was being caressed by a bikini-clad girl. The caption in the ad read, "Are you big enough to ride the Wild One?" The *Life* cutline explained, "Sales appeal is woman's great contribution to the modern economy. Her body serves as bait to lure buyers to other, less erotic consumer products." In a companion article entitled "Where did it all go wrong?" Richard Gilman stated, "the nature of most languages tells us more about the hierarchical structure of male-female relationships than all the physical horror stories that could be compiled. ... But that our language employs the words "man" and "mankind" as terms for the whole human race demonstrates that male dominance, the *idea* of masculine superiority, is perennial, institutional and rooted at the deepest levels of our historical experience.

"Whether or not it is unjust is another question. And whether or not, if it is unjust, it can be overthrown is still another" (pp. 40-55).

1971. "Contempt for women can be discerned in a purer form in the use of female terms as abuse for pusillanimous or incompetent men. 'You girl,' say the Londoners, in a tone of deepest contempt," wrote Germaine Greer in a chapter entitled "Abuse" in *The Female Eunuch*. She went on to say, "Feminists might like to consider the gratuitous attribution of the female sex to unspecified objects and creatures, as in this headline which identified the Loch Ness Monster as female, 'If Nessy's there *she's* got a sonar shock coming.' Perhaps we can deduce the latent motive for the attribution from the sadism of the context" (p. 264).

Greer also showed that such a term as *witch* is negative only when applied to a woman. Other words with negative connotations developed into exclusively feminine words. For example *hag* used to "apply to a direct satanical manifestation of peculiar grisliness,"

a *termagant* in early Christian plays was a disagreeable Moham-
medan deity, *harlot* became exclusively feminine in the seventeenth
century, *bawd* in the eighteenth century, and *hoyden* in the
nineteenth (pp. 259-60).

October 29, 1971. "An Airline's Ad Encounters Some Turbulence" was the heading *Life* magazine gave to its story about the
protests and the picketing that National Airlines' "I'm Cheryl. Fly
Me" advertising campaign was eliciting. Feminists protested that
the sexual connotations of this slogan were offensive and in-
appropriate. However their protests did not keep the advertisers
for Continental Airlines from coming up with an even sexier ad,
"We really move our tail for you!" (pp. 75-76).

Winter 1971. "The vocabulary of the radical women's movement generally employs terms and usages common to the rhetoric
of New Left protest movements which developed in the 1960's,"
wrote Margaret B. McDowell in an article titled "The New
Rhetoric of Woman Power" *Midwest Quarterly*, (12:2, pp. 187-98).
As evidence, she cited (1) the large percentage of nouns ending in
tion or *sion*, e.g., *confrontation, liberation, exploitation, agitation,
intimidation, subjugation, discrimination, oppression,* and *coer-
cion;* (2) nouns ending in *-ism* such as *Americanism, capitalism,
commercialism, tokenism, sexism, racism,* and *chauvinism;* (3)
nouns or verbs used as adjectives, as in *encounter* groups, *life* styles,
movement women, and *subsistence* wages; obscene or vulgar nouns
used as adjectives, as when housework is called *scut*-work or *shit*-
work; (4) a preference for heavy, academic adjectives; for example,
women's problems are not *personal* or *individual* but *societal* and
political because they result from *hierarchical* ordering of people,
or they are *socio-political* or *economico-social;* (5) a preference for
extreme words over moderate ones; for example, women who
experienced *discontent, frustration,* and *boredom* in Betty Friedan's
1963 rhetoric now are *unfulfilled.*

April 16, 1972. "One Small Step for Genkind," a five-page
article by Casey Miller and Kate Swift, appeared in the *New York
Times Magazine* (pp. 36ff). Although their concluding suggestion
that *gen* be coined as an alternate for generic *man* has shown little
likelihood of catching on, their article was nevertheless significant,
because for the first time key issues, treated in a serious manner,

were brought before a large general audience. Among the points made and illustrated with good examples were the following:

The English language assumes people in general to be male unless otherwise identified; women are subspecies.

Male and *female* are not sexist words, but *masculine* and *feminine* are, since it is practically impossible to use them without involving cultural stereotypes.

Many English words contain a subtle disparagement of females and approbation of males.

Long-standing conventions of the news media keep women from being taken seriously in the news.

The Judeo-Christian tradition springs from a male patriarchy and the language, including pronouns, is used to construct a reality that simply mirrors society's assumptions.

April 1972. The American Heritage School Dictionary was published with the claim that it was "the first reference book to seriously consider the problem of sexism in school materials and to take considered steps to solve the problem." The publishers advertised that their editorial staff was divided equally between men and women, comparable male and female terms such as *waiter/waitress* and *gentleman/gentlewoman* were given the same definition, an effort was made to find and give explanations of words that derived from names of real women such as *bloomers* from Amelia Jenks Bloomer and *curie* (a unit of radioactivity) from Marie Curie, an effort was made to write nonstereotyped illustrative sentences, and new words such as *Ms., sexism,* and *male chauvinist* were defined.

June 24, 1972. George Malko writing in *Saturday Review* on "How to Get Interviewed by Dick Cavett—in Several Tricky Lessons," quoted one of the pre-interviewers, who was giving her criteria for selecting guests. "First of all," she said, "if we find a pretty girl who also talks, she can almost invariably get on a talk show. We're forever looking for pretty girls who can talk because the *Cavett Show,* if you've noticed, very rarely has girls. There aren't very many girl talkers. There're occasional women talkers, like Margaret Mead, but there aren't many young, pretty girls who also can hold a conversation with Cavett. Johnny Carson can fool around with them, act sexy, look down their dresses, make a couple of sly remarks, roll his eyes, and get an interview out of that. Cavett

BRIDWELL LIBRARY
SOUTHERN METHODIST UNIVERSITY
DALLAS, TEXAS 75275

doesn't do that. He tries to find a girl he can have an intelligent conversation with" (pp. 5-7).

Summer 1972. "We should not set out to change the language at all. Instead, we may take people to task for what they say, not because the language itself is sexist, but because those people are continuing to think in sexist ways without being conscious of it, and they should be made aware of their attitudes," stated Dorothy Hage in an article in *Aphra* entitled "There's Glory for You" (3:3, pp. 2-14).

In talking about the definitions society gives to the words *feminine* and *masculine*, she said, "So strong are these definitions of male and female roles in society that when women strive to redefine the term 'feminine' to allow it to include strength, courage, vigor, etc., it is the women themselves who end up being redefined." She went on, "No matter how many women and girls are aggressive, strong, and independent, they will all be called unfeminine—and hence, for lack of a better term perhaps, masculine. . . . In the process of freeing ourselves and redefining our role in society, we must make sure that society does not redefine us. When our activities are called unwomanly let us insist on the fact that, by definition, nothing done by women is unwomanly."

August 1972. "The Liberated Lady Has a Dirty Mouth" was the catchy title of a one-column piece in *Psychology Today,* which told about Robin Lakoff's work at the University of California at Berkeley. Freedom of language is a barometer of the degree to which women are becoming emancipated, noted Lakoff. But she added that as emancipation moves forward, the linguistic change-over is a one-way street: women adopt more and more of men's cuss words but few men adopt words traditionally favored by women, such as *fine, chic,* and *divine* (p. 16).

August 1972. At the American Sociological Association Annual Meeting in New Orleans Joseph W. Schneider and Sally L. Hacker of Drake University presented a paper, "Sex Role Imagery and Use of the Generic 'Man' in Introductory Texts: A Case in the Sociology of Sociology." To study the effect on students of the word *man,* they had enlisted the help of college students from campuses other than their own in collecting photographs, cartoons, and other popular

FONDREN LIBRARY
SOUTHERN METHODIST UNIVERSITY
DALLAS, TEXAS 75275

culture illustrations appropriate for a proposed introductory text in sociology. Half of the students were given proposed chapter titles containing *man*; the other half were given alternate titles which relied on the word *people* to express the same concept. The students with the *man* titles brought in a significantly larger number of all-male or mostly male pictures than did the students with the *people* titles (*American Sociologist*, 8:8, pp. 12-18).

September 1972. "Guidelines for Improving the Image of Women in Textbooks" was published by Scott, Foresman and Company. This eight-page booklet was prepared by the Sexism in Textbooks Committee of Women at Scott, Foresman. Half of the booklet was devoted to recommendations for avoiding sexist language in three different categories: omission of women, demeaning of women, and sex-role stereotyping.

Fall 1972. The following riddle made the rounds on television talk shows and was published in several newspapers and magazines:

> Ann and her father are both seriously injured in a highway collision. Ann is taken by ambulance to one hospital; her father to another. When Ann is wheeled into the operating room, the shocked surgeon says,
> "I cannot operate on this girl. She's my daughter." Who is the surgeon?
> Answer: Ann's mother. And if you didn't get it, you haven't come a long way, baby.

Another witticism being quoted at this time was the question, "Are women really revolting?"

March 4, 1973. In a column that was either humor or ridicule, Russell Baker writing for the *New York Times* replaced *man* with *person* in all the words he could think of. He came up with such paragraphs as "When you begin to brood about Halderperson, the futility of personal labor and the Weatherpersons, warm up the phonograph, put on Benny Goodperson playing, "In Old Personhattan" or "Can't Help Lovin' That Person of Mine," sip a little glass of Personischewitz, and you'll lose that murderous impulse to rush into the streets shouting, "Yo ho ho and a bottle of rum, fifteen persons on a dead person's chest!" Although he probably offended many feminists, he did make the point that replacing *man* with *person* was not as simple a solution as it might at first appear.

Spring 1973. In the Wee Pals comic strip a baseball game was being organized. One boy said, "I'm gonna be the third baseman!" Another said, "I'll be the first baseman! What about you, Connie?" Connie answered with, "I'll be the second base person!"

October 1973. Dr. Spock's *Baby and Child Care* is about to be liberated from the tyranny of infantile male chauvinism, declared Patti Hagan of the *New York Times* News Service. She explained how Dr. Spock after 27 years, 201 printings, and 23,445,781 copies of his famous Baby Bible, revised his pronoun usage, which referred to the baby as *he, him,* or *his* roughly ten thousand times. In the new edition, Dr. Spock relies on the sexless *they, them, their,* except where the plural is exceptionally awkward. Then, as a balance to the old book, he uses *she, her,* or *hers.* In defense of his original book, Dr. Spock pointed out that even in 1946 before most people were thinking of such things, he prefaced *Baby and Child Care* with a word of apology to the parents "who have a girl and are frustrated by having the child called *him* all through this book. It's clumsy to say *him* or *her* every time, and I need *her* to refer to the mother."

1973. "Men tend to talk as though they were bigger, and women as though they were smaller," observed Jacqueline Sachs, Philip Lieberman, and Donna Erickson in a study entitled "Anatomical and Cultural Determinants of Male and Female Speech." They recorded samples of the speech of 14 boys and 12 girls between the ages of four and 14. The children were preadolescent, so that they had larynxes of the same size relative to weight and height, etc. Yet 83 adult judges listening to the recordings could "reliably and validly identify the sex of the children from their voices." Possible explanations explored by the researchers were that there may be differential use of anatomy, or perhaps hormonal control over certain aspects of the motor output; that the children could be learning culturally determined patterns that are viewed as appropriate for each sex; or that the judges may have drawn on other cues to identify the sex of the child speaker; e.g., it seems that "boys had a more forceful definite rhythm of speaking than girls."(Shuy and Fasold, 1973, pp. 74-84).

Fall 1973. "From a feminist point of view, dictionaries are museum pieces of an archaic culture. Yet they are a powerful reinforcing expression of men's prejudice against women, and if they cannot be rewritten at once, a general awareness of their sexism must weaken their authority," declared Ruth Todasco in the introduction to *An Intelligent Woman's Guide to Dirty Words, Volume One* (pp. ii-iii). The fifty-page booklet lists epithets and their dictionary definitions under six classes: Woman as Whore, Woman as Whorish, Woman as Body, Woman as Animal, Woman as *-ess*, Woman as *-ette*. *Playboy* gave the booklet a write-up, complete with a photograph of a small busted (at least by *Playboy* standards) nude absorbed in reading. The title was "Lib Service" and the concluding note was addressed to one of the compilers, Jessie Sheridan, who had pointed out that "almost every word in the English language that has to do with women has some degrading meaning." "Maybe so, Jessie," wrote the editor,"but did you know that *Webster's* definition of feminine is still *passive?*"

November 1973. A statement on page 18 of the Linguistic Society of America bulletin said the Women's Caucus rejoiced that "the offensive term *manpower* had been dropped from the title" of the committee on personnel resources. But on page 12 of the same bulletin was a headline reading "Interim Report on the Manpower Survey."

November 1973. Listed on the program for the National Council of Teachers of English convention in Philadelphia were more than two hundred chairmen, almost equally divided between male and female. Fewer than half a dozen people were listed as *chairwomen* or chairpersons; all were female. At the opening session, the featured speaker, Monroe Beardsley, congratulated the membership for their good sense in retaining the clear, efficient, and pleasant-sounding word *chairman* rather than changing to *chairperson.*

December 28-30, 1973. At the Linguistic Society of America meeting in San Diego, three of six papers in a session on Language

and Social Roles dealt with sexism, and a special session on the
subject was sponsored by the LSA Women's Caucus. In the newsletter preceding this convention, a program committee report
stated that since LSA had adopted the plan of selecting program
participants from abstracts identified by number rather than by
name, a significantly higher number of women were being included as program participants.

Trends toward more women participants and acceptance of
linguistic sexism as a serious topic for research could be seen
during the following years at national meetings of the Modern
Language Association, American Dialect Society, National Council
of Teachers of English, and Teachers of English to Speakers of
Other Languages.

December 1973. In the Modern Language Association newsletter, Deborah Rosenfelt and Florence Howe complained in a note
titled "Language and Sexism": "Attempts to change sexist usage
meet not merely with resistance, but with ridicule. It is odd that
such ridicule often comes from the very people who profess their
faith in the power of the word—linguists, literary critics, members
of the MLA."

January 1974. Peter Farb in his best-selling *Word Play: What
Happens When People Talk* included a "Linguistic Chauvinism"
chapter discussing several kinds of political chauvinism. "Closely
related to the unequal treatment of a minority language by a
majority language," he explained, "is the unequal treatment many
languages give to the two sexes. The Bible regards Eve as merely an
offshoot from Adam's rib—and English follows suit by the use of
many Adam's-rib words" (p. 141).

Later, he wrote," ... *Female* originally was a non-sexist Middle
English word, *femelle*, meaning "small woman," he said, but
popular speech changed it to *female* because of its apparent resem-
blance to the word *male*. On the other hand, *woman* originated as an
Adam's rib word, derived from the Old English *wife* plus *man* (p.
142). Farb went on to discuss whether the status of women would be
improved by changing the language. His conclusion: "The fact is
that language merely reflects social behavior and is not the cause of
it. The problem of woman's status in English-speaking communities will not be solved by dismantling the language—but by
changing the social structure. Even if it were in our power to

legislate changes in the platitudes of words, the attitudes would nevertheless remain" (p. 144).

Consistent with his attitude, Farb went on to entitle the following chapter "Man at the Mercy of Language," and a later chapter "Man the Talker."

January 28, 1974. Time magazine, which has frequently expressed the opinion that English is perfectly adequate as it is and that feminists are being foolish to ask for changes, apparently is not really convinced that masculine pronouns are generic. In the cover story, "A Telltale Tape Deepens Nixon's Dilemma," the editor wrote, "Until someone within the White House steps forward to admit that *his or her* (italics mine) fingers pushed those keys to wipe out the conversation, the cover-up cannot, indeed, be considered to have ended" (p. 13). In a departure from *Time* style, the writer used both pronouns, probably to make sure that readers thought of feminine as well as masculine fingers, since Rose Mary Woods was a prime suspect.

May 1974. "Dirty Words *Can* Harm You," said Barbara Lawrence writing in *Redbook*. She stated that the systematic derogation of women implicit in many obscenities involves origins and imagery with "undeniably painful, if not sadistic, implications, the object of which is almost always female." It is interesting, she noted, that the same people who are offended and shocked by racial or ethnic obscenities do not take any special note of obscenities which derogate women (p. 33).

June 1974. Editors of *Psychology Today* gave Chris Kramer's three-page article on folk linguistics the title, "Wishy-Washy Mommy Talk" (pp. 82-85). Kramer's argument was that *attitudes* toward sex differences in language use may be just as important as actual differences. We expect certain expressions to be uttered by one sex or the other, and this colors our perceptions. By asking people to identify speakers as male or female in cutlines from covered-up cartoons, she found that people had definite ideas about masculine and feminine speech. There was a high percentage of agreement as to whether a male or a female was speaking. But when Kramer presented individual males and individual females with identical pictures and asked them to describe the contents, she found that male and female speech did not differ as much as might have been expected. For example, men used as many adjectives as women.

July 1974. Among observations Robin Lakoff made in a *Ms.* magazine article, "You Are What You Say," was a comparison of the two terms *lady* and *woman.* Lakoff pointed out that *lady* once was used as a euphemism for *woman.* It was a polite and respected term because it was cognate with *gentleman.* But it has now been used so much in terms like *cleaning lady, saleslady,* and *lady of the evening,* etc., that it is no longer a term denoting special respect. For example: "The decision to use *lady* rather than *woman,* or vice-versa may considerably alter the sense of a sentence, as the following examples show:

> a. A woman (lady) I know is a dean at Berkeley.
> b. A woman (lady) I know makes amazing things out of shoelaces and old boxes.

The use of *lady* in (a) imparts a frivolous, or nonserious, tone to the sentence: the matter under discussion is not one of great moment. Similarly, in (b) using *lady* here would suggest that the speaker considered the 'amazing things' not to be serious art, but merely a hobby or an aberration."

If *woman* were used, the idea could be communicated that she was a serious sculptor. *Lady doctor* is condescending since we don't say *gentleman doctor* or *man doctor.* And when the *San Francisco Chronicle* referred to Madalyn Murray O'Hair as "the *lady atheist*" it was an intentional put-down (pp. 63-67).

October/November 1974. The newsletter of the New York State NOW chapter carried an announcement of "Woman's Place is in the World" T-shirts. The sizes offered were *Men's* Small, Medium or Large.

November 1974. A draft of proposed "Guidelines for Combating Sexism in Language" was distributed in the exhibit hall at the convention of the National Council of Teachers of English by the NCTE Committee on the Role and Image of Women in the Council and the Profession. The draft described sexism in language as (1) the assumption that a person's sex determines the appropriate speech for that person to either hear or use; (2) English usages which imply that things masculine are superior to things feminine, for example, a *man-sized* job as important whereas *woman's work* is trivial; (3) use of a masculine word such as *chairman* in a generic sense, a practice which causes females to be unintentionally excluded from the thought. Among "thought-provoking questions for English teachers" were the following:

> Do you personify bad practices in English teaching as always female, i.e., Miss Fidditch or Mrs. Grundy?
>
> In literary criticism, do you use the word *masculine* as a positive term meaning *strong*, and *feminine* as a negative term meaning *weak*?
>
> Do you support the *men of letters* stereotype by going along with publishers who hide the fact that an author is a woman by using either masculine-sounding pen names or initials?
>
> Do you teach your students to exclude women, at least mentally, from the business world by heading all letters either *Gentlemen* or *Dear Sirs*?

December 1974. "We will hire the most qualified person regardless of his sex," is one of the quotes Sol Saporta gave in a paper, "Language in a Sexist Society," before the Modern Language Association meeting in New York. "It seems that language is to sexism as symptom is to disease ... flu is presumably diagnosed on the basis of a set of symptoms of which fever is one." Saporta concluded: "The more institutionalized a particular phenomenon becomes, the less visible, and, presumably, the more resistant it is to change.... Given the data, then, one can ask, is language sexist or are people sexist or is society sexist? The probable answer, regrettably, is all three."

Spring 1975. In *Male/Female Language*, the first of several books treating sexism in language, author Mary Ritchie Key brought together examples, anecdotes, and formal research. In her concluding chapter, "An Androgynous Language," Key wrote, "An androgynous language will be complementary rather than divisive. It will find balance and harmony in its completeness. It will establish an equilibrium in its unity rather than invidious separation. It will combine the abstract with the concrete; feeling with logic; tenderness with strength; force with graciousness. It will be a balanced tension—supporting rather than opposing. It will be exuberant and vibrant, leaving out the weak and the brutal. It will not tolerate the simpering, helpless, bitchy sweetness of the *feminine* language. Nor will it tolerate the overwhelming smash of the opinionated and blustering *masculine* language. It will move away from the cruel distinctions that have wounded both male and female human beings" (p. 147).

April 6, 1975. "The woman's rights movement has won a dubious victory in Indiana," stated an editorial in the *Los Angeles Times*. "The grand dragon of the Ku Klux Klan there has let it be known that from now on his bullyboys want to be known as Klanspersons. Although manic terrorism is still in, male chauvinism is out. The prospect of a non-sexist KKK raises two burning questions, and we hope the answer to both is yes. Has membership fallen to such a low point that the nightriders must recruit a ladies' auxiliary or face extinction?

"Will the ladies decline and tell their Klansperson husbands to take off those silly hoods and robes and spend their nights doing something useful—like cleaning out the garage?"

Spring 1975. The U.S. Department of Labor brought out a 363-page book entitled *Job Title Revisions to Eliminate Sex- and Age-Referent Language from the Dictionary of Occupational Titles, Third Edition* (1965). Although the whole book was devoted to changing such terms as *craneman* to *crane operator, stewardess* to *flight attendant*, and ____*master* to ____*supervisor*, the cover clearly stated that the book comes from the U.S. Department of Labor and *Man*power Administration (italics added).

The list of job title changes included such gems as *odd-shoe girl*, now *odd-shoe examiner; knock-up man* (woodworking), now *knock-up assembler; sauce girl*, now *sauce canner*; and *blow-up boy* (glass manufacturing), now *blow-up worker*. A survey of terms in the 1965 *Dictionary* is less amusing. In a casual perusal, I found hundreds of *man* terms and dozens of *boy* and *girl* terms (mostly for menial jobs), but not a single *woman* term.

Spring 1975. Robin Lakoff's paper, "Language and Woman's Place," originally printed in *Language and Society,* came out in paperback from Harper & Row. Lakoff pursued the point that society has given women certain roles to fill, and the language that goes with these roles serves to perpetuate the system. Discussing "woman's language," Lakoff wrote, "So a girl is damned if she does, damned if she doesn't. If she refuses to talk like a lady, she is ridiculed and subjected to criticism as unfeminine; if she does learn, she is ridiculed as unable to think clearly, unable to take part in a serious discussion: in some sense, as less than fully human. These two choices which a woman has—to be less than a woman or less than a person—are highly painful" (p. 6).

May 1975. "How Serious Is Sex Bias in Language?" asked Muriel R. Schulz in *College Composition and Communication* (pp. 163-67). She asked whether we really respond to *man* as "male human being" in such words as *chairman, congressman,* and *workman* where the ending rhymes with *one* rather than *fan.* "Eventually, if the words systematically refer to women as well as men," she said, "the semantic tie with *man* may be broken, as has happened in such words as *daisy* (from *day's eye*), *holiday* (from *holy day*), and *alone* (from *all one*)." She pointed out problems inherent in trying to rid the language of the *man* suffix. For example, if men resist being called *chairperson* so that the word is used only for women, nothing has been gained. And as long as *he* remains the generic pronoun, we get ourselves into a bind by creating sentences like "Every chairperson will have ____ own office."

Among solutions available within the system, Schulz mentions using *they, them,* and *their* as androgynous pronouns, using *he or she* with moderation, pluralizing whenever possible, rewriting so that a pronoun is not necessary, and accepting *he* as a true generic.

May/June 1975. "Person the lifeboats!" commanded Boyd Wright, "The language is sinking!" Wright, associate editor at *Women's Wear Daily*, wrote in a half-page feature in the *Columbia Journalism Review*: "*Man*, as all dictionaries agree, can be as much a generic, sexless word as *horse* or *dog*. We have not yet resorted to *racemare* or *seeing-eye bitch*. Why, then, *chairwoman* or the even clumsier chair*person?*" He went on to ask if women consider themselves safe from "jaws" because everyone knows that sharks are, after all, only man-eaters? He gave several similarly amusing examples and then concluded with "The irony is that violating the language in this fashion undermines the cause of women's liberation, in whose name this battle is being waged. The result is not a more adequate recognition of women's equality, but a verbal ugliness that makes a valid cause seem unnecessarily dubious" (p. 32).

May/June 1975. The problem that is "tearing newsrooms apart" was discussed in the *Columbia Journalism Review* under the title "Kissing 'the girls' Goodbye: A Discussion of Guidelines for Journalists" (pp. 28-33). In 1974 a Stanford University student group called the Women's News Service developed eleven "Guidelines for Newswriting About Women." Because, as the CJR editor said, "any set of guidelines is bound to be controversial," a panel of journalism professors, editors, reporters, and news directors was brought together to discuss the guidelines. Included in the highlighted comments were these statements: "I'm not particularly anxious to use the tremendous power of the press to change language just because a number of people think it's socially useful," and "Who's described physically? Usually the women. And who are they described for? Usually the men."

June 1975. *The American Psychologist* published guidelines drawn up by a seven-member task force "To offset language bias and to present several alternatives for nonsexist writing."

"The purpose of these stylistic guidelines," the editors wrote, "is to overcome the impression presently embedded in the English language that (a) people in general are of the male gender and (b) certain social roles are automatically sex-linked. Another purpose is to insure that psychological writing does not degrade or circumscribe human beings" (p. 682).

June 24, 1975. At the International Women's Year meeting in Mexico City, the Committee on Language Revision passed a proposal calling on the media, educational institutions, and all individuals to effect change in language so that it will express the equality of the sexes.

July 1975. "Feminist Writers, Hanging Ourselves on a Party Line?" was the title of an article by Vivian Gornick in *Ms.* magazine (pp. 104-07). She cautioned against a situation in which feminists "use the word sisterhood like a club over the heads of all women whose thought and action follow the dictates of individual conscience rather than those of what has quickly become a closed system of response." In contrasting *live* responses to automatic responses, she used the term *consciousness raising* as an example. "After five years of regular exposure to the phrase in the pages of *Time* and *Newsweek* is there a woman in the country who would come to the experience with the freshness and emotional 'ignorance' required for original discovery?" She went on to write about "the potency of our ideas drowning in a welter of words that once held living meaning and have now become automatic slogans that begin to deprive us—rather than support us—in our struggle to change our lives.

"Today terms like *MCP* and *sexual object* are jargon and carry with them all the dangers of jargon. For jargon, after all, is shorthand; and the danger of shorthand is that it short-circuits thought..."

September 14, 1975. A Sunday feature in the *Los Angeles Times* was an article, "Still Fighting Prejudice: Women in the Law," by Pat B. Anderson.

Los Angeles Superior Court Judge Joan Dempsey Klein reported that most judges "still find women lawyers unusual. They have a 'stop and think' rather than a routine reaction to them. Some of the judiciary still refer to them as 'madame' instead of addressing them as 'counsel' the same as the man attorney."

A male public defender explained the difference in attitudes by saying, "We were raised by women and we don't want them soiled by the things that are part of criminal law—stabbings, murders and even dirty words."

One of the difficulties of fitting into the expected courtroom scene was mentioned by a female lawyer in a San Francisco firm, who said, "Your voice takes on a certain bitchy tone you can recognize when you try to make a legal point." She added that she thinks it is easier for younger women, who were not raised to be dependent on men, to be assertive without being aggressive.

October 1975. The new *Harper Dictionary of Contemporary Usage*, edited by William and Mary Morris, included several discussions on changes being made at least partially because of the feminist movement. One of the longest entries was "Sexism in Language," which discussed the issue of guidelines (pp. 549-53).

Fall 1975. "This book rides in on the first crest of what we expect to be an ocean of interest in the topic," said Barrie Thorne and Nancy Henley in the preface of *Language and Sex*, published by Newbury House. The book began with twelve papers, many previously published, on such topics as differences between male and female speech, relationships between prestige and speech forms, the difficulties of making a "non-sexist" dictionary, and cultural attitudes about males and females reflected in language use and metaphor. An annotated bibliography listed approximately 230 studies of vocabulary and syntax, phonology, conversational patterns, women's and men's languages, dialects, multilingual situations, language acquisition, verbal ability, and nonverbal aspects of communication.

Winter 1975-76. Articles in popular magazines reflected increased awareness of the issue of women's assertiveness through speech. They included "My Husband Wanted a Silent Partner" and "How Much Should a First Lady Say?" (*McCall's*, February 1976), plus "How Nursery Schools Teach Girls to Shut Up" (*Psychology Today*, December 1975).

February 1976. Henry Maloney was interviewed by David Sohn in the "Viewpoint" column of NCTE's *English Journal* (p. 9). Without mentioning *Miss Fidditch* or *Mrs. Grundy* and without using feminine pronouns, the two men managed to put across the old stereotype that women are responsible for bad English teaching practices:
Maloney: ... There was some notion that existed in the English teacher's mind as to just how you were supposed to speak, how you were supposed to write. I think a lot of this notion was a kind of elitist, "Vassar-trained," carefully speaking person who could write with elegance. The substance of the messages was lost in this scramble for great form.
Sohn: Did you ever run into any Vassar-trained teachers who could write with elegance?
Maloney: By their definition of elegance, I think so. Their sentences had nice balance, and they didn't use words such as *nice*. They were very conscious of their vocabulary.
Sohn: They wrote nicely, in other words.
Maloney: Yes. But I want to move on to something else. ...

June 1976. Winners of an in-house contest in which employees competed to find the best written examples of sexism in the English language were announced by Doubleday & Company. First place went to Amoy Allen and Elena Scotti, who both turned in an ad from the May 4 *New York Times*. Under the pre-Mother's Day caption, "Give your Mother the World," was an advertisement for the Harcourt Brace Jovanovich book by Irving Howe, *World of Our Fathers: The Journey of the East European Jews to America and the Life They Found and Made.* The book title was cited as an example of the patriarchal assumption of our Judeo-Christian culture that the world is made and inhabited by males only. Bill Strachan won a prize for noticing an ad for the First Women's Bank in the *New York Post* of February 27, 1976. The ad read in part, "And if you need a loan just ask one of our experts. He keeps Excedrin in his desk." Five days later the same ad ran in the *New York Times* with copy changed to read: "And if you need a loan just ask for one of our experts. (They keep Excedrin in their desks.)".

A Report on a Survey

If change occurs in any language, it is the users of that language who determine the direction of that change. In an attempt to predict possible changes in our language, the authors made a survey of people's attitudes on the issue of sexism and American English.

Approximately two hundred one-page questionnaires were sent out early in 1976. One hundred of these went to editors of books, magazines or newspapers. The editors queried were those whose names appeared near the middle of every fourth page of the 1973 edition of *Writer's Market.* A similar process was used to choose approximately twenty-five members from the directories of three professional organizations: the National Council of Teachers of English, Teachers of English to Speakers of Other Languages, and the Linguistic Society of America. In addition, the questionnaire was sent to twenty-five members of NCTE's Committee on the Role and Image of Women in the Council and in the Profession.

Over eighty of the questionnaires were returned by the deadline date. Many more trickled in over the following months, and some of the comments are included in this book, but numerical responses on late questionnaires were not counted. The people who received the questionnaires were asked to note their reactions to sentences illustrating certain generic usages and to give an indication of their views on language issues which have arisen within the last few years. They were also invited to add comments on any aspect of linguistic sexism which particularly interested them. From the quality of the comments received, it was obvious that most of the respondents—all of whom work professionally with the English

Statement	Number of Responses			
	A. Good change	B. Probable change	C. Impractical change	D. Impossible change
1. In newspapers, etc., listing women's names as *Mrs. Mary Sue Smith* rather than *Mrs. John D. Smith*, etc.	57	9	2	2
2. Replacement with *Ms.* of the terms *Miss* and *Mrs.*	41	23	10	6
3. The retention by married women of their maiden or birth names	36	23	10	6
4. The use of *person* in place of *man* as in *chairperson*, etc.	27	30	6	11
5. Ridding the language of derogatory sexist terms such as *sissy*, *bastard*, *cuckold* for men and *slut*, *bitch*, and *chick* for women	26	4	9	35
6. Development of dual pairs of words such as *policeman/policewoman*, *chairman/chairwoman*, etc.	29	24	13	13
7. Replacement with a neutral form such as *tey* of the masculine pronoun *he* when it is used in the generic sense	11	25	31	29
8. Replacement with a neutral form such as *gen* of the morpheme *man* when used in the generic sense as in *man*kind, *man*power, etc.	9	9	30	25

Fig. 1. Opinions on tactics for solving problems of linguistic sexism

language—had given thought to the matter of linguistic sexism long before they received the questionnaire.

Probably the most interesting aspect of the responses was the diversity of opinion and the firmness with which these opinions were stated. As expected, members of the Women's Committee were the most in favor of trying to change the language, while members of the Linguistic Society were the least in favor of such "tampering."

A substantial difference in attitude between male and female respondents was shown, for example, in the following two letters, which came back in the same envelope:

> We have made few, if any, changes and do not plan to do so. Perhaps this is because our readers . . . are over 95 percent male.
>> editor

> This is a note from _____'s secretary. His answers and the deletion of his name speak for themselves. I'm working on him.
>> Sincerely,
>> editorial secretary

A much bigger and more carefully controlled sample would have to be surveyed to find out whether the differences in male and female attitudes among my respondents were due entirely to the fact that women are more sensitive to sexist language than are men. Perhaps my sampling of females was weighted by questionnaires sent to members of the NCTE Women's Committee, who might have stronger feelings about the matter than do female language teachers and/or editors at large.

In the first part of the questionnaire there were eight statements relating to suggestions for solving problems of linguistic sexism that have appeared in recent articles and/or speeches. Respondents were asked to tell whether they thought each suggestion was:

A A good change which we should encourage
B A change that will probably come with time
C A fair idea but too impractical to work
D An impossible change

The suggestions and reactions are listed in Figure 1. Those ideas which were acceptable to the most respondents appear first.

Statement 5, about ridding the language of derogatory terms, elicited the greatest divergence of opinion, with only thirteen respondents holding middle-of-the-road positions. The rest were at the two extremes. Twenty-six people thought it was a good change which should be encouraged and thirty-five thought it was an impossible change. The latter group were much more vociferous in

Sentence	Number of Responses		
	A. Perfectly acceptable	B. Acceptable	C. Deviant
1. Suzy got her bachelor's degree in 1971.	64	9	3
2. In the 1960s Jacqueline Kennedy was a highly effective patron of the arts.	58	18	4
3. Nursing mothers experience a warm feeling of fellowship as attested by the clubs they belong to.	50	19	7
4. The agriculture department shipped in over a million male ladybugs.	33	27	14
5. I think Margaret Chase Smith was a true statesman.	30	30	16
6. My niece wants to be a fireman when she grows up.	27	51	7
7. Each of the students in the home ec. class brought his own ingredients.	22	35	19
8. My daughter was a ballboy for Billie Jean King.	11	32	32
9. My aunt got the Junior Chamber of Commerce Man-of-the-Year award.	6	27	51

Fig. 2. Reactions to sentences involving words with masculine-sounding affixes

expressing their opinions through comments, all of which appeared to come from males.

The second part of the questionnaire dealt with the problem of masculine-sounding affixes, which is indeed a troublesome area. Some—but not all—words with these affixes trigger some—but not all—speakers to think specifically of males, while other words that technically appear equally masculine do not. On the questionnaire, nine sentences were listed and respondents were asked to indicate whether the sentence was:

> A. "Perfectly acceptable—I would probably not even notice the use of a generic term."
> B. "Acceptable, although I might notice the apparent contradiction between sex and gender."
> C. "Deviant—I would be startled to hear this sentence."

Reactions are tabulated in Figure 2. Some respondents quarreled with the categories, saying, for example, that although they wouldn't be startled to hear a particular sentence, they might consider it awkward or poor composition. Others skipped sentences that didn't seem to fit into one of the categories; thus, the numbers of people responding for each sentence are not necessarily consistent throughout the study. The sentences were not ranked in the following order on the questionnaire, but here they are listed with the most "acceptable" sentences first and the most "deviant" last.

The sentence that provoked the most specific comment in the margin was #4, about the "male ladybugs." One person wrote "Silly!", another person wrote "laughable," and several made question marks. Apparently it is a surprise to find a feminine-sounding word that is in fact generic. The accompanying tables give an indication of current feelings about the relative acceptance of some usages and some ideas; they also illustrate the diversity of opinion that exists.

But I think the real value of the survey is in the freewheeling opinions people expressed, either on the back of the survey form or in separate letters. These proved more interesting and informative than any number of checkmarks. Some of these comments appear at beginnings of chapters in this book. Those included best express personal viewpoints, give new insights, or illustrate the diversity of opinion among professional people of good will. An effort has been made not to quote people out of context in ways that would misrepresent either attitudes or opinions. Respondents who preferred to remain anonymous are so listed.

We are strongly opposed to the introduction of superfluous new pronouns or neutral morphemes into the language; it doesn't need them. What it perhaps *does* need is the elimination of artificial "feminine" forms like "chairwoman" or "poetess," coupled with a new understanding . . . that "man" does in fact mean "human being," and that if members of the male sex have borrowed it to mean themselves, that is simply an historical arrogance which has become an innocuous linguistic tradition . . . .

. . . Derogatory sexist terms belong in the language as much as derogatory religious or racial terms do. We may abhor them, . . . but they are a part of the richness of the language. Anyway, I am extremely skeptical of the notion that any language can be "rid" of any sort of slang or derogatory terms. So far, at least, there's no way to apply a blue pencil to the spoken word . . . . in sum . . . we feel that critics or foes of linguistic sexism should be at least as concerned about language as they are about sexism.

Colman Andrews
editor

Rather than use *chairperson*, which is not in the dictionary, create a word like *official*. And if *spokesman* bothers someone, use *representative*. If *newsman* is bothersome, use *journalist*. . . . There are sufficient words in the English language to permit us to communicate properly.

Mike Weingart
editor

What are you suggesting for the salutation of business letters written to a company rather than an individual? Obviously the conventional *gentlemen* won't do. When I came to that problem, I recommended simply omitting the salutation, since very few companies are very *dear* anyway.

Elisabeth McPherson
teacher, writer

Sexism as Shown through the English Vocabulary

Alleen Pace Nilsen

Over the last hundred years, American anthropologists have travelled to the corners of the earth to study primitive cultures. They either became linguists themselves or they took linguists with them to help in learning and analyzing languages. Even if the culture was one that no longer existed, they were interested in learning its language because besides being tools of communication, the vocabulary and structure of a language tell much about the values held by its speakers.

However, the culture need not be primitive, nor do the people making observations need to be anthropologists and linguists. Anyone living in the United States who listens with a keen ear or reads with a perceptive eye can come up with startling new insights about the way American English reflects our values.

Animal Terms for People—Mirrors of the Double Standard

If we look at just one semantic area of English, that of animal terms in relation to people, we can uncover some interesting insights into how our culture views males and females. References to identical animals can have negative connotations when related to a female, but positive or neutral connotations when related to a male. For example, a *shrew* has come to mean "a scolding, nagging, evil-tempered woman," while *shrewd* means "keen-witted, clever, or sharp in practical affairs; astute... businessman, etc." (*Webster's New World Dictionary of the American Language*, 1964).

A *lucky dog* or a *gay dog* may be a very interesting fellow, but when a woman is a *dog*, she is unattractive, and when she's a *bitch* she's the personification of whatever is undesirable in the mind of the speaker. When a man is self-confident, he may be described as *cocksure* or even *cocky*, but in a woman this same self-confidence is likely to result in her being called a *cocky bitch*, which is not only a mixed metaphor, but also probably the most insulting animal metaphor we have. *Bitch* has taken on such negative connotations— children are taught it is a swear word—that in everyday American English, speakers are hesitant to call a female dog a *bitch*. Most of us feel that we would be insulting the dog. When we want to insult a man by comparing him to a dog, we call him a *son of a bitch*, which quite literally is an insult to his mother rather than to him.

If the female is called a *vixen* (a female fox), the dictionary says this means she is "an ill-tempered, shrewish, or malicious woman." The female seems both to attract and to hold on longer to animal metaphors with negative connotations. A *vampire* was originally a corpse that came alive to suck the blood of living persons. The word acquired the general meaning of an unscrupulous person such as a blackmailer and then, the specialized meaning of "a beautiful but unscrupulous woman who seduces men and leads them to their ruin." From this latter meaning we get the word *vamp*. The popularity of this term and of the name *vampire bat* may contribute to the idea that a female being is referred to in a phrase such as *the old bat*.

Other animal metaphors do not have definitely derogatory connotations for the female, but they do seem to indicate frivolity or unimportance, as in *social butterfly* and *flapper*. Look at the differences between the connotations of participating in a *hen party* and in a *bull session*. Male metaphors, even when they are negative in connotation, still relate to strength and conquest. Metaphors related to aggressive sex roles, for example, *buck, stag, wolf,* and *stud*, will undoubtedly remain attached to males. Perhaps one of the reasons that in the late sixties it was so shocking to hear policemen called *pigs* was that the connotations of *pig* are very different from the other animal metaphors we usually apply to males.

When I was living in Afghanistan, I was surprised at the cruelty and unfairness of a proverb that said, "When you see an old man, sit down and take a lesson; when you see an old woman, throw a stone." In looking at Afghan folk literature, I found that young girls were pictured as delightful and enticing, middle-aged women were sometimes interesting but more often just tolerable, while old women were always grotesque and villainous. Probably the reason for the negative connotation of old age in women is that women are valued for their bodies while men are valued for their accomplishments and their wisdom. Bodies deteriorate with age but wisdom and accomplishments grow greater.

When we returned home from Afghanistan, I was shocked to discover that we have remnants of this same attitude in America. We see it in our animal metaphors. If both the animal and the woman are young, the connotation is positive, but if the animal and the woman are old, the connotation is negative. Hugh Hefner might never have made it to the big time if he had called his girls *rabbits* instead of *bunnies*. He probably chose *bunny* because he wanted something close to, but not quite so obvious as *kitten* or *cat*—the all-time winners for connotating female sexuality. Also *bunny*, as in the skiers' *snow bunny*, already had some of the connotations Hefner wanted. Compare the connotations of *filly* to *old nag*; *bird* to *old crow* or *old bat*; and *lamb* to *crone* (apparently related to the early modern Dutch *kronje, old ewe* but now *withered old woman*).

Probably the most striking examples of the contrast between young and old women are animal metaphors relating to cats and chickens. A young girl is encouraged to be *kittenish*, but not *catty*. And though most of us wouldn't mind living next door to a *sex kitten*, we wouldn't want to live next door to a *cat house*. Parents might name their daughter *Kitty* but not *Puss* or *Pussy*, which used to be a fairly common nickname for girls. It has now developed such sexual connotations that it is used mostly for humor, as in the James Bond movie featuring Pussy Galore and her flying felines.

In the chicken metaphors, a young girl is a *chick*. When she gets old enough she marries and soon begins feeling *cooped up*. To relieve the boredom she goes to *hen parties* and *cackles* with her friends. Eventually she has her *brood*, begins to *henpeck* her husband, and finally turns into an *old biddy*.

How English Glorifies Maleness

Throughout the ages physical strength has been very important, and because men are physically stronger than women, they have been valued more. Only now in the machine age, when the difference in strength between males and females pales into insignificance in comparison to the strength of earth moving machinery, airplanes, and guns, males no longer have such an inherent advantage. Today a man of intellect is more valued than a physical laborer, and since women can compete intellectually with men, their value is on the rise. But language lags far behind cultural changes, so the language still reflects this emphasis on the importance of being male. For example, when we want to compliment a male, all we need to do is stress the fact that he is male by saying he is a *he-man*, or he is *manly*, or he is *virile*. Both *virile* and *virtuous* come from the Latin *vir*, meaning *man*.

The command or encouragement that males receive in sentences like "Be a man!" implies that *to be a man* is to be honorable, strong, righteous, and whatever else the speaker thinks desirable. But in contrast to this, a girl is never told to be a *woman*. And when she is told to be a *lady*, she is simply being encouraged to "act feminine," which means sitting with her knees together, walking gracefully, and talking softly.

The armed forces, particularly the Marines, use the positive masculine connotation as part of their recruitment psychology. They promote the idea that to join the Marines (or the Army, Navy, or Air Force) guarantees that you will become a man. But this brings up a problem, because much of the work that is necessary to keep a large organization running is what is traditionally thought of as *women's work*. Now, how can the Marines ask someone who has signed up for *a man-sized job* to do *women's work*? Since they can't, they euphemize and give the jobs titles that either are more prestigious or, at least, don't make people think of females. Waitresses are called *orderlies*, secretaries are called *clerk-typists*, nurses are called *medics*, assistants are called *adjutants*, and cleaning up an area is called *policing* the area. The same kind of word glorification is used in civilian life to bolster a man's ego when he is doing such tasks as cooking and sewing. For example, a *chef* has higher prestige than a *cook* and a *tailor* has higher prestige than a *seamstress*.

Little girls learn early in life that the boy's role is one to be envied and emulated. Child psychologists have pointed out that experimenting with the role of the opposite sex is much more acceptable for little girls than it is for little boys. For example, girls are free to dress in boys' clothes, but certainly not the other way around. Most parents are amused if they have a daughter who is a *tomboy*, but they are genuinely distressed if they have a son who is a *sissy*. The names we give to young children reflect this same attitude. It is all right for girls to have boys' names, but pity the boy who has a girl's name! Because parents keep giving boys' names to girls, the number of acceptable boys' names keeps shrinking. Currently popular names for girls include *Jo, Kelly, Teri, Chris, Pat, Shawn,*

Toni, and *Sam* (short for *Samantha*). *Evelyn, Carroll, Gayle, Hazel, Lynn, Beverley, Marion, Francis*, and *Shirley* once were acceptable names for males. But as they were given to females, they became less and less acceptable. Today, men who are stuck with them self-consciously go by their initials or by abbreviated forms such as *Haze, Shirl, Frank*, or *Ev*. And they seldom pass these names on to their sons.

Many common words have come into the language from people's names. These lexical items again show the importance of maleness compared to the triviality of the feminine activities being described. Words derived from the names of women include *Melba toast*, named for the Australian singer Dame Nellie Melba; *Sally Lunn cakes*, named after an eighteenth century woman who first made them; *pompadour*, a hair style named after Madame Pompadour; and the word *maudlin*, as in *maudlin sentiment*, from Mary Magdalene, who was often portrayed by artists as displaying exaggerated sorrow.

There are trivial items named after men—*teddy bear* after Theodore Roosevelt and *sideburns* after General Burnside—but most words that come from men's names relate to significant inventions or developments. These include *pasteurization* after Louis Pasteur, *sousaphone* after John Philip Sousa, *mason jar* after John L. Mason, *boysenberry* after Rudolph Boysen, *pullman car* after George M. Pullman, *braille* after Louis Braille, *franklin stove* after Benjamin Franklin, *diesel engine* after Rudolf Diesel, *ferris wheel* after George W.G. Ferris, and the verb *to lynch* after William Lynch, who was a vigilante captain in Virginia in 1780.

The latter is an example of a whole set of English words dealing with violence. These words have strongly negative connotations. From research using free association and semantic differentials, with university students as subjects, James Ney concluded that English reflects both an anti-male and an anti-female bias because these biases exist in the culture (*Etc.: A Review of General Semantics*, March 1976, pp. 67-76). The students consistently marked as masculine such words as *killer, murderer, robber, attacker, fighter, stabber, rapist, assassin, gang, hood, arsonist, criminal, hijacker, villain*, and *bully*, even though most of these words contain nothing to specify that they are masculine. An example of bias against males, Ney observed, is the absence in English of a pejorative term for women equivalent to *rapist*. Outcomes of his free association test indicated that if "English speakers want to call a man something bad, there seems to be a large vocabulary available to them but if they want to use a term which is good to describe a male, there is a small vocabulary available. The reverse is true for women."

Certainly we do not always think positively about males; witness such words as *jerk, creep, crumb, slob, fink,* and *jackass.* But much of what determines our positive and negative feelings relates to the roles people play. We have very negative feelings toward someone who is hurting us or threatening us or in some way making our lives miserable. To be able to do this, the person has to have power over us and this power usually belongs to males.

On the other hand, when someone helps us or makes our life more pleasant, we have positive feelings toward that person or that role. *Mother* is one of the positive female terms in English, and we see such extensions of it as *Mother Nature, Mother Earth, mother lode, mother superior,* etc. But even though a word like *mother* is positive it is still not a word of power. In the minds of English speakers being female and being powerless or passive are so closely related that we use the terms *feminine* and *lady* either to mean female or to describe a certain kind of quiet and unobtrusive behavior.

Words Labelling Women as Things

Because of our expectations of passivity, we like to compare females to items that people acquire for their pleasure. For example, in a recent commercial for the television show "Happy Days," one of the characters announced that in the coming season they were going to have not only "cars, motorcycles, and girls," but also a band. Another example of this kind of thinking is the comparison of females to food since food is something we all enjoy, even though it is extremely passive. We describe females as such delectable morsels as a *dish,* a *cookie,* a *tart, cheesecake, sugar and spice,* a *cute tomato, honey, a sharp cookie,* and *sweetie pie.* We say a particular girl has a *peaches and cream complexion* or "she looks good enough to eat." And parents give their daughters such names as *Candy* and *Cherry.*

Other pleasurable items that we compare females to are toys. Young girls are called *little dolls* or *China dolls,* while older girls— if they are attractive—are simply called *dolls.* We might say about a woman, "She's pretty as a picture," or "She's a fashion plate." And we might compare a girl to a plant by saying she is a *clinging vine*, a *shrinking violet*, or a *wallflower*. And we might name our daughters after plants such as *Rose, Lily, Ivy, Daisy, Iris*, and *Petunia*. Compare these names to boys' names such as *Martin* which means warlike, *Ernest* which means resolute fighter, *Nicholas* which means victory, *Val* which means strong or valiant, and *Leo* which means lion. We would be very hesitant to give a boy the name of something as passive as a flower although we might say about a man that he is a *late-bloomer*. This is making a comparison between a man and the most active thing a plant can do, which is to bloom. The only other familiar plant metaphor used for a man is the insulting *pansy*, implying that he is like a woman.

The Language of English Teaching

In the teaching profession, language usage also reflects the correlation of masculinity with positive qualities. For example pedagogical journals make references to hypothetical teaching situations. When a good teaching practice is described, the masculine pronoun is used. This is because somewhere out there good teaching is the general rule. Many people are doing it, so we follow the rule that says when the sex of the referent is both male and female or is unknown, the masculine pronoun is appropriate. But when a contrasting example of bad teaching is given, a different situation is described. It is a much more specific situation in which only one teacher would make this particular mistake. And since it is now a specific incident, the teacher is referred to with a feminine pronoun or with our infamous fictionalized name for a bad English teacher: *Miss Fidditch*. Or perhaps we use the names *Mrs. Grundy* or *Miss Thistlebottom* to represent prudishness.

This repeated usage may contribute to the way we view men and women teachers; the professor is nearly always thought of as *he* and the teacher as *she*. As English teachers we extend masculine and feminine differences to literary criticism. We describe poetry by contrasting *masculine rhyme* (of stressed syllables) with "weak" or *feminine rhyme* (flatter/matter). We talk about *men of letters*, and many women writers have reported that men seem to think they are giving a high compliment when they say "You write like a man." Perhaps the implication is that the woman is not only *pregnant with ideas*, but she is also *a seminal thinker*. The definition of *seminal* as a small idea destined to grow bigger goes back to the belief that the man with his semen provides the seed for a new baby and the woman with her womb provides the nurturance.

How the English Vocabulary Defines Sex Roles

One of the greatest problems with sexism in English relates to gender which will be talked about more in the next chapter. But as for the lexicon, the concept of gender affects a surprisingly large number of words. By skimming through the 1964 college edition of *Webster's New World Dictionary of the American Language*, I found 517 words which had either masculine or feminine markers of this type. Of these words, 385 had masculine markers and 132 had feminine markers. This was roughly a ratio of three masculine words to every one feminine word. This is a ratio we might expect, because historically men have played more varied and active roles than have women and words were needed to describe these roles. Besides, it was men who were making up the language and recording it.

By analyzing these 517 words according to such semantic features as /person in the generic sense, /occupation, /prestige, /negative connotation, /human, /abstract, /unusual age, and /family relationship, we can get insights into societal roles assigned on the basis of sex. For example, these words show that males have more occupations than females, because among words describing occupations there were five masculine to every one feminine word. However, a larger proportion of the masculine words than of the feminine occupational terms are archaic or rare, for example, *bowman, huntsman, headman, bargeman, bellman, chapman, coachman, cragsman, hackman, wheelsman, yeoman,* etc. Perhaps as *horsepower* and automation replace the traditional *manpower*, women as well as men are physically capable of performing most jobs so new occupations are less apt to be titled ... *man*.

In analyzing the terms for /prestige, I used as a definition of prestige any denotation of either skill or power over others whether of a positive or negative nature. The masculine words outnumbered the feminine words six to one. Masculine words included such terms as: *alderman, Apostolic Fathers, best man, choirmaster, chairman, concert master, country gentleman, craftsmanship, favorite son, grand duke, horsemanship, journeyman, kingly, knight-*

ly, manly, master (*builder, craftsman, mason,* etc.) *old master, sportsmanlike, warlord, white man's burden,* and *workmanship.* Feminine terms included *Alma Mater, first lady, forewoman, gold star mother, grand duchess, lady luck, ladyship, maid of honor, May queen, motherhood, mother lode, mother superior, mother country, queen's English,* and *schoolmistress.*

When the words with negative connotations were analyzed, feminine words outnumbered masculine words 25 to 20. This is more striking when we remember that the overall ratio of masculine to feminine words was three to one. Many of the negative feminine words were occupational terms such as *alewife, fishwife, chambermaid, charwoman, call girl, gun moll, hausfrau, housewife, sob sister, washerwoman,* and other words such as *madwoman, old maid, old wives' tale,* and *weird sisters.* The masculine words included such items as *chapman, fall guy, hangman, junkman, ragman, madman, son of a gun,* etc.

The ∤human and ∤abstract sets of words were made up of terms no longer referring to people. Through a process of either metaphor or lexical complication, these words came to refer to inanimate or abstract items, although they still carry the ∤masculine or ∤feminine marker. There were more than twice as many masculine as feminine words in these sets. Many of the terms were adjectives or words describing qualities or states. An informal observation is that the feminine words tended to deal with aesthetically pleasing little things, for example *ladybird, lady's slipper, ladyfinger, maidenhair fern, granny knot, Queen Anne's lace,* etc., while the masculine words were more serious or powerful such as *white man's burden, brotherhood, fraternalism, statesmanship, kingship evil,* etc.

Among words containing some marker of age, feminine words appeared more often than masculine words. There were 34 feminine terms and 27 masculine terms. This supports the idea mentioned earlier in relation to animal metaphors. Age is more important with females than with males. Terms marking age included *old man* and *old woman,* which depending on their context could have either positive, neutral, or negative connotations. The masculine *old master* nearly always has positive connotations while the feminine terms *old lady, old maid, old wife, old wives' tale,* and *old womanish* nearly always have negative connotations. For the latter five terms there were no equivalent masculine terms, unless we want to count *grandfatherly advice* as parallel to the feminine *old wives' tale.* If we look at these as matching terms, we can see an extreme difference in the amount of respect triggered in the listener's mind.

Of greatest interest to students of sexism are the numerous words with an overt marker of masculine which are sometimes used in the generic sense:

bachelor's degree

baseman

bedfellow

brotherhood

caveman

clansman

committeeman

common man

congressman

countryman

craftsman

craftsmanship

draftsman

Englishman

fellow man

fellowship

fellow traveler

flagman

forefather

fraternalism

fraternize

freeman

freshman

gentleman's agreement

horsemanship

inner man

journeyman

juryman

kinsman

layman

manikin (mannequin)

(to) man *v.*

man-hours

man

mankind

manpower

manslaughter

marksmanship

master

(to) master *v.*

master craftsman

masterful

masterliness

mastermind

masterpiece

master's degree

master stroke

middle man

one-man show

patronize

penmanship

salesmanship

seamanlike

seamanship

self-mastery

showman

showmanship

spokesman

sportsman

sportsmanlike

sportsmanship

statesman

statesmanlike

statesmanship

straight man

straw man

stunt man

townsman

tribesman

underclassman

upperclassman

(to) unman *v.*

weatherman

whipping boy

white man's burden

workmanlike

workmanship

workmen's compensation

yachtsmanship

yes man

Undoubtedly not everyone would have chosen the same words I selected as generic, because this is a changing area in English, and as with all language change, it is not occurring at the same time or in the same way in all dialects. Historically, probably all of these words did refer specifically to males. But through changes in the culture they came to include females as well as males. For example, it was not until the late 1800s that many females were allowed to go to college, so naturally, the educational terms *freshman, underclassman, upperclassman, penmanship, bachelor's degree, fraternity,* and *master's degree* all meant specifically male. They have now been used for so long to refer to people of both sexes that most people are surprised when reminded that these words are just as masculine as the more controversial *chairman.*

People have invented feminine counterparts for some of the words that I have listed as generic. But having masculine and feminine counterparts does not necessarily guarantee linguistic equality. Usually the masculine word is thought to be more basic and when lexical incorporation occurs, it is the masculine word that travels into other words. For example we have *craftsman/craftswoman/craftsmanship* but not *craftswomanship.*

Another set of words, illustrated below, lacks the specifically masculine marker, yet the feeling that these are masculine words is so strong that feminine counterparts have been created, comparable to our contemporary usages, *lady lawyer, woman doctor, woman truckdriver,* etc.

actor/actress	hunter/huntress
administrator/administratrix	instructor/instructress
adulterer/adulteress	major/majorette
adventurer/adventuress	masseur/masseuse
ambassador/ambassadress	poet/poetess
ancestor/ancestress	protector/protectress
author/authoress	sculptor/sculptress
aviator/aviatrix	seducer/seductress
benefactor/benefactress	seer/seeress
conductor/conductress	songster/songstress
comedian/comedienne	sorcerer/sorceress
director/directress	tempter/temptress
/directrix	tiger/tigress
executor/executrix	usher/usherette
governor/governess	waiter/waitress
heir/heiress	warder/wardress

In this list, the difference between the importance of the

masculine word and the feminine word is apparent. In some cases
the meanings are not the same. For example a *majorette* is not really
a female *major*, nor is a *governess* a female *governor* in the usual
sense of the term. While puzzling over this list wondering why
feminine counterparts would have been created for these particular words, I noticed that most of them end in an *-er* or *-or* sound. In
English, traced back to Latin, we use the *-er* or *-or* suffix to mean *do*
(a *farmer* is one who farms, a *writer* is one who writes, a *sweeper* is
one who sweeps, etc.). Perhaps the feeling that males are the active
doers in society has contributed to the idea that the *-er* sound is a
kind of male suffix. For example in the very few incidents when we
wanted to make a masculine word, this is the suffix we chose, as in
widower adapted from the feminine *widow*. And when in the 1800s
speakers wanted to make a more genteel word than *roost cock*, they
came up with *rooster*.

But there are still many *-er* words which seem feminine—*mother*,
dancer, *teacher*, *cleaner*, etc.—so something more than the *-er*
ending must have inspired speakers to create feminine forms. It
might be that because many of the words are high-prestige terms,
both sexes felt it advantageous to clearly identify the sex of the
referent. In the more specialized or even pretentious words we
separate males and females. For example, English has only the
single term *writer* but the double terms *author/authoress* and
poet/poetess. The same goes for *art*, in the pair, *sculptor* and
sculptress. And in music there is only *singer* or *player*, but both
songster and *songstress* and *conductor* and *conductress*.

What has happened in the past with words like this is that the
feminine form is used as much to indicate triviality as to indicate
sex. For example, in a newspaper article about a woman con-
ducting high-altitude tests for NASA, the headline called her an
aviator. Just a few days later the same newspaper had an article
about a woman participating in a small-time air show. In contrast,
the headline labelled her an *aviatrix*. When Barbara Walters was
doing the Johnny Carson show, she did not call herself the *hostess*.
Instead, she announced that she was going to *host* the show,
probably because she felt she was doing something different from
catering to people's physical comfort, the usual role of a hostess.
Harriet Tubman is called a *conductor*, not a *conductress*, of the
underground railway. Related to this idea of seriousness vs.
triviality is the fact that a serious writer usually does not want to be
labelled *poetess* or *authoress*.

In linguistic situations which deal with actual sex differences, different masculine and feminine words serve a useful purpose. For example, if one's desire in going to a massage parlor is to be sexually stimulated, one has to distinguish between a *masseur* and a *masseuse*. There is an actual sex-related difference involved in being in a *paternity suit* and in a *maternity suit*, and if the purpose of a girl marching in front of a band is sex related, then it is appropriate that she be distinguished from a *drum major* by having her own title of *majorette*. But in areas which are not actually connected to sex differences, the system of separate male and female terms usually shortchanges women, who end up with the less prestigious titles. But, of course, in a changing culture with changing attitudes, this may not happen in the future.

The Vocabulary through Feminine Eyes

The problem of positive vs. negative connotations is important in relation to guidelines and language change. Many feminists have quite recently decided that they are not included as referents in any word that has a masculine marker. Yet many of these words with masculine markers are the high-prestige terms. This is a hotly debated issue and no one has come up with a really workable solution. To illustrate the complexity of the problem, let me show you the restrictions that would be placed on my daughter if the language stays the same as it is and if, at the same time, we decide she *cannot be included* as a referent in masculine-sounding words.

First, she could have no rights of property or citizenship. In fact, she would have no legal rights at all, since our entire form of government is outlined in a language relying almost exclusively on masculine pronouns. Among the peculiar restrictions placed on her would be that she could never really participate in the *brotherhood* of *mankind*. If she were a twin, she would have had to be an identical twin since she couldn't have been a *fraternal* twin. And regardless of what her *forefathers* were, she couldn't have been born an *Irishman*, a *Frenchman*, a *Scotsman*, an *Englishman*, or a *Dutchman*.

At school she would have to learn early that she could serve on committees but never be the *spokesman* or *chairman*. She could participate in sports, but she could not practice *sportsmanship*. In baseball, she could be a pitcher or a catcher, but not the *ballboy* or the *first baseman*. In the classroom, she could practice handwriting, but only the boys could practice *penmanship*. When she reaches high school, it's obvious that she will have to skip her *freshman* year, but how can she ever get to be an *upperclassman* if she can't first be an *underclassman*? When it's time for college, she can't apply for a *fellowship* to help her get her *bachelor's degree*. I suppose that she can get into a sorority, but I had hoped that she would be invited to join an honorary *fraternity*. The point of an education is the development of the *inner man* and of *self mastery*. I wonder if she can make it without ever participating in a *bull session* or going on to get her *master's degree*.

I wonder what she'll do when she's ready to join the *manpower* of the world. Naturally she can't be a skilled *craftsman* or *journeyman* or *foreman*. Will she be eligible for *workmen's compensation*? With all the problems related to *man and his environment* and the big urban squeeze, maybe she'll turn to rural America, but she can't be a *frontiersman* or a *gentleman farmer*. She can be a cowgirl, although this doesn't mean that she will do the same things that a *cowboy* does, or that she can develop the necessary *horsemanship* to become a first rate *cattleman*.

Perhaps she will be interested in art. If so, I'll feel bad that all she can create are paintings instead of *masterpieces*. Or maybe she will want to be a writer. Some journalists have started out as *copy boys*, but she couldn't do this. Nor could she be a *deskman* or a *rewriteman*. New careers are opening to TV *newsmen, soundmen*, and *anchormen*. But since she couldn't try out for these, she would have to be satisfied with getting a job as a TV weathergirl or as a newspaper sob sister. Or if this fails, maybe she can get a job as a salesgirl, but she doesn't have much chance for success, since she couldn't practice *salesmanship*. If she worked in the post office she could become a *postmistress*, but here, too, she would be limited; she couldn't go to the top, since it would have to be a male filling the role of *postmaster general*.

Even if she rose to real power in the world and became a *queen*, she couldn't rule because there are only *kingdoms*—no queendoms. It's too bad she won't be able to get together with some *fellow* feminists and *mastermind* a plan for electing a woman President. It would be especially hard since she couldn't start out with such a traditional job as city *councilman* or *congressman*. But at least I wouldn't have to worry about the implications of the old saying,

"Politics makes for strange *bedfellows*," nor whether or not her companions are *men of their word*. She couldn't count on their coming to a *gentlemen's agreement* and making her their *favorite son* candidate. But if by some happenstance, she did succeed in gaining power in government, the real tragedy is that she could never be a *statesman*—only a politician!

I've been skeptical about actually changing the language by conscious effort, yet encouraged at the widening awareness people are coming to have, through feminist urgings, of the premises that often go along with such simple matters as pronoun reference. Just having to think twice before saying "the student . . . he . . . " is a good change in attitude . . .

Richard Ohmann
teacher-editor

Problems with sexism in English are helped by current acceptance of plural pronouns with antecedents which are sexually neutral, but grammatically singular—the "everybody . . . they" type. Since the language in use has been moving in that direction, maybe NCTE should nudge it along; after all, people who have insisted on the singular pronouns have chiefly been English teachers (many of whom have been female).

Bruce Cronnel
educational researcher and
developer

I prefer *one* term for men and women: not policeman and police-woman, but police officer. . . . terms denoting male and female will continue to divide people, rather than letting them be thought of as *person* first, and man or woman second.

Patrice Harper
editor

Efforts to get rid of the combining form -*man* in words like chairman I regard as trivial and pointless. As a linguist I recognize unstressed -man/mən as down-graded from a base to a suffix which simply means "person." I generally still use the traditional terms in these instances.

William Stryker
teacher

Shakespeare used "everyone to *their* heart's desire"—so I use it too and will not correct on student papers.

Nancy Wells
teacher

Gender-Marking
in American English:
Usage and Reference

Julia P. Stanley

Natural and Grammatical Gender

The distinction between "natural" and "grammatical" gender in linguistic analyses has a long and confusing history, so confusing that a thorough examination of the subject is beyond the limits of this chapter. Nevertheless, some discussion of the distinction is necessary as an introduction to the problem of gender-marking in English. The acceptance of the distinction between "natural" and "grammatical" gender as valid has flawed descriptions of our language, and obscured the ways in which biological sex and the social roles associated with it influence the structure of English.

Grammatical gender refers to the three main noun-classes recognized in Greek and Latin, "feminine," "neuter," and "masculine," and at least part of the confusion derives from the traditional use of sex-linked terminology to designate noun classifications. As Lyons (1969, p. 283) points out, this terminology reflects "the association which traditional grammar established between sex and gender." The term *gender* is derived from Latin *genus*, "class" or "kind," and the classification of nouns into three genders accounted for pronominal reference and adjectival concord (Lyons). Theoretically, grammatical gender is independent of sex.

Natural gender refers to the classification of nouns on the basis of biological sex, as female or male, or animate and inanimate. According to grammarians, English is a language in which natural gender determines pronominal reference. As Lyons has expressed it: "Gender plays a relatively minor part in the grammar of English.... There is no gender-concord; and the reference of the pronouns *he*, *she*, and *it* is very largely determined by what is sometimes referred to as 'natural' gender—for English, this depends upon the classification of persons and objects as male, female or inanimate" (1969, pp. 283-84). Later in this chapter, I will demonstrate how "natural" gender fails to accurately describe noun classifications and reference in American English.

Even in languages such as French, in which both "grammatical" and "natural" gender function as the bases of noun classification, problems arise in usage that require circumlocution and some awkwardness. In his discussion of the "clash" between "natural" and "grammatical" gender, Lyons (1969, pp. 286-87) uses the example of *professeur*, which is classified as masculine, although it may refer to either a woman or a man. In French, there is no problem with concord within the noun phrase, whether the noun refers to a woman or a man, and we find in *le nouveau professeur* that the masculine article and the masculine form of the adjective agree with the masculine grammatical gender of the noun *professeur*. However, if *professeur* refers to a woman, and an adjective which would normally agree with it occurs in the predicate of the sentence, there is a clash between the masculine gender of the noun and the female sex of the individual referred to by the noun.

> Neither the masculine form of the adjective (e.g., *beau*) nor its feminine form (*belle*) can be used appropriately in these circumstances without resolving, as it were, the "conflict" between "grammatical" and "natural" gender. Neither *Le nouveau professeur est beau* (which necessarily refers to a man) nor **Le nouveau professeur est belle* (which is ungrammatical) is possible. The "conflict" is resolved with a sentence like *Elle est belle, le nouveau professor* ("She is beautiful, the new teacher").

Lyons goes on to observe that such examples suggest that grammatical cohesion may be stronger within the noun-phrase than between the subject and the predicate of a sentence, and also show "that there is indeed some 'natural' basis for the gender systems of the languages in question." He does not, however, elaborate further on this observation.

Lyons (1969, p. 288) concludes his discussion of gender by saying, "Gender-concord is a 'surface-structure' phenomenon of certain languages. It is clearly the pronominal function of gender which is of primary importance in communication." In these two sentences, Lyons effectively evades the problem of gender and its role in communication: If the primary function of "grammatical" gender is pronominal agreement with an antecedent noun, how are we to describe a language like English, which does not have "grammatical" gender? Even if one is willing to claim, as I am not, that

English relies on "natural" gender, then gender-concord must be something more than "a 'surface-structure' phenomenon."

Otto Jespersen (1964, p. 347) described at some length the extent of our reliance on gender-marking.

> Most English pronouns make no distinction of sex: *I, you, we, they, who, each, somebody,* etc. Yet, when we hear that Finnic and Magyar, and indeed the vast majority of languages outside the Aryan and Semitic world, have no separate forms for *he* and *she*, our first thought is one of astonishment; we fail to see how it is possible to do without this distinction. But if we look more closely we shall see that it is at times an inconvenience to have to specify the sex of the person spoken about.

Perhaps some speakers of English are uncomfortable when they have to specify the sex of someone they're talking about, but I suspect that most of us feel comfortable only when gender-marking is used. Consider, for example, the following passage from *The Cook and the Carpenter*, in which the author created neutral pronouns, *na* and *nan*.

> The carpenter knew na had foolishly wasted most quarter-hours on the same quarter-acres, not even counting the disproportionate time allotted to the milli-mile, nan bed; na had failed to prepare naself at all for the cook's assumption ("Carpenter," 1973, pp. 3-4).

My own discomfort with this passage illustrates for me the difficulties involved in trying to alter the thinking with which I am most comfortable, the sex-role dichotomy perpetuated by our society and embedded within our language. It is important to us to know the sex of people because we decide how to relate to them on that basis. When we try to relate to other people outside of the socially accepted sex-role stereotypes, we are lost, our definitions blur. For example, a colleague once asked me how I dealt with students if I didn't know their sex. (We were discussing the unisex phenomenon, and he was upset because he often had trouble deciding the sex of some of his students.)

Q: "What do you do when you can't tell if a student is male or female?"

A: "Why is that important to you?"

A: "How else will I know how to relate to them?"

This exchange reveals the extent of our dependence on culturally defined norms in our personal relationships, and gender-marking in English provides us with the necessary cues in linguistic communication.

In this brief introductory section, I have tried to sketch the accepted definitions of grammatical and natural gender as they are used by grammarians and linguists, and to illustrate some of the inaccuracies introduced into linguistic descriptions because of this distinction. Because English is thought to be a language that has "natural" gender, I will set aside further discussion of grammatical gender. In the remainder of this chapter, I will demonstrate that English does not, in fact, even have natural gender as a grammatical classification for nouns. Instead, the semantic space of English is structured in accordance with the sex-role stereotypes of our society.

Definition of Sex Roles

Recent linguistic research on English, although often insightful and thought-provoking, has barely begun in-depth analysis of the internal structure of our vocabulary. We still know very little about the organizational principles inherent in English semantics, primarily because we have failed to perceive the existence of semantic "sets" other than the easily recognized ones, such as kinship terms, color terms, and counting systems. As a matter of fact, one lexicographer has claimed that English does not have well defined semantic sets like those found in other languages. Clearly, such a statement is too general and oversimplified. If linguists have somehow failed to provide a convincing analysis of English semantics, it is because we have failed to perceive the obvious and to use it as a starting point for our descriptions.

The definitions that follow, taken from the *Random House Dictionary of the English Language*, make explicit the ways in which one portion of the English lexicon is divided into two gender-defined vocabularies. (I chose RHD as my source for these definitions because the editor, Jess Stein, was "guided by the premise that a dictionary editor must not only record; he must also teach." With respect to individual words, Stein had this to say: "In man's language is to be found the true mirror of man himself. His lexicon is an index to his ideas and passions, his inventions and achievements, his history and hopes." This statement makes the definitions found in RHD of special interest.) The terms for which I have provided definitions are: *feminine/masculine, womanly/manly, effeminate/mannish*. (The comments on *effeminate* were found under the definition for *female*; those for *mannish*, under *manly*.) These adjectives describe that portion of our lexicon which refers to the behaviors held to be "appropriate" for women and men in our culture. Even the phrasing and word choices in the definitions reveal the cultural value attached to each of the words.

> **feminine** ... 1. pertaining to a woman or girl: *feminine beauty*; *feminine dress*. 2. like a woman; weak; gentle; *feminine delicacy*.
>
> **masculine** ... 1. having the qualities or characteristics of a man; manly; virile; strong; bold; *a deep masculine voice*. 2. pertaining to or characteristic of a man or men: *masculine attire*.
>
> **womanly** ... 1. like or befitting a woman; feminine; not masculine or girlish.... **Syn** ... WOMANLY implies resemblance in appropriate, fitting ways: *womanly decorum, modesty*. WOMANLIKE, a neutral synonym, may suggest mild disapproval or, more rarely, disgust: *Womanlike, she (he) burst into tears*. WOMANISH usually implies an inappropriate resemblance and suggests weakness or effeminacy: *womanish petulance*.
>
> **manly** ... 1. having the qualities usually considered desirable in a man; strong; brave; honorable; resolute; virile.... **Syn** ... MANLY implies possession of the most valuable or desirable qualities a man can have, as dignity, honesty, directness, etc., in opposition to servility, insincerity, underhandedness, etc. ... It also connotes courage, strength, and fortitude: ... MANNISH applies to that which resembles man: ... Applied to a woman, the term is derogatory, suggesting the aberrant possession of masculine characteristics ...
>
> EFFEMINATE is applied reproachfully or contemptuously to qualities which, although natural in women, are seldom applied to women and are unmanly and weak when possessed by men: *effeminate gestures; an effeminate voice*. FEMININE, corresponding to masculine, applies to the attributes particularly appropriate to women, esp. the softer and more delicate qualities. The word is seldom used merely to denote sex, and, if applied to men, suggests the delicacy and weakness of women: *a feminine figure, point of view, features.*

These definitions capture the cultural assumptions regarding the "true nature" of both women and men, and they describe the behaviors for which our culture rewards us. Women are supposed to be delicate, petulant, liable to burst into tears with little provocation; we are supposed to possess "decorum"—have you ever heard anyone speak of *masculine decorum*? Women must be modest, weak, and gentle. In the definitions for the adjectives that refer to female behavior, the editors of RHD make it clear that the "standard" for human behavior is male, and women cannot, and must not, measure "up" to that standard. The language of these definitions for women is cast negatively; our behavior is that *which is not masculine*. The definition for the word *mannish* explains to us that women who possess such attributes as strength, fortitude, honesty, courage, directness, and bravery are "aberrant"!

During moments of unbridled optimism, we might be tempted to ignore Jess Stein and the editors of RHD, and dismiss their definitions as either inaccurate or exaggerated. But I think that their definitions of terms like *feminine* and *masculine* do reflect the meanings of these words, as they are understood and used by speakers and writers of English. The following passages from popular prose illustrate the usage of *feminine* and *masculine* in context. (Italics have been added for emphasis.)

1.a.   Difficult as the master's role may be, it is even more disquieting to admit to masochistic tendencies, since they involve *dependence* and *helplessness*, those *"feminine"* traits. Leather men abhor effeminacy, ... (Richard Goldstein, "S & M: The Dark Side of Gay Liberation," *Village Voice*, July 7, 1975, p. 10).

   b.   She seemed *smaller, softer*, more *feminine* and *compliant* than the Amazon who had fired arrows into a beast a hundred times her size less than two hours before (Robert A. Heinlein, *Glory Road*, p. 175).

2.a.   ... she found herself resenting Leo [a woman] more than the book itself; for taking everything as a matter of course, for being always unembarrassed, for being able to discuss books like this in terms of royalties and serial rights in the same voice as if they were bottled beer; for the whole *armour of masculine impersonality* which Elsie sensed without knowing what it was that she had felt and resented; ... (Mary Renault, *The Middle Mist*, pp. 125-26).

   b.   The surgeons sat around, reading the newspapers, discussing the stock market and their golf games. ...
        She was the only woman in the room, and her presence changed the *masculine* atmosphere subtly (Michael Crichton, *The Terminal Man*, p. 63).

The adjective *feminine* is also used in some contexts in which it contrasts *negatively* with those things of the world conventionally regarded as masculine; although the word *masculine* is not explicit, it is implied in the context. The two quotations that follow, both taken from Ursula K. LeGuin's *Left Hand of Darkness*, illustrate the negative connotations associated with the human behaviors defined by *feminine*.

> The guards were seldom harsh and never cruel. They tended to be stolid, slovenly, heavy, and to my eyes effeminate—not in the sense of delicacy, etc., but in just the opposite sense: a gross, bland fleshiness, a bovinity without point or edge. Among my fellow-prisoners I had also for the first time on Winter the sense of being a man among women, or among eunuchs. The prisoners were hard to tell apart; their emotional tone seemed always low, their talk trivial (p. 170).
>
> b. Ignorant, in the Handdarn sense: to ignore the abstraction, to hold fast to the thing. There was in this attitude something feminine, a refusal of the abstract, the ideal, a submissiveness to the given, which rather displeased me (pp. 202-03).

The last two passages in this section illustrate usages of both *feminine* and *masculine* in contexts where the author has used the polarization inherent in the two terms in order to express the contrasting values attached to the two sets of behavior patterns.

> 4.a. Otherwise it was identical with the floor below, except for the differences trivial but enormous, which marked the transit from a feminine to a masculine world. Down there the doors had had a guarded look, an air of preserving, watchfully, small face-savings and shifts from a prying eye; here they were slammed for quiet or stood carelessly open (Renault, *The Middle Mist*, p. 180).
>
> b. "But the loss of—of everything feminine—of delicacy—and the loss of masculine self-respect—You can't pretend, surely, in *your* work, that women are your *equals*? ... "
> "Of course, I have known highly intelligent women, women who could think just like a man, ... " (Ursula K. LeGuin, *The Dispossessed*, p. 14).

In each of these excerpts, the author has made use of the cultural values that are the denotative meanings of both *feminine* and *masculine*, and the negative and positive connotations of each term respectively. I am not saying that these passages reflect directly on any of the authors, only that the polarization represented in these adjectives is available in the language, that as writers and readers in English all of us know the meanings of these words and the values attached to each of them, and that, in fact, the words would not exist if it were not for their usefulness and inherent cultural meanings. The last example, from *The Dispossessed*, illustrates the use of males as the *standard* for human behavior, and how the behavior of women must always stand in only a comparative or contrastive relationship to that standard.

Feminine and *masculine* are only the two most obvious adjectives that define the characteristics attributed to the two biological sexes. Around these two cluster other adjectives that are selectively used for either of the sexes, and their usage is gender-marked. For example, consider the adjectives *pretty, beautiful*, and *handsome*. *Pretty* can only be used for a woman, and it refers to her physical attractiveness. When *beautiful* refers to physical attractiveness, it is used for women, but when it denotes a spiritual or personal quality it may refer to persons of either sex. (I should say here that *pretty* can refer to males, but only in the phrase *pretty boy*, which is derogatory and implies that the male is a homosexual, through the adjective *pretty*; *boy* clearly contrasts with the norm represented in the noun *man*.) When we speak of a male as being attractive, we use the adjective *handsome*, and we do not use the word for an attractive woman unless she is over forty. To speak of a woman as "handsome" implies that she is older, perhaps more mature, and it may be "safer" to attribute a masculine adjective to a woman when she is past the age of childbearing.

Keeping firmly in mind the meaning and usage of the adjectives I have discussed and the dichotomy introduced into the semantic structure by the existence of words like *feminine* and *masculine*, let us explore the ways in which our usage of nouns, e.g., *man, mankind, child, kids, sociologist, woman*, etc., follows the pattern established by sex-role stereotyping, and how the reference of such nouns indicates the prevalence of the male as our social standard.

The Myth of Generics

The recent controversy concerning the use and reference of so-called "generics" in English reveals the extent, if not the nature, of the political investment at stake in attempts to preserve the myth of a "generic person" in our language. Those who would like to maintain the use of masculine nouns as nouns of general reference are relying on popular beliefs, *not* linguistic evidence. If the history of English can tell us anything about the outcome of this controversy, I have to conclude that popular misconceptions (those definitions with the most political power supporting them) will prevail, and neither traditional authorities, nor linguistic analysis,

nor actual usage will influence those who wish to believe that
English has a generic person.

At this point I must define what I mean by "popular misconceptions," because the term "popular" is probably misleading.
When I speak of "popular misconceptions," I am referring to the
widespread belief of those self-appointed guardians of the "purity"
of the English language, those men, and some women, who have
access to the media and thereby have the opportunity to offer their
opinions as the final word on a given topic to many people. In
general, the suggestion that English does not have a generic person
has been dismissed as "msguided" and categorized as illicit
"tampering" with the language, or as a "fad," or as a grotesque
"error" in the same class as *ain't* and double negatives. The specific
accusation varies with the degree to which the writer identifies
her/himself as the last bastion in the defense of the English
language against barbarism and/or change.

One writer has called feminist analyses of English "the new
Sispeak" (Kanfer: 1972, p. 79), while L. E. Sissman, in his article
"Plastic English," says that such tampering with language is as
threatening as the American Communist Party. He goes on to say
that feminists "distort and corrupt further the language already
savaged by the Establishment politicians when they conspire to
eliminate the innocuous, and correct, locution, 'Everyone knows *he*
has to decide for *himself*,' and to substitute the odious Newspeakism
'chairperson' ... (Sissman: 1972, p. 37). Perhaps the best evidence
for the angry determination to defend male dominance in English
can be seen in the violent reactions to the 1972 McGraw-Hill
Guidelines for the Equal Treatment of the Sexes published in the
New York Times.

The individuals who have committed themselves to defending
their belief that English possesses a generic person must ignore
statements by traditional authorities on English and the ways
native speakers of English use the language. When I speak of
"popular misconceptions," I do not mean the ways that the woman-
in-the-street thinks about English. Those who would defend English against degeneration are protecting their own interests
against those of us they have defined as "the enemy." Such people
feel comfortable fighting a change that has already occurred.

The arguments advanced in favor of *man* and *mankind* as the
generic person are not substantive; they are political. The *Oxford
English Dictionary* states clearly in its definition of *man* that

generic usage of this noun is "obsolete," and the editors go on to note that "in modern apprehension *man* as thus used primarily denotes the male sex, *though by implication referring also to women.*" (Italics added.) Note that women are included in *man* as referents only by implication, *not inference!* Unless there is some indication in the immediate context in which *man* is used that the writer/speaker *intends* for it to refer to persons of both sexes, we cannot pretend that it does. With respect to the phrase, *a man*, the OED is equally explicit: The phrase is used "quasi-pronominally" for *one*, or *any one*, but it "implies a reference to the male sex only." As early as 1924, Otto Jespersen observed that "The generic singular *man* sometimes means both sexes . . . and sometimes only one." Because of its ambiguity of reference, Jespersen was blunt in his judgment of *man* as the generic person: "This is decidedly a defect in the English language," and he went on to mention that "the tendency recently has been to use unambiguous, if clumsy expressions like *a human being*" (1964, p. 231). That was in 1924, and "the tendency" to use *human being* never did catch on.

I doubt that anyone would argue that speakers of English have no use for a generic person. There are too many contexts in which we wish to speak about people in general. But *man* and *mankind* do not fulfill this expressive function. Jespersen (1964, p. 231) compares English *man* to German *mensch*, Danish and Norwegian *menneske*, and Swedish *människa*. In the strictest etymological terms, the comparison is accurate. But it ignores one important fact about the history of the English language: In Old English, *wer* and *wif* served as the sex-specific terms; *man* was the generic. But at some time prior to 1000 AD *man* began to be used in its present meaning, a male human being, and *wer* was subsequently lost. (It remains only in the compound *werewolf*.) Then, as now, male control of the media and important social institutions evidently made it easy for men to acquire what had once been a generic for their own term.

One other aspect of English has obscured the situation: the distinction between "formal" and "colloquial" styles. Most of us, in our everyday use of language, do not use *man* or *mankind*, nor do we say, "Everyone . . . he . . ." We use words such as *people, person, someone*, etc., and in informal speech when we use *everyone* or *everybody*, the pronoun that follows is most often the plural *they*. Of course, the traditional grammarians have been consistent in their efforts to eradicate this usage by labeling it as "incorrect." I suspect that we still use *they* because we know more about our language than those who would protect us from error.

What do we, as writers and readers of English, understand as the referent of the nouns *man* and *mankind* in common usage? What do these two nouns mean to us? In some usages, it is clear from the context that the writers are using *man* and *mankind* as pseudo-generics, and that, in fact, the actual meaning is *male* human being. In the passages that follow, especially the last one, we can see how women have been cognitively excluded.

5.a.   A knife is an extension of the brain and eye, a tool, a weapon, a friendly and intimate presence, a romantic symbol, an object of repellent fascination, an atavistic expression of the aggressor and penetrator in man (Jack McClintock, "Blades with Class," *Esquire*, July 1975, p. 138).

b.   It seemed to Mare Dante that the ocean was the same on any world. It was the womb, the all-encompassing mother where men migrated at least once in their lives— ... (Dean R. Koontz, "Soft Come the Dragons," *The Liberated Future*, p. 199).

c.   Mankind has, ever since he began to think, worshipped that which he cannot understand. As millenia have passed he has understood an ever-increasing amount about the world around him. He has even hoped, in his most optimistic moments, to comprehend it all. Yet man is now in the position of facing the ultimate unknowable, which can never be penetrated as long as he remains in his present physical form. ... The constantly augmenting knowledge of the world has only been achieved by centuries of dedicated work by men of science. ... It is as if man departs from his mother's womb to enter straight into another one created by the scientists. ... Even before birth new drugs are used to help the foetus survive. Once born and for the whole of his life medical discoveries allow him to drug himself, have bad parts cut out of his body, or good ones transplanted into it. ...
   When he has grown safely to adulthood he can wake up in the morning in his heated or air-conditioned house, use the latest techniques to prepare food for himself, drive off in his heated or air-conditioned car, and spend the day in a glass and plastic office ... or even exceptionally be one of the select few who have voyaged to the moon. And to cap it all he may, if he really so desires, stay at home and change into a she! (John G. Taylor, *Black Holes*, pp. 11-12).

I have quoted the last passage at such length in order to demonstrate the way a particular use may at first sound as though *man* or *mankind* (or both) is being used generically. At the beginning of 5.c, we find "Mankind ... he." If we believe that this is a generic reference, we're not likely to become suspicious as we read through the first paragraph, although we might find the use of *penetrate* as a metaphor slightly strange. In the next sentence we find the phrase *men of science*, which I'm sure is not a generic use, who provide "man" with a synthetic womb as comfortable as "his mother's." The last excerpt from *Black Holes*, the description of the fabricated womb created by technology, contains the sentence that betrays the male reference implicit in the rest of the quotation. It is still possible for the reader to imagine that Taylor's uses of the masculine *man, mankind,* and *he* include women in their referential scope.

A generous reader might continue to give Taylor the benefit of the doubt until the last sentence because women also live in "heated or air-conditioned" houses; we prepare food for ourselves using "the latest techniques"; we drive in "heated or air-conditioned cars"; and some of us spend our days "in a glass and plastic office." When the author said, "he may, if he really so desires, stay at home and change into a she!" and dropped the pretense of his inflated prose, he revealed to his readers the cognitive content of *man, mankind,* and *he*: male human beings. I don't think it's accidental, either, that this quotation contains phrases that echo the content of my first two examples in this section. Taylor is so secure in the universality of masculine reference that he also signals to his readers his negative attitude toward "the second sex," and toward any male stupid enough to voluntarily accept a subordinate role, in his use of the adverb *really*, which implies that he can't quite understand such a thing, and with the exclamation at the end of the sentence, which again underscores the paradox of such a decision.

As we all know, examples that are as obvious as the three I have offered here are not the rule. Most writers are clever enough to make their usage more ambiguous and their prejudice less apparent. But there are examples of sex-specific reference in contexts in which we might expect to find more inclusive terms. Each of the following quotations contains a noun of masculine reference in a context in which some other noun, such as *person, human being,* or *people* could have been used equally as well. After each example, I have provided a rewritten version of the passage to illustrate alternatives available to the writers.

6.a.   He rides a skateboard like *no other man!* (Ad for Schmidt's Beer, Channel 2, New York City, July 6, 1975).

  a.   He rides a skateboard like *no one else!*

  b.   *The man* who'd rather drive a truck would rather drive a Dodge (TV ad, Nashville, used during 1975).

b.   *The person* who'd rather drive a truck would rather drive a Dodge.

c.   It is again very likely that such conditions have a far greater bearing upon the level of *man's* use of the sea than upon the shark's behavior once it meets *a man* in the water (H. David Baldridge, *Shark Attack*, p. 82).

c. It is again very likely that such conditions have a far greater bearing upon the level of humanity's use of the sea than upon the shark's behavior once it meets a person in the water.

d.   Among the many famous *men of history* who employed astrology to guide their destinies was Adolf Hitler.... Take our leading presidential candidates. For the guidance of inquiring voters, herewith their astrological signs so that we will know what kind of *man* we are electing.... Aries—*Males* of this persuasion are forceful, overbearing exponents of *masculinity* at any price....
     Before voting, then, study the candidates' astrological charts so you can wisely determine the kind of *man* you are choosing for your leader. (Arthur Hoppe, "It Beats Listening to Speeches, Anyhow," *Nashville Banner*, Sept. 19, 1975, p. 9)

d. Among the many famous *historical figures* who employed astrology.... so that we will know what kind of *person* we are electing. Aries—*Persons* of this persuasion are forceful, overbearing exponents of *aggression* at any price.... so you can wisely determine the kind of *person* you are choosing for your leader.

e.   Wisdom is not addictive; its maximum is that of the wisest *man* in a given group (Heinlein, *Glory Road*, p. 262).

e. Wisdom is not addictive; its maximum is that of the wisest *individual* in a given group.

f.   I was being nasty as only *a man* can be who has had *his* pride wounded (Heinlein, *Glory Road*, p. 241).

f. I was being nasty as only *people* can be who have had *their* pride wounded.

g.   *A man* makes art because he has to (LeGuin, *The Dispossessed*, p. 169).

g. *People* make art because *they* have to.

h.   "You can't tell *a man* to work on a job that will cripple *him*."
     "But then why do people do the dirty work at all?..."
     "... People take the dangerous, hard jobs because they take pride in doing them.... Hey, look, *little boys*, see how strong I am! You know? A person likes to do what *he* is good at doing.... One's own pleasure, and the respect of one's *fellows*...."
     "Does everybody work so hard, then?" Oiie's wife asked. "What happens to *a man* who just won't cooperate?"

> "Well, he moves on. The others get tired of *him*, you know."
> (LeGuin, *The Dispossessed*, pp. 120-21).

h. "You can't tell *someone* to work on a job that *is crippling*."
> "...Hey, look, *kids*, see how strong I am! ...*People* like to do
> what *they* are good at doing.... One's own pleasure, and the respect
> of one's *community*. ..."
> "What happens to *people* who just won't cooperate?"
> "Well, *they* move on. The others get tired of *them*, you know."

Examples like the preceding force us to ask: What is the content
of the noun *man* and the related noun phrases, *a man* and *the man*.
Note that the rewritten versions of the excerpted passages do alter
the meaning of the originals. When the specifically masculine
reference, *man, a man*, or *the man*, is deleted, the positive
connotations of strength associated with these phrases are also
removed. As the OED editors observed: *a man* "implies a reference
to the male sex only." Nor is it an accident that each quotation is
concerned with subjects like *competence, power,* or *leadership.* The
two television advertisements appeal directly to the association in
our minds between maleness and competence. The example from
The Dispossessed is particularly interesting in this respect, because
in this science fiction novel, LeGuin created a social order in which
people were not bound by the sex-role stereotypes many of us take
for granted as inherent aspects of biological sex. Throughout the
passage she uses *people* and *one* in alternation with *a man* and *he.* As
readers we might be tempted to grant that her usage here is
generic, were it not for one significant slip in her language, when
her major character, a male physicist, is allowed to say that the
people in his society show off for *little boys*! Such usage, in a novel
written to exemplify a utopian society, indicates the extent to which
our cognitive space is occupied by male visions of male importance
and superiority.

The usage of the English speakers I have quoted up to this point
illustrates how the male sex continues to dominate the media to
which we are exposed every day. Whenever the topic is important,
involving an active, rather than a passive, role in society—when
decision-making and competence are involved—we are presented
with a male authority figure as the only "appropriate" possibility. It
is not surprising, then, that we find males cast as the "generic
person" in English in those contexts associated with male behavior
and male concerns such as anger, control, autonomy, history, and
dignity. All of these areas are potentially *human* concerns, but they

are traditionally associated with men, as the following quotations illustrate:

7.a. By questioning the control exercised by autonomous *man* and demonstrating the control exercised by the environment, a science of behavior also seems to question dignity or worth (B. F. Skinner, *Beyond Freedom and Dignity*, p. 21).

b. A small step for *man*, a giant step for *mankind*! (astronaut Neil Armstrong)

c. The history of anger is the history of *mankind*. *Man* has been exposed to the effects of anger, others' as well as *his* own, since *he* was first placed on earth (Leo Madow, *Anger*, p. 1).

d. Those who manipulate human behavior are said to be evil *men*, necessarily bent on exploitation (Skinner, *Beyond Freedom and Dignity*, p. 41).

Any attempt to claim that any of these uses could be interpreted in the sense of a "generic person" would necessarily have to acknowledge that in each one we are dealing with either an event or a context in which men have been involved. In b., of course, it was males who stepped onto the moon's surface. In c., the statement is almost literally true; history is concerned with the events that were the consequences of male anger. And in d., it would be difficult to interpret Skinner's use of *men* as anything but sex-specific.

One last example of the generic use of *man* may serve to illustrate the OED editors' reason for labeling it *obsolete*:

8. Archeologists announced today that they have discovered evidence of *man's* existence as far back as 3,000,000 years ago, based on the dating of a woman's skeleton (Radio news report, Knoxville, April 1975).

Here, the explicit semantic contrast introduced by the use of *woman* makes the attempt to interpret *man* as a generic impossible, and even humorous.

Finally, there are those contexts in which we find specific reference to women, because women *are* the persons about whom the writer is speaking. And, as with the examples of *man* and *men*, which occur when the subject is traditionally associated with male interests, the noun *woman* is used, with both abstract and concrete reference, when the topic is regarded as a specifically female behavior or interest.

9.a.   As *Woman*, she would have been happier had she continued
       enshrined in the privacy of domestic love and domestic duty
       (Helen B. Andelin, *Fascinating Womanhood*).

  b.   This comprehensive book of one hundred embroidery stitches will
       be useful not only to teachers and students but to *women* of all ages
       who are interested in embroidery (*100 Embroidery Stitches*).

  c.   *Women* unconsciously prefer to fulfill their maternal role and to be
       loved by a man. *Woman* is intended for reproduction (Frank Caprio,
       Female Homosexuality).

  d.   The right idea for today's creative *woman* from the Cooking and
       Crafts Club (Book-of-the-Month Club flyer for a subsidiary division).

These quotations contain explicit references to women because the
topic in each instance, whether it is food, nurturing, or embroidery,
is one assumed to be of interest only to women. I would like to
emphasize the terms that *do not* appear, as I did with the examples
in Section 6. We do not find a "generic person" such as *person,
human being, people,* or *individual*; nor do we find the pseudo-
generics *man* or *mankind*. This, in spite of our training in
traditional grammar, where we learned that we had to use a
masculine term as long as there was *one* male in the group about
which we were speaking. In fact, 9.b. was given to me by a male who
enjoys embroidery; he was upset to find that the writer of the book
on embroidery had excluded him from consideration by using the
female-specific *women*.

A semantic parallel to the examples *man* and *a man* in Section 6,
the passages in which we might have expected to find uses of more
general terms for people, can be found in contexts where the
writer/speaker has used the word *woman* to carry all the connotations associated with our sex—those characteristics that males
would have us believe inhere in our nature because of our sex. So we
find examples like those below; instead of words like *person, human
being,* or *individual*, the noun *woman* is used as a self-contained
explanatory term for a restricted set of human behaviors such as
eccentricity, housecleaning, effortlessness, cowardice, and triviality—personality traits that are certainly *not* possessed *only* by
women.

10.a.   There's no law that says a *woman* has to do housework all the time!!
         [This ad begins with a woman standing in a kitchen; when she
         delivers this line, she is holding a baby. Moral: Women have other

things to do besides cleaning house; we also have our nurturing
function to fulfill!] (Television ad for Fantastic spray cleaner, New
York City, July 14, 1975; Nashville, Oct. 25, 1975).

b.   Helen had the looks, and the definable aura of success, which enable
a woman to convey by acquiescence the idea that she is making no
effort (Renault, *The Middle Mist*, p. 223).

c.   Eccentricity in *women* always boiled down to the same thing. She
wanted a man (Renault, *The Middle Mist*, p. 231).

d.   "We shall call a council of warriors tonight from all the canyons . . . "
"You are turning into *women* . . . . " (Mary Staton, *From the
Legend of Biel*, p. 163).

e.   High fashion has always struck me as a monumental bore and of
inherent interest only to *women* without much on their minds (Merle
Miller, "From Madcap to Dowager," *Saturday Review*, May 3, 1975,
p. 23).

All of the passages I have quoted in the course of this discussion of
the "generic person" in English illustrate the fact that our language
does not have a generic, and that writers and speakers of English
use a gender-specific term, usually either *man* or *woman*, depending upon the subject with which they are concerned. The next
example from *The Dispossessed* is a passage in which the author
uses both *woman* and *man* precisely; we cannot possibly mis-
interpret her meaning.

11.   He simply had not understood that the purpose was to enable *men*
with machine guns to kill unarmed *men* and *women* easily and in
great quantities when told to do so (p. 245).

But perhaps the clearest and most convincing example of how
man always refers to male persons and *woman* refers to female
persons is the new television advertisement for the Alka Seltzer
"Cold Kit." On the screen we see a male cartoon figure with an
umbrella, galoshes, and an overcoat. A male voice tells us that *man*
is the most intelligent of all the animals, but that *he* is also the most
vulnerable. In the picture we see the male figure sloshing through
snow and sneezing. The male voice tells us that when *man* needs
help, he turns to another intelligent animal, *woman*. A smiling
woman appears on the screen, holding the Alka Seltzer Cold Kit.
The last picture shows a woman and a man, cartoon figures again;
the woman is nursing the man, who is sitting in a chair, wrapped in
a blanket.

The "Generic" He

Uses of the so-called "generic *he*" have occurred often in the excerpts accompanying my discussion of the "generic *man*." Because males have reserved for themselves most of the activities considered important in the "world"; their language follows the behavioral dictates of the male social order. In general or abstract discussions, we find the pronoun *he* used to replace the antecedent noun; we use the "feminine" pronoun *she*, only in situations in which we are referring to a specific female. Two writers explained this usage in a footnote to their readers: "The common pronoun 'he' refers to persons of either sex except when 'she' is definitely applicable" (James & Jongewald, 1973, p. 2).

Of course, this usage, and its corresponding "rule," (the rule that justifies the usage), contradict most of the theoretical statements of linguists concerning the function of both "grammatical" and "natural" gender and all of the definitions of pronouns provided in traditional texts. In *Theoretical Linguistics*, Lyons claimed that the primary function of both "natural" and "grammatical" gender was their role in determining pronominal reference. A standard traditional text defines pronominal agreement in the following way: "When a pronoun has an antecedent, it agrees with that antecedent in gender, number, and person" (Birk & Birk, 1951, p. 735).

All of us agree that English does not have "grammatical" gender, and I am demonstrating here that our language does not have "natural" gender, either. Unless we are all males. In order to justify the occurrence of *he* as a "common" pronoun in abstract or general discussions, almost every noun in English must be marked as a masculine noun. If it is true that pronouns agree with their antecedent nouns in gender, number, and person, then *he* can only replace a noun that carries the feature [+masculine]. Otherwise, the argument based on pronominal reference fails as a description of English structure. In this section I will discuss a few examples in which *he*, or *she*, or both pronouns occur.

The following excerpted passage from Simone de Beauvoir's "preface" to *La Bâtarde* illustrates the use of *he* for a common noun and *she* for specific reference.

12.   It is said that the unrecognized writer no longer exists; anyone, or
        almost anyone, can get *his* books published .... Violette Leduc does
        not try to please; *she* doesn't please .... "I am a desert talking to
        myself," Violette Leduc wrote to me once .... And whoever speaks

to us from the depths of *his* loneliness speaks to us of ourselves. Even
the most worldly or the most active *man* alive has *his* dense thickets,
where no one ventures, not even *himself*, but which are there: ... A
woman is descending into the most secret part of *herself* and telling
us about all *she* finds there with an unflinching sincerity, ... (p. 7).

In this example we find the possessive pronoun *his* replacing both
writer and *anyone*; *she* functions as the replacement for the proper
noun, Violette Leduc, in accordance with "natural" gender. Then
his replaces *whoever*, its antecedent indefinite pronoun. So far, so
good. De Beauvoir (or her translator) is simply following traditional rules. But the semantic contrast in the next two sentences
reveals the thinking that lies behind usage of *he* as a "common"
pronoun, or perhaps the sort of thinking that is the result of
centuries of the "generic" *he*. In one breath de Beauvoir is telling us
about the "most active man"; in the next she is speaking about "a
woman." Her use of *he* leads her into using *man* in her general
statement, a usage parallel to that illustrated in Section 6.

My next example comes from the writing of John Ciardi, who,
while expressing his sympathy for Women's Liberation, nevertheless maintains that it is easier to change attitudes than it is to
change the English language. I do not think that either of these is
amenable to change, and this quotation illustrates how language
and social attitudes are mutually reinforcing in perpetrating male
dominance in our thinking.

13.   The test of a writer, once *he* has learned something about language
as a medium, is invention: .... What does *he* imagine into place that
meets the demands of what he has already written ...
     Given a talented student, a writing coach can be useful in
developing the talent. *He* cannot make a gift of it. *He* cannot be more
than tentative about it. *He* can read the manuscripts ... *He* can help
the writer get outside *his* own writing ....
     The writer must learn for *himself*, but a coach can prod *him* to
views and to questions *he* might not have come to for years if left
unprodded ....
     ... A writer may be *a man* who has labored to make *himself*
unemployable and who must, therefore, take what comfort *he* can in
his decision. But, teacher, let it be *his own* life decision (John Ciardi,
"Manner of Speaking: Creative, Uh, Writing," *Saturday Review*,
May 3, 1975, p. 26).

In Ciardi's writing we find the same gradual progression, a drift
from the general "person" to a specifically male reference. His first
use of *he* replaces the antecedent *writer*. In the next paragraph, *he*

substitutes for two preceding references, the *student/writer* and
(*writing*) *coach*. This use of *he* for dual reference results in an
ambiguous sentence, "*He* can help the writer get outside *his* own
writing." Out of context, *his* can refer to either antecedent. Toward
the end of his article, Ciardi uses the indefinite masculine singular,
a man, as did de Beauvoir; a few sentences later, the indefinite
becomes the definite noun phrase, *the man*. This passage is a good
example of the way in which the masculine gender encourages
writers and speakers of English to perceive the male sex as the
social standard.

Because males have managed to reserve most of the semantic
space of English for their own, we often find the definite masculine
singular without any antecedent pseudo-generic, as in this example
from the Metropolitan Museum of Art.

> 14.   The assembled pieces are now ready for the *glazier—the man* who
> joins them together. *He* bends the soft lead strips ... (Stained glass
> exhibit, Metropolitan Junior Museum, New York City, June 1975).

If we are to believe that *glazier* is a common noun, what is the
content of *the man*, which immediately follows it? What is the
purpose of a definite noun phrase, especially one that is sex-specific
when the writer might just as well have said, "The assembled pieces
are now ready for the *glazier*—who joins them together." The use of
a masculine antecedent indicates that the pronoun *he* is not generic;
it is clearly a sex-specific reference.

My last example of the usage of the so-called "generic" *he* also
calls into question the use of compounds with masculine markers as
nouns of general reference.

> 15.   (*Man* prefers to adapt environments to *himself*, although some
> scientists now question whether this is the more practical way to
> survive.) ....
>   Modern *man's* impact on butterflies, as well as other harmless
> insects, is of deep concern to many scientists today.... About the
> only way *man* can totally eliminate a butterfly or moth species ... is
> by destroying its habitat....
>   Butterfly nuts all belong to the same species, but they divide into
> several subspecies.... They may be wealthy *business* or *professional*
> *men* who collect butterflies with much the same zeal as they would
> stamps or fine paintings.... (*Men* have caught and killed millions of
> butterflies in the last three centuries; ...)
>   The collector breeder stores *his* chrysalids and cocoons in boxes

and baskets.... (Paul Showers, "Signals from the Butterfly," *New York Times Magazine*, July 27, 1975, pp. 10, 42-43).

Again, we find usage of *man* and *men* that some readers would regard as "generic," and *his* as the pronominal replacement for "collector breeder." What casts doubt on the validity of this interpretation occurs in the third section of the excerpt, the splitting of the compound *businessmen* in the phrase "business or professional *men*." The writer's division of what is generally labeled as a "common" compound reveals that it is cognitively a male-specific noun, and establishes that his use of *his* toward the end of the passage quoted is also a male-specific reference.

For those who still want to maintain that *he* is generic in usage, the following examples with *she* as the pronoun will demonstrate that *she* occurs in what ought to be general contexts. If *she* is a sex-specific pronoun, then we should not find it used as an abstract substitute. Such examples indicate that a small portion of the English vocabulary contains nouns marked for female referents, nouns other than *mother* and *wife*.

16.a.   A doorkeeper will sit for hours in the entrance hole. *She* admits only members of *her* community demanding entrance by taps with their antennae, and these only if *she* can also recognize their smell (Karl von Frisch, *Animal Architecture*, p. 103).

b.   Other species hide their egg cocoons instead of carrying them about. Still others attach them without concealment to a leaf or some other surface....
One remarkable spider lives its entire life underwater and yet remains an air-breathing animal; ... This spider always carries *her* own supply of air about with *her*.... *Her* home is an air-filled underwater balloon held in place between aquatic plants (von Frisch, p. 34).

c.   Our America is singing!
In *her* schools and colleges
on *her* streets and in *her* camps,
on *her* wheatfields and on *her* ships,
because of *her* sweet Liberty,
our America is singing....
Listen to the song of *men*....
A day is near, we pray,
when *men* schooled in working and
        playing together
shall help their *brothers* join
        hands around the world, ...

> Some day we'll bequeath it [the world]
>   with pride
> to our children
> as our *fathers* did to us.
>   (McKeesport High School Yearbook, 1944, p. 91)

d.   On the pasture lands each stock beast was accompanied by *her* young (LeGuin, *The Dispossessed*, p. 166).

e.   This breakdown of the reliance on dogma in Europe ushered in the scientific revolution, and allowed Western *man* within the last three centuries to gain the power over nature which has led us to where we are today, in the technological society.... Simultaneously, the world's power requirements are far outstripping *her* capacity; ... (Taylor, *Black Holes*, p. 20).

f.   A nurse is many things ... *She's* sympathy with hope in *her* eyes ... Love with *her* fingers on the pulse of life (Dan Valentine, *American Essays*, p. 12).

g.   *She's* America's most popular career girl ... *She's* the office favorite ... *She* runs the office for *men* who run the world ... *She's* a secretary ... (Valentine, *American Essays*, p. 21).

The first example from *Animal Architecture*, in which *she* refers to the antecedent *doorkeeper*, informs us that the doorkeeper in an ant colony is female, although in context we know this *only* from von Frisch's use of the sex-specific pronoun. The next quotation from von Frisch is a fascinating illustration of the way in which the dominant sex within a species becomes the standard in "scientific" writing. Without explanation, without apology, von Frisch uses *she* as a "generic" for the species of spiders he describes. In the first excerpt on spiders, notice that he discusses how "species" hide their "egg cocoons." In the second paragraph quoted here he uses the possessive *her* to refer to the antecedent "remarkable spider." In the case of spiders, the female is evidently the most important to scientists, and it is her activities that scientists observe. Why? Because the female spider kills the male after mating. In our own species, the male locks the female in "his" house after mating, whenever possible, and, as a consequence, scientific observers comment most often on the more interesting activities of the male of the species. Perhaps there is a lesson that women could learn from the spider.

Example 16.c contains the traditional use of *she* to refer to a country; of special interest is the shift to the male gender as soon as the writer begins to speak of who does the singing and who holds the power in this country. The same semantic contrast is used in 16.e; the world is female, but it is *man* who has gained "power over nature." The last two examples illustrate the use of the generic *she* to replace "common" nouns, *nurse* and *secretary*. Of course, neither of these nouns functions as a general referent, and *she* is not "generic" by any stretch of the imagination; both nouns are female-specific in their reference, because nursing and secretarial work are two of the nurturing occupations open to women.

To conclude this section, here are two more passages that would be unremarkable, probably, in any other discussion of English structure. Such examples are so common that we let them pass without comment in much of our reading and listening; they seem so "natural" to us that we internalize the pronominal usage found in them without thinking. Once again, we find the masculine pronoun when the activities described are important, and therefore within the male domain of our cognitive space, and the female pronoun when the activities are defined as either trivial or subordinate.

17.a.   Wishful thinking is believing that when *a man*, about to become President, swears to uphold the Constitution, *he* will grow in stature when *he* assumes the awesome power of that office.
    Wistful thinking is fantasizing that when the next President to assume the awesome power of that office swears to uphold the Constitution, *she* will grow in stature.... The if-ful thinker, when *he* "ifs" a posture, is pragmatic, an activist who points up a lesson to be learned from our former mistakes.... Wishful thinking is the art of self-hypnosis, wherein one is convinced that a good fairy will soon fly nonstop across the land, in the nonsmoking section, and with a wave of *her* wand will suddenly restore our life of overabundance.... The wishful thinker holds that we must send them money because America has never turned *her* back on an ally.... The if-ful thinker digs deeper. *He* points out that if we had learned our lesson.... (Goodman Ace, "Top of My Head: The If-ful Thinker," *Saturday Review*, May 3, 1975, p. 10).

b.   When *Man* and *Nature* are in Harmony the World is a Happy Place!
    —But *people* no longer love the *Earth* as they once did. *Her* waters are polluted, *her* air and soil poisoned, *her* resources wasted.
    —*Man* in *his* ignorance has assumed that the *Earth* will always heal *herself*, no matter what *he* did. This is not so! The *Earth* can lose *her* resiliency. And in destroying *her*, we destroy ourselves.
    —The men and women known as the Wicca still call the *Earth* their *Mother*, revere *Nature* and teach *her* secrets (Flyer posted in a bookstore in Athens, Georgia, May 1975).

In this section, I have provided examples of the ways in which the principle of pronominal agreement in English operates in terms of sex-specific activities, at least as they are traditionally defined for us by our culture. If we always found the male singular pronoun *he* in abstract or general discussions, it would at least be possible to regard it as a quasi-generic, since it's the closest thing to a generic in English. However, the current and continuing occurrence of *she* in those general contexts defined as female makes such a claim doubtful. Clearly, speakers and writers of English recognize, at some level, that most of the nouns in English are defined as inherently masculine, and a smaller group of nouns is marked as inherently feminine. Furthermore, this small group of nouns contains those which refer to the socially-defined activities and functions of women. At the center of the female semantic space we might place *wife* and *mother*, both nurturing, supportive, and subordinate roles. Around these two words, we can then list occupational terms such as *nurse, secretary*, and *prostitute*, which incorporate the core meanings of *wife* and *mother* as part of their meaning.

By extension, these nouns and their meanings can be graphically surrounded by the metaphors usually characterized as female-specific, *land, earth, nature, cars, boats* and *ships*, and the *good fairy*. In conclusion, I would like to suggest that one way of accounting for these metaphorical extensions of female-specific reference derives from the male point of view, which assumes male dominance and male control of the earth, the world, all the land, and the oceans. All of these things are regarded as their possessions. As one legal textbook defines the situation: "land, like woman, is for possessing."

Male Semantic Space in English

As I have suggested throughout this discussion of gender-marking in English, to the extent that we can talk about a gender system in the language, our vocabulary is divided into two separate and unequal portions. The smaller group of nouns, marked as [+female], consists of those words that refer to culturally-defined female activities and interests. As others have observed, men have been the doers and the actors, the central figures in their histories, and those nouns that refer to active occupation in the world, especially the socially prestigious and financially rewarding endeavors, carry the semantic feature [+male] as part of their meaning, e.g., *doctor, lawyer, judge, chairman.** Only a few nouns carry the feature [+female] (or [-male] as Geoffrey Leech: 1969, p. 20, would mark them), e.g., *prostitute, nurse, secretary, housewife, spider.*

As a consequence, when women move into activities outside their roles of wife and/or mother, we move into *negative semantic space,* semantic space that does not exist for us, because it is already occupied by the male sex. When a woman becomes a professional in one of the fields usually reserved for males, she does not move into the corresponding semantic space covered by the noun conventionally used as its label. Instead, her anomalous position must be marked by the addition of a special, female-specific marker; for nouns such as *doctor, lawyer, surgeon,* or *sculptor,* we feel uncomfortable unless we place some qualifier such as *woman/ female/lady* in front of the occupational term. In our usage, then, we are accustomed to talking about the *lady doctor,* a *female surgeon, woman lawyers,* and *lady sculptors.* Those occupations that have less social prestige are marked with a special "feminine" suffix, e.g., *waitress, authoress, poetess,* or *majorette.* We understand any noun that occurs in its "unmarked" form to refer to a male, and failure to provide the information that the person referred to is a woman, in the given context, often results in confusion for the hearer, and the conversation must begin again once the gender is made explicit.

For example, if I tell a friend that I've found a good doctor/ lawyer/therapist, she will assume that that person is male, and indicate her assumption in her response by using the masculine singular pronoun, "Oh, do you feel like you can trust *him*?" or "Do you think *he* could help with my problem?" On the other hand, those occupations reserved for women in our society, e.g., *prostitute, nurse, secretary,* require a sex-specific semantic feature in those contexts in which they refer to males. Thus, in common usage, we speak of *male nurses, male secretaries,* and *male prostitutes.* There are fewer examples in this instance since men have not shown as much interest in traditionally "female occupations" as women have shown in those of men, perhaps because the jobs that women hold pay less money.

In addition, when a given noun must be explicitly marked for

*This description of feature-marking is inaccurate, but for the sake of simplicity, I chose to use the term *marking* in its more general sense. In linguistics, however, *marking* has a specialized use; it is more accurate to say that *male,* the semantic feature, is the *unmarked* feature for most human nouns in English, and that *female* is the *marked* feature. Those features that are regarded as inherent meanings of a sex, it acquires a negative connotation, the price for moving out of one's socially defined semantic space, as though there were something "not quite right" with such an individual. That we need to mark occupational terms for sex indicates to me that our semantic space is rigidly structured and maintained by culturally defined sex roles, and when one of us goes beyond the boundary of the space provided for us within the English vocabulary, we move into negative semantic space, and special linguistic accommodations must be made.

As my next set of examples will show, women have read themselves into participation in more nouns in the English language than just those usually regarded as "generic." We have wanted to believe that common nouns included us as part of the human population in other areas of life, and we have assumed that we were referents in a general sense in nouns like *children, kids, people, person, individual, teacher, sociologist,* and *surgeon.*

In 1924, Otto Jespersen made a similar observation, although he did not make a judgment about the fact he was describing: "While a great many names for human beings are applicable to both sexes, e.g., *liar, possessor, inhabitant, Christian, fool, stranger, neighbor,* etc., others, though possessing no distinctive mark, are as a matter of fact chiefly or even exclusively applied to one sex only, because the corresponding social functions have been restricted either to men or to women. This is true of *minister, bishop, lawyer, baker, shoemaker* and many others on the one hand, *nurse, dressmaker, milliner,* on the other" (1965, p. 232). In 1975, things are pretty much the same. The following example from a well known text on role analysis makes the point implicitly, because the author has accepted as given social distinctions.

> 18. Usually, however, role analysis is pitched in terms of the roles of some particular category of person, such as doctor or female (Erving Goffman, *Encounters*, p. 91).

John Lyons (1969, p. 287), using the French word *enfant* (child) as his example, observed that gender is only "semantically relevant" in the case of those nouns usually described as having "common gender." In English, *child* is regarded as a "common" noun, and Lyons' remarks with respect to *enfant* are generally believed to describe the semantic status of our corresponding word: "...*enfant*... is inherently indeterminate with regard to gender,

word do not need to be marked; since *maleness* is an inherent feature of most human nouns, it is the *unmarked* feature in English. For this reason, Leech can linguistically justify his semantic features, [+male] and [-male], as the most efficient description of the English lexicon, because such a semantic description is the most economical, and introduces less redundancy into the linguistic model.

but is determined as either masculine or feminine according to the sex of the child referred to." In those situations in which we are referring to a specific child, of course, this description holds true. However, in those contexts in which we are speaking or writing about children in general, the male sex is the referent. And I am not speaking here about uses of the masculine "generic person." The evidence for my observation comes from the surrounding context in which the "common" noun is used. I offer these examples to you without further comment; I don't think I could add anything that would enhance the statement made by the examples of usage themselves.

19.a. *2001*: two thousand *astronauts* and one girl ... what to do? (*Peabody Post*, Sept. 10, 1975, p. 2).

b. For the merry-go-round *rider*, for example, the *self* awaiting is one that entails a *child's* portion of bravery and muscular control, a *child's* portion of *manliness* ... (Goffman, *Encounters*, p. 98).

c. There were two *people* from the rad lab doing a radiation check; there was one *girl* drawing blood for the chem lab, to check steroid levels; there was an EEG technician resetting the monitors; ...
One of the rad-lab *men* had hairy hands ... (Crichton, *The Terminal Man*, p. 133).

d. She had been the only *woman* among the six or seven *people* there, ... (Renault, *The Middle Mist*, p. 191).

e. American middle-class *two-year-olds* often find the prospect too much for them. They find their parents at the last moment to avoid being strapped into a context in which it had been hoped they would prove to be little *men* (Goffman, *Encounters*, p. 105).

f. *First Satirist*: A satirist can't teach *people* anything if he offends *them*.
Second Satirist: I offend *them*. *They* love it. I make fun of *their* wives (Jules Feiffer, *Feiffer's Album*, p. 2).

g. Nevertheless, he [Kahane] is capable of a shrewd public-relations humor, as when he demanded additional hiring of *Jews* in New York City.
"*Jews* for years have suffered the disability of Jewish mothers who insisted that they get an education. Because of this, *they* have been disadvantaged, unable to compete with other *groups* in athletics. Under the merit system *they* are unfairly excluded from full participation in American life. We demand that the Mets immediately agree to a roster that will include 26.2 per cent *Jews*" (Herbert Gold, review of *The Glory of the Jewish Defense League* by Meir Kahane, *New York Times Book Review*, June 8, 1975, p. 5).

h. Our *people* are the best gamblers in the galaxy. *We* compete for power, fame, *women* (*Star Trek*).

i. When I was going to school I spent most of my time talking to *teachers* and *their wives* (Edward Albee, in an interview, *New Yorker*, June 3, 1974, p. 29).

j. When the white man came to America, the *Indians* were running it. There were no taxes, no debts, the *women* did all the work. And, dopes that *we* were, *we* thought *we* could improve on a system like that! (Dial-a-Joke, New York City, July 9, 1975).

k. And what is one to think of our *fellow citizens* and their passivity? *They* will take anything! It's enough to make you wonder whether someone has relieved *them* of *their manly* attributes.
    Attributes of which she, on the other hand, clearly had plenty, despite her sex (Robert Merle, *Malevil*, p. 340).

l. We find that *holders of the MA and MS* who enter this department do well in graduate work here. *Their* applications, like those of *women*, and of members of minority groups, are welcome (Flyer, Department of Psychology, University of Tennessee, Knoxville, 1975).

m. Happy hour for *fishermen and their wives* (Poster in a Provincetown store window)

n. Bullworker helps turn *kids* into powerful *he-men* (Margrace Corp. mail brochure).

o. Even in the most serious of roles, such as that of *surgeon*, we yet find that there will be times when the full-fledged *performer* must unbend and behave simply as a *male* (Goffman, *Encounters*, p. 140).

p. My heroes have always been the kind of men who act on impulse and instinct, who don't see ambivalence and ambiguity—*people* who follow *their cocks* (Richard Goldstein, "S & M: The Dark Side of Gay Liberation," *Village Voice*, July 7, 1975, p. 10).

q. *Sociologists qua sociologists* are allowed to have the profane part; *sociologists qua persons*, along with other *persons*, retain the sacred for *their* friends, *their wives*, and *themselves* (Goffman, *Encounters*, p. 152).

r. This kind of equipment is to the *homecraftsman* what washing machines, clothes dryers, etc., are to the *housewife* (*Woodworking*).

s. A *child's* anxiety over physical danger, for example, may be explained in psychoanalytic terms as a fear of *castration*. And the psychoanalyst genuinely means that the *child* has an unconscious fear *his penis* will be cut off (*Sigmund Freud and the Psychoanalytic Theory of Development*, p. 310).

t. We also played what some *kids* called "capping" or the "dozens." This is a game of verbal assault, in which *kids* insult each other by talking about *sexual liberties they have taken with the opponent's mother.* It is a very common game in the Black community (Huey Newton, *Revolutionary Suicide*, p. 26).

u. Like all the *students* and *professors*, he had nothing to do but his intellectual work, literally nothing. ... And no *wives*, no families. No women at all (LeGuin, *The Dispossessed*, p. 104).

v. It is here, in this personal capacity, that an *individual* can be warm, spontaneous, and touched by humor. It is here, regardless of *his* social role, that an *individual* can show "what kind of a *guy he* is" (Goffman, *Encounters*, p. 152).

w. The history of lynching in the South shows that *Blacks* of mixed blood had a much higher chance of surviving racial oppression than their all-Black *brothers.*

  In any case, my father's pride meant that the threat of death was always there; yet it did not destroy his desire to be a man, to be free. Now I understand that because he was a man he was also free (Newton, *Revolutionary Suicide*, p. 33).

x. If there are *people* who don't like Anarres, let 'em go. ... But if *they* try to come sneaking back, there's going to be some of us there to meet *them.* ... And they won't find us smiling and saying "Welcome home, *brothers.*" *They*'ll find *their* teeth knocked down *their* throats and *their* balls kicked up into *their* bellies (LeGuin, *The Dispossessed*, p. 287).

y. Ordinary walking may have to be put on, too, especially, presumably, by the *half* of our population whose appearance is, and is designed to be, appreciated by *all* and savored by *some*: ... (Goffman, *Relations in Public*, p. 272).

Gender-marked Usage of the "Impersonal" You

The last example in the preceding section on gender-marked usage of "common" nouns, in which the indefinite pronouns *all* and *some* clearly refer to a male image in the writer's mind, raises the question of gender-marking in our uses of other pronouns, such as *we* and *you.* There have been some occurrences in previous sets of examples of the use of *we* to refer only to males (cf. 19.j). The final series of quotations, presents uses of the "impersonal" *you* in contexts where it is clearly marked for gender. In each of these passages, the author has decided which sex the book will appeal to, and the direct address to the reader, *you*, occurs in a context in which the writer reveals the sex of her/his projected audience. As in the cases of gender-marking of "common" nouns, sex-specific usage of *you* reflects the sex-role stereotypes prevalent in our society.

20.a. *You're* a mother and a wife, and *your* men count on *you*. So take One-a-Day Vitamins with iron for the people who count on *you* (Television advertisement, 1975).

b. WOULD LOOKING YOUNGER HELP *YOU* LAND THAT JOB? *You've* brushed up on *your* typing. *You've* put together a wardrobe that looks perfect for a working woman . . . Yet you still find it a little scary competing with all those young *girls* just out of school . . . If you think it might help in your job-hunting to look as young as you can (and honestly, could it hurt?) . . . (Ad for Oil of Olay, *TV Guide*, Aug. 23, 1975).

c. Surprise *your husband* with a pair of well-turned legs (Ad for chicken in a grocery store).

d. What it does mean is that *you* should be alert to *your* family's needs not only day by day but meal by meal. When you know that *your husband* is going to come home hungry on Tuesday after his after-work bowling league, have a little extra ready for the beginning of the meal (Gene Kowalski, *How to Eat Cheap But Good*).

e. Is *your wife* slippin' around? Not if she's on Armstrong tires (Billboard in Knoxville).

f. And there are the coquettish *girls* who give *you* a shy look, drop their gaze, and put their hands behind the back, which causes their breasts to protrude (Nierenberg and Calero, *How to Read a Person Like a Book*).

g. Look, *Mac*, when *you* are having the most gorgeous dream of *your* life and just getting to the point, do *you* stop to tell yourself that it is logically impossible for that particular babe to be in the hay with *you*? (Heinlein, *Glory Road*, p. 60).

h. . . . *your* biceps and forearms can start bulging and rippling with the bone-crushing strength that *girls* love to feel around them (Margrace Corp. mail brochure).

i. Remember back when people carried a rabbit's foot, and called avocados 'alligator pears'; . . . *Remember squiring Lucy* to the soda fountain: this years before anybody could hope to take *her* to bed? Nevertheless, *we* knew as *we* watched her licking vanilla from a long-handled spoon that to provide such fare was a form of possession. Already *we* had some sense that sex itself must be a feast, or if not that, at least a meal. At any age it still is an intimate business *to furnish* food to a woman, *to be cooked for* by *her*, like lying next to each other for a little (Edward Hoagland, "Survival of the Newt, *New York Times Magazine*, July 27, 1975, p. 6).

j. Now for the important question: What can *you and your husband* do

to aid your pre-school youngsters in progressing normally through
this family romance . . . (Fitzhugh Dodson, *How to Parent*, p. 193).

The lengthy quotation from Hoagland's article, "The Survival of
the Newt," was included in this selection of illustrations because the
implied you of the imperative *remember* is an intended male
reference on the part of the writer, as the second sentence makes
obvious. This passage, however, becomes more and more interesting as we follow the cognitive progression of male reference. The
indefinite pronoun *anybody* refers to males, as do the three uses of
the inclusive pronoun *we*, that usage which brings the reader into
the discourse as a participating observer. From a linguistic point of
view, the most fascinating aspect of this passage is to be found in the
final sentence of the paragraph. Syntactically, the infinitive *to
furnish* has a deleted subject of male reference, but according to
syntactic theory, the subject can only be deleted after the occurrence of an identical noun that is coreferential; in this case, the
implied male from the first sentence is the *only* possible coreferential noun. The same is true for the deleted logical object of the
passive phrase "to be cooked for by her." Throughout the passage is
the implicit *you*, the male audience for whom Hoagland is writing.
The entire quotation provides an excellent example of how women
are invisible in the contemporary media, and how the male
perspective dominates in subtle ways.

Conclusions

We clearly have a problem in English with gender-marking,
particularly in the many instances when we wish to talk about
people in general. However, even using nouns like *person* and
people is suspect, as the examples in Section 19 illustrate. In fact, in
the language uses I've been hearing lately, *people* is being used to
refer to groups that are either exclusively female or exclusively
male. For example, on a recent Saturday, Howard Cosell was
describing the lineup for a football team that was preparing to
receive a kickoff. How did Cosell refer to the situation? "The
Longhorns have three *people* back to receive the kick." In a moment
of generosity, of course, I might consider interpreting the use of
people to refer to groups composed of one sex as a welcome stage in
the neutralization of English reference. But I am not feeling

generous, and the examples I have provided in this chapter do not encourage optimism. On the contrary, I suspect that I am hearing more sex-specific uses of *people* and *person* because no one is willing to admit that there are sex-specific uses. Everyone seems to be embarrassed, or at least intimidated. I hope.

It is unfortunate that English does not have a generic person comparable to the French *on*, but I am certainly tired of having *man* passed off as its equivalent. I would like to be able to talk about people, but I'm no longer sure who I'd be referring to. Where does one go from here? What are we to do when we have to continue to use a language in which the semantic space is dominated by males? For the time being, I suggest that we mark gender explicitly, in those cases when it is possible, creating pairs of terms; e.g., *chairwoman/ chairman, spokeswoman/spokesman, saleswoman/salesman*. The use of neutralized terms perpetuates the invisibility of women in positions outside their traditionally defined roles, and the tendency to assume that such roles are filled by males has been illustrated amply in these pages.

Our language is sexist because our society is sexist, and until there is a significant reversal of the prevalent attitudes toward women, we cannot hope to accomplish much. The often virulent attacks on those of us who wish to eliminate sexism from English are misdirected and based largely on ignorance. Removing sexist words, phrases, comparisons, jokes and the like is NOT *changing* the English language. We recommend alternatives *already* extant in the language and in use among people. *Chairwoman* has been in the language for at least fifty years, although it has not been needed often enough. *Humanity, people, persons,* and *human being* are not new additions to the English vocabulary, although *astronaut, x-ray* and *bwana* are.

Those who oppose the removal of sexist relics in English hope to obscure the real issues, which have to do with political power. For example, *they* has been in use as a replacement for indefinite pronouns at least since Chaucer. Only the influence of the tradi-tional male grammarians has kept it out of so-called Formal English. Male omnipresence in our vocabulary is only one of the ways in which women have been kept invisible in our society when they moved beyond their traditional roles. If sexist terms are really so innocuous and trivial, why is everyone so anxious to protect them?

We have human rights legislation in Nova Scotia which prohibits specifying a preference for men or women [in hiring], but there are various interesting linguistic ways of circumventing [it]. . . . Ads for girl Friday and seamstress are marked m/f, . . . The same applies to the word *manager*, which is shown with no sex marking, and the word *manageress*, which is designated m/f. Needless to say, the position of manageress pays far less . . .

> Janet Carney
> government consultant

Language is not a tool which we send back to the workshop when it needs spare parts. Language is the dimension in which we exist, a continually changing medium that should also be profoundly conservative, since its task is to preserve the history of the race. Arbitrary, "mandated" changes of language are a regular feature of totalitarian regimes . . .

> D. S. Carne-Ross
> teacher-writer

As a feminist, I think it [combating linguistic sexism] is *the* most important aspect of the movement. We think in language and the political importance is incalculable. We know that Americans tried to denigrate the suffragists by calling them suffragettes.

> Nancy Wells
> teacher

My field is religious publishing. I suppose the increased emphasis on women's rights and roles . . . has led me to wince when I hear sentences like "God loves all *men*." . . . I am in favor of admitting the problem and of seeing what one can do about it in one's own writing and in the writing of others which one is called upon to edit. But, good grief, let's have a sense of proportion about it. . . . when I am editing a manuscript, falsehoods, bad logic, sloppy thinking and sloppy language, and indeed sexism itself seem much more critical targets than, for example, unaccented "-man" suffixes.

> Marlin J. VanElderen
> editor

Sexism in the Language of Legislatures and Courts

Haig Bosmajian

Our attitudes, thoughts, beliefs, and behavior are affected by the language used in several societal institutions: religion, law, education, politics, media such as the newspapers, magazines, and television. The teachings of our religion, what the law demands, what we are taught in our schools, the political status attributed to various groups—all have profound effects on the values, qualities, and characteristics we attribute to others. Legal, political and religious language: the words, names, labels, phrases, definitions we use when we talk and write to and about each other influence how we see ourselves and how others perceive us. If the words of the law say that the woman has lesser rights than the man, then our attitude and behavior towards women will be different from that towards men. If the words of our religion place women in a status inferior to men, our beliefs and behavior towards the female will be different from those towards the male. Political rights granted to men but not to women influence our perception of women and their status in society.

The purpose of this chapter is to demonstrate how the language of the law and politics has treated women as inferior to men and hence systematically "kept women in their place." More specifically, an examination of the language of the courts and legislatures will show that women have been defined, labeled, and stereotyped as (1) mother and wife, (2) infantile and incompetent, (3) seductive and immoral, and (4) nonpersons and nonentities. The materials are both historical and contemporary, for it is important to know how the language of sexism has evolved over the years to its present uses.

There is no doubt about the power of the law to control our lives. Laws are meant to be obeyed and those persons who break them are penalized, fined, imprisoned. We do not send people to jail for any other reason than for violating the law. So the language of the law must be part of our considerations of the language of sexism.

In a variety of ways, the courts, the judges, the legislators have defined and labeled women as inferior and subservient to men. As Supreme Court Justice William J. Brennan, Jr. said in *Frontiero v. Richardson* (1973):

> There can be no doubt that our nation has had a long and unfortunate history of sex discrimination. Traditionally, such discrimination was rationalized by an attitude of "romantic paternalism" which, in practical effect, put women, not on a pedestal, but in a cage.... Our statute books gradually became laden with gross, stereotyped distinctions between the sexes and, indeed, throughout much of the nineteenth century the position of women in our society was, in many respects, comparable to that of blacks under the pre-Civil War slave codes. Neither slaves nor women could hold public office, serve on juries, or bring suit in their own names, and married women traditionally were denied the legal capacity to hold or convey property or to serve as legal guardians of their own children.

Justice Brennan then went on to state that "it can hardly be doubted that, in part because of the high visibility of the sex characteristic, women still face pervasive, although at times more subtle, discrimination in our educational institutions, in the job market and, perhaps most conspicuously, in the political arena."

The language of the law has traditionally relegated the female to second class status and this in effect has determined to a great extent the perception of males and females towards women. This perception in turn has been reflected in the law. Robert Sedler, in "The Legal Dimensions of Women's Liberation: An Overview," has stated: "Since law theoretically reflects societal values, it is not surprising that American law has never reflected the value of sexual equality. To the contrary, sex-based distinctions in law are pervasive and to a large extent serve to implement the societal determination that a woman's primary role is that of 'wife and mother.'"

The editors of the *Valparaiso University Law Review* said in the prefatory comments to their 1971 Symposium on Women issue:

> It is undisputed that women comprise the majority of American citizenry. Yet, equality in many areas of human endeavor is reserved for the male minority—the same minority that creates and interprets law and ultimately justifies its validity. The claim is forcefully presented that the Anglo-American legal system has perceived and personified the woman as inferior to man, limited by her ascribed

biological and social function to propagating the species and maintaining the basic family unity.

The dismal record of the courts in the area of sex discrimination led John Johnston and Charles Knapp to conclude in their 1971 article "Sex Discrimination by Law: A Study in Judicial Perspective" that

> ... by and large the performance of American judges in the area of sex discrimination can be succinctly described as ranging from poor to abominable. With some notable exceptions, they have failed to bring to sex discrimination cases those judicial virtues of detachment, reflection and critical analysis which have served them so well with respect to other sensitive social issues.... "Sexism"—the making of unjustified (or at least unsupported) assumptions about individual capabilities, interests, goals and social roles on the basis of sex differences—is as easily discernible in contemporary judicial opinions as racism ever was.

Since so much of our law and legislation is a reflection of our religious beliefs and values and a matter of legal precedent, we need to look back into some of the sexist language appearing in the early legal and religious documents expressing the idea that women were not entitled to the same rights as men because of the doctrine of *propter defectum sexus,* "because of the defect of sex." The oldest written English law, Ethelbert's dooms of 600 AD, as W. J. V. Windeyer has observed in his *Lectures on Legal History,* was "given by a Christian king to a Christian people; and in tracing the development of the law of England from that date, when by the orders of a petty chieftain in Kent some primitive rules were committed to writing, to the time when more than half the world was to be ruled by English law, it is important that we should remember that throughout the intervening centuries, that law has been developed by men in close contact with the moral and intellectual traditions of the Christian Church" (p. 3). The sentiments that have been expressed in American legislatures and courts regarding the place of women reflect a variety of centuries-old religious beliefs designating the female subservient to the male. The woman's inferior status, as stated in *The Interpreter's Dictionary of the Bible,* is reflected in Hebrew laws "which show discrimination: A daughter is less desirable than a son (Lev. 12:1-5); she could be sold for debt by her father (Exod. 21:7; ch. Neh. 5:5); she could not be freed at the end of six years, as could a man (Lev. 25:40). She could be made a prostitute by her father (Judg. 19:24;

but ch. Lev. 19:29). The man had the right of *divorce*. The valuation of a man differs from that of a woman when a special vow is made" (Lev. 27:1-7). In 1 Timothy the woman is to keep silent and is the transgressor: "In like manner also, that women adorn themselves in modest apparel, with shamefacedness and sobriety; not with broided hair or gold, or pearls, or costly array; But (which becometh women professing godliness) with good works. Let the woman learn in silence with all subjection. But I suffer not a woman to teach, nor to usurp authority over the man, but to be in silence. For Adam was first formed, then Eve. And Adam was not deceived, but the woman being deceived was in the transgression." (1 Tim. 2:9-14)

Women, like children in some instances, were to be seen, not heard. In 1 Corinthians it is clearly stated: "Let your women keep silence in the churches; for it is not permitted unto them to speak; but they are commanded to be under obedience, as also saith the law. And if they will learn anything, let them ask their husbands at home; for it is a shame for women to speak in the church" (1 Cor. 14:34-35).

Earlier in 1 Corinthians, the superiority of the man over the woman is established: "But I would have you know, that the head of the woman *is* the man; and the head of Christ *is* God. Every man praying or prophesying, having *his* head covered, dishonoureth his head. But every woman that prayeth or prophesieth with *her* head uncovered dishonoureth her head; for that is even all one as if she were shaven. For if the woman be not covered, let her also be shorn; but if it be a shame for a woman to be shorn or shaven, let her be covered. For a man indeed ought not to cover *his* head, forasmuch as he is the image and glory of God: but the woman is the glory of the man. For the man is not of the woman; but the woman is of the man. Neither was the man created for the woman; but the woman for the man" (1 Cor. 11:3-9).

The superiority of the man then implies the submission of the woman. In Ephesians the submission appears to be complete: "Wives, submit yourselves unto your own husbands, as unto the Lord. For the husband is the head of the wife, even as Christ is the head of the church: and he is the saviour of the body. Therefore as the church is subject unto Christ, so let the wives be to their own husbands in every thing" (Ephesians 5:22-24).

This perception of woman as inferior, subservient, silent, and obedient became part of English law and Blackstone, in his eighteenth century *Commentaries on the Law of England*, a document which had great impact on the American legal system, describes women (as summarized in a 1961 brief by the American Civil Liberties Union for Gwendolyn Hoyt, who had been tried and found guilty in Florida by an all-male jury)

> as chattels, in effect slaves, their legal existence suspended during marriage, with limited freedom of movement, little right to property or earnings, no control over their children, and no political or civil rights, of any kind. Blackstone's quip (slightly paraphrased) that "Husband and wife are one and that one is the husband," was no idle jest. At the very moment when a man met his bride at the altar and said to her, "With all my worldly goods I thee endow," he was actually taking every cent she possessed. . . . He could beat her with a stick "no bigger than the wedding ring." All this on account of her "defectum sexus."

Since Blackstone's *Commentaries* have been so influential on American law, the following excerpts from that document appear below, demonstrating the language used by Blackstone in defining women as inferior to men:

> By marriage, the husband and wife are one person in law; that is, the very being or legal existence of the woman is suspended during the marriage, or at least is incorporated and consolidated into that of the husband, under whose wing, protection, and cover, she performs everything; and is, therefore, called in our law—French a *feme-covert, foemina viro co-operta*; is said to be *covert-baron*, or under the protection and influence of her husband, her *baron*, or lord; and her condition, during her marriage, is called her coverture. Upon this principle, of an union of person in husband and wife, depend almost all the legal rights, duties, and disabilities, that either of them acquire by the marriage. I speak not at present of the rights of property, but of such as are merely personal. For this reason, a man cannot grant anything to his wife, or enter into covenant with her, for the grant would be to suppose her separate existence. . . .
>
> But, though our law in general considers man and wife as one person, yet there are some instances in which she is separately considered, as inferior to him, and acting by his compulsion; and therefore all deeds executed, and acts done by her, during her coverture, are void. . . . She cannot by will, devise lands to her husband, unless under special circumstances; for at the time of making it she is supposed to be under his coercion. And in some felonies, and other inferior crimes, committed by her, through constraint of her husband, the law excuses her, but this extends not to treason or murder.
>
> The husband, also, (by the old law) might give his wife moderate correction; for, as he is to answer for her misbehavior, the law thought it reasonable to intrust him with this power of restraining

her, by domestic chastisement, in the same moderation that a man is allowed to correct his apprentices or children; for whom the master or parent is also liable in some cases to answer. But his power of correction was confined within reasonable bounds, and the husband was prohibited from using any violence to his wife.... Yet the lower rank of people, who were always fond of the old common law, still claim and exert their ancient privilege; and the courts of law will still permit a husband to restrain a wife of her liberty, in case of any gross misbehaviour.

There are the chief legal effects of marriage during the coverture; upon which we may observe, that even the disabilities which the wife lies under are, for the most part, intended for her protection and benefit. So great a favorite is the female sex of the laws of England!

Such was the language of Blackstone's *Commentaries*, submerging the woman's identity into that of her husband. She was defined as infantile and incompetent; she was labeled as weak and needed the protection of men; she was helpless and imperfect. The sentiment that "the disabilities which the wife lies under are for the most part intended for her protection and benefit" was to be the bane of women two centuries to come.

The Destiny of Woman to Be Wife and Mother

This perception of the woman, this language of sexism, became an integral part of many judicial opinions which denied certain rights and privileges to women. In 1872, the United States Supreme Court decided in *Bradwell v. The State of Illinois* that Illinois could deny a woman a license to practice law in that state. In the words of Supreme Court Justice Joseph Bradley:

...the civil law, as well as nature herself, has always recognized wide difference in the respective spheres and destinies of man and woman. Man is, or should be, woman's protector and defender. *The natural and proper timidity and delicacy which belongs to the female sex evidently unfits it for many of the occupations of civil life.* The constitution of the family organization, which is founded in the divine ordinance, as well as in the nature of things, indicates the domestic sphere as that which properly belongs to the domain and functions of womanhood. ...

It is true that many women are unmarried and not affected by any of the duties, complications, and incapacities arising out of the married state, but these are exceptions to the general rule. *The paramount destiny and mission of woman are to fulfill the noble and benign offices of wife and mother. This is the law of the Creator.* And the rules of civil society must be adapted to the general constitution of things, and cannot be based upon exception cases. (Italics added.)

Having labeled the woman as "naturally" timid, delicate, mother and wife, it was easy enough for Justice Bradley to conclude that women should not be allowed to practice law and a variety of other "occupations of civil life." If it is the "destiny and mission of women" to become wives and mothers, and this "is the law of the Creator," there obviously is no place for the woman in the profession of law and, by extension of the argument, in any of the other professions. With his words, with his definition, Justice Bradley placed limits on the options and freedom of women to choose their occupations; he took out of the hands of women the opportunity to determine their own destinies.

Defining and limiting the roles of females as mother and wife led to their being denied access not only to certain occupations but also being denied various rights. As wife and mother the woman had no place in the political process; she had no right to vote; she could be prohibited from jury duty.

During the Congressional debates on whether women should be granted the right to vote, the woman's role as wife and mother was invoked again and again as a reason for denying her suffrage. After arguing that "women are essentially emotional," Senator George Vest declared in the halls of Congress on January 25, 1887:

What we want in this country is to avoid emotional suffrage, and what we need is to put more logic into public affairs and less feeling. There are spheres in which feeling should be paramount. There are kingdoms in which the heart should reign supreme. That kingdom belongs to women. The realm of sentiment, the realm of love, the realm of the gentler and the holier and kindlier attributes that make the name of wife, mother, and sister next to that of God himself. . . .

It is said the suffrage is to be given to enlarge the sphere of woman's influence. Mr. President, it would destroy her influence. It would take her down from that pedestal where she is today, influencing as a mother the minds of her offspring, influencing by her gentle and kindly caress the action of her husband toward the good and pure.

On January 12, 1915, Congressman Frank Clark of Florida stood up in the House of Representatives arguing against suffrage for women:

Mr. Speaker, there can be no possible mistake as to the part which woman is to play in the activities of the human race. God has decreed that man is to be the head of the family and woman is to be his "helpmeet," and any attempt to change this order of human affairs is an attempt to change and to overthrow one of the solemn decrees of God Almighty. In every well-regulated Christian family the wife is the "helpmeet" of the husband. She is, and should be, his equal, his copartner, and where genuine love reigns she is exactly this. But, Mr. Speaker, *she is not to go out in the world to meet its trials, engage in its struggles, and fight its battles, and I venture to remark, without the slightest fear of successful contradiction, that no instance in American life can be found where any woman ever did this voluntarily who had a husband who was "worth the powder and lead which would be required to kill him."* (Italics added.)

Having confined the woman to the household and after citing the Biblical passage that it is "shameful for woman to speak in the church," Congressman Clark continued: "Ah, Mr. Speaker, if it is shameful for a woman to speak out in public in the service of the Master, what is it in the sight of God for her to stand upon a goods box on the corner and appeal to the gaping crowd for votes? *To give her the ballot is to unsex her and replace the tender loving, sweet-featured mother of the past with the cold calculating, harsh-faced, streetcorner scold of politics."* (Italics added.)

Congressman Clark concluded by labeling the woman as the "queen of the household," "the loveliest of all creation," and "undisputed dictator of the destiny of man":

I am absolutely safe in asserting that practically all the women in America who are happily married are opposed to suffrage. In opposing this measure, I am speaking for that vast multitude of American wives and mothers who love their husbands and their children and who prefer to reign as queen of the home rather than to grovel in the slums of politics. ... *I have a supreme contempt for the vigorous, healthy man who permits his wife to go forth in the world to labor for the family support, and I have the most thorough disgust for the married woman who lavishes all her affection on a poodle dog. Mr. Speaker, women who have husbands, children, and happy homes have no time to monkey with politics or to fondle poodle dogs.* They occupy the proudest and most influential position in all the world. "The hand that rocks the cradle is the hand that rules the world" is as true today as when it was first uttered. *Let us, then, leave woman where she is—the loveliest of all creation, queen of the household, and undisputed dictator of the destiny of man.* (Italics added.)

In effect, Congressman Clark defined all those women who

argued for woman suffrage as unhappily married, unsexed and childless. He equated women getting involved in politics with women fondling their poodles. He labeled the woman "queen of the household" and "undisputed dictator of the destiny of man," portraying her as someone with great power and hence not needing the right to vote or to get involved in politics to exert her power. Obviously, queens and dictators should not be concerned with mundane matters like suffrage for themselves.

Other legislators, because of their asserted high regard for American women as wives and mothers, echoed Clark's sentiments. North Carolina's Congressman Edwin Webb almost outdid his colleague's representation of women as powerful potentates:

> Mr. Speaker, I am opposed to woman suffrage, but I am not opposed to woman. *I respect her, admire her, reverence her, because of the sacred position she occupies in all human life and growth.* It is because of this respect, admiration, and reverence that I am opposed to woman suffrage. *Nature destined woman to be the home maker, the child rearer, while man is the money maker.* The most sacred and potential spot on earth is the fireside shrine. Here the child receives its morals, its religion, its character; *and over this shrine the devoted mother presides as the reigning sovereign, the uncrowned queen;* but her influence is more powerful, her edicts more important than the acts of all the throned monarchs of earth. *I am unwilling, as a southern man, to force upon her any burden which will distract this loving potentate from her sacred, God-imposed duties.* (Italics added.)

Again, having defined the woman as destined by nature to be the homemaker, having labeled her the "reigning sovereign, the uncrowned queen," and "loving potentate," it became obvious that such a powerful individual, such an influential class needed the right to vote. Also, we have the anomaly of a class of people, females, being designated as queens, potentates, reigning sovereigns, all carrying with them the connotations of competence and intelligence and leadership and at the same time this class being denied a role in political decision making which would benefit from these very characteristics.

One legislator from Texas, Congressman Martin Dies, revealed not only his sexist attitudes but also his racist views when he stated in the House of Representatives on January 12, 1915:

> I am opposed to it [women's suffrage] because it would thrust the ballot into the hands of millions of ignorant negro women of the South and force unsought political burdens upon millions of home

> makers throughout the land who are at present more profitably
> employed than in running after politics. I still adhere to the old-
> fashioned belief that the hand that rocks the cradle wields a better
> and a stronger influence upon the Nation than the hand that writes
> the ballot. ... *A nation that has good mothers to mold the boys will
> never want for good men to make the ballots. I wish to speak against
> this amendment on behalf of the millions of American mothers who are
> detained at home on more important business. No doubt some of these
> absent mothers are busy extracting splinters from the toes of future
> Congressmen, hearing the lessons of future supreme court judges,
> boxing the ears of future generals, buttering the bread for future
> Senators, or soothing with a lullaby the injured feelings of future
> Presidents.* (Italics added.)

It is not clear at all why "queens," "potentates," and "reigning
sovereigns" should be bothered with such common chores as taking
out splinters, boxing the ears of future generals, and buttering
bread; further, it is not clear who is taking care of all those little
girls while mothers are concentrating their attention and care on
the little boys who are to be the future judges, senators, and
presidents. The future motherly "potentates" and "queens" apparently can take care of themselves as little girls, buttering their
own bread, taking out their own splinters.

After telling his fellow legislators that God "gave strength and
courage to man and upon woman He bestowed grace and beauty,"
Congressman Dies informed them that *to man God "gave strong
reasoning powers and a keen sense of justice; to woman He gave
unfailing intuition and kindly sympathies."* (Italics added.) Then
the Congressman from Texas brought the House down with
laughter:

> I have no doubt that if women handled the cleaver at the beef stalls
> we would get cleaner steaks; but what man wants to court a butcher?
> [Laughter] No doubt women would make excellent peace officers;
> but what man wants to marry a policeman? [Laughter] It may be
> that the entrance of pure women into dirty politics would have a
> cleansing effect upon the politics, but I can not believe that it would
> have that effect upon the women. And in a case of that kind we had
> better have soiled linen than soiled laundresses.

Through some odd transformation the "undisputed dictator of
man" has become the "soiled laundress." Congressman Stanley
Bowdle of Ohio was interrupted with applause again and again
during his speech in the House of Representatives on January 12,

1915, when he spoke against granting the vote to women. After speaking against women's suffrage he followed with a condemnation of the idea of women being jurors or judges. In fact, according to Mr. Bowdle, women on trial would prefer to be judged by men: "I was saying a moment ago that the women who are opposed to suffrage oppose it because of the necessary change of status that will ensue to them. It ought to be apparent to any man that the power to create institutions implies the power to manage them. *Now, women do not wish their rights to be passed upon by women. Women uniformly prefer men judges and men jurors. What woman in a criminal case would take a woman jury? They know the leniency of men.*" (Italics added.)

The pregnant woman simply was not the type of person to act as a judge or juror, according to Bowdle:

> Mr. Speaker, *the functions of women are of a character that disqualifies them from acting as jurors or judges. If I were to defend a man on a capital charge and a woman were to offer herself as a juror, there are some very intimate questions that I should insist on putting to her. And that man or woman does not live who would submit his or her personal or property rights to a judge or juror who was with child. Her condition at such a time rendered her peculiarly sacred under Roman law and under our law.* (Italics added.)

Congressman Bowdle saw the man as king and the woman as queen, but their domains were significantly different: "*Women— have they a mission? Yes; it is to rule in the world of love and affection—in the home. It is not to rule in the State. They have a function to perform which precludes the latter sort of rule. Man is king of this universe; woman is queen. The queen rules when the king is dead, or becomes a mollycoddle, and the American man is not that yet, [Applause.]*" (Italics added.)

These definitions of women, used to deny them the right to vote until 1920, continued to be used in the second half of the twentieth century to exclude women from juries. In 1959, the Florida Supreme Court upheld Florida's statute providing that while jurors are to be taken from male and female electors, "the name of no female person shall be taken for jury service unless said person has registered with the clerk of the circuit court her desire to be placed on the jury list," the effect being largely all male juries. The Florida court stated that

> *whatever changes may have taken place in the political or economic*
> *status of women in our society, nothing has yet altered the fact of their*
> *primary responsibility, as a class, for the daily welfare of the family*
> *unit upon which our civilization depends.* The statute, in effect,
> simply recognizes that the traditional exclusion was based not upon
> inherent disability or incapacity but upon the premise that such
> demands might place an unwarranted strain upon the social and
> domestic structure, or result in unwilling participation by those
> whose conflicting duties, while not amounting to actual hardship,
> might yet be expected, as a general rule, to affect the quality of their
> service as jurors. (*Hoyt v. State*, 1959. Italics added.)

Because of this system of jury selection, Gwendolyn Hoyt, who
had killed her husband during a period of prolonged marital dis-
cord and alleged infidelities on his part, was tried and found guilty
of second degree murder by an all-male jury. She appealed to the
United States Supreme Court.

In its brief presented to the highest court in the land, the state of
Florida argued that whatever changes may have taken place in our
society, the woman's place was still in the home:

> Ever since the dawn of time conception has been the same. Though
> many eons may have passed, the gestation period in the human
> female has likewise remained unchanged. Save and except for a
> number of beneficial precautions presently available, parturition is
> as it well may have been in the Garden of Eden. *The rearing of*
> *children, even if it be conceded that the socio-psychologists have made*
> *inroads thereon, nevertheless remains a prime responsibility of the*
> *matriarch. The home, though it no longer be the log cabin in the*
> *wilderness, must nevertheless be maintained. The advent of "T.V."*
> *dinners does not remove the burden of providing palatable food for the*
> *members of the family, the husband is still, in the main, the bread-*
> *winner, child's hurts are almost without exception, bound and treated*
> *by the mother.* (Italics added.)

It was precisely this same argument which was used a half century
earlier to deny suffrage to women.

The United States Supreme Court found against Gwendolyn
Hoyt in 1961, the high court stating that

> despite the enlightened emancipation of women from the restric-
> tions and protections of bygone years, and their entry into many
> parts of community life formerly considered to be reserved for men,
> *woman is still regarded as the center of home and family life.* We
> cannot say that it is constitutionally impermissible for a State,
> acting in pursuit of the general welfare, to conclude that a woman

should be relieved from the civic duty of jury service unless she herself determines that such service is consistent with her own special responsibilities.

In 1966, the Mississippi Supreme Court in upholding a statute which excluded women from jury duty declared in *State v. Hall* that *"the legislature has the right to exclude women so they may continue their service as mothers, wives, and homemakers, and also to protect them (in some areas, they are still upon a pedestal) from the filth, obscenity, and noxious atmosphere that so often pervades a court-room during a jury trial."* (Italics added.)

A woman who unsuccessfully challenged in 1970 New York's statute permitting women to claim exemption from jury service argued that while the population of New York was about evenly divided between men and women, only about twenty percent of the women were available for possible jury service. In the words of Justice George Starke, "the bone of her contention is that if less women were exempted, more would serve, and she would thus have a jury of her own peers." In finding against Maria DeKosenko, Starke wrote an opinion which was sexist in the extreme. Said Starke:

> Her plea is indeed strange. What woman would want to expose herself to the peering eyes of women only? But it is not novel. For we learn from Blackstone's *Commentaries* that "when a widow feigns herself with child, in order to exclude the next heir, and a suppositious birth is suspected to be intended; then upon the writ de ventre inspiciendo (of inspecting pregnancy), a jury of women is to be impaneled to try the question, whether with child or not.

Plaintiff's entreaty is, from her viewpoint, rather modest. She does not ask for a female judge. Although that we have. She does not request female court attendants. That too, we have. She does not seek to declare the Declaration of Independence unconstitutional because it prescribed that only "all men are created equal." All she wants is a "jury of her peers," emblazoned as if it came straight out of the Magna Charta. . . .

Following this sarcasm, Justice Starke declared that "this court agrees wholeheartedly with the Attorney General's statement: 'Plaintiff desires to have the Court declare that women are no different from men. To this, the Legislature has said 'Vive la difference.' It was declared that women should not be subjected to jury duty against their will.'"

Judge Starke's concluding paragraph can only be described as blatant sexist language: "Plaintiff is in the wrong forum. Her lament should be addressed to the 'Nineteenth Amendment State of Womanhood' which prefers cleaning and cooking, rearing of children and television soap operas, bridge and canasta, the beauty parlor and shopping, to becoming embroiled in plaintiff's problems with her landlord."

John Johnston, Jr. and Charles Knapp said of Starke's 1970 opinion: "In *DeKosenko v. Brandt*, plaintiff, a female tenant suing her landlord, also challenged New York jury law on constitutional grounds, claiming that it would deprive her of a fair jury. Her claim was denied by the New York County Supreme Court in an opinion defective in so many different ways that no description here could possibly do it justice." (*New York University Law Review*, October 1971) After observing that any statute automatically exempting black persons or all white persons from jury service would be held unconstitutional, Johnston and Knapp state:

> Is a blanket exemption for all females any more justifiable? Granted that many females have work or child care responsibilities (or health disabilities) which might justify excusing them from service, it is difficult to imagine any excuse ... which could not also be advanced by a man similarly situated. How then is it possible to maintain that an exemption for every woman—including even the childless, single woman, and the working wife or mother—is not an arbitrary discrimination when based solely on her sex? Such a scheme, we submit, is based—and court opinions right up to the present day support our contention—on an additional assumption: that women are delicate creatures to be encouraged to stay at home and be protected from the hard, cruel world—and incidentally, as long as they *are* at home, to do the cooking, mending and ironing for those of us who do have the affairs of the world to attend to.

In a 1970 case, *Reed v. Reed*, in which a woman challenged Idaho's statute that stipulated males must be preferred to females in the administration of the estate of a person dying intestate (having made no will), the Idaho Supreme Court found the statute constitutional; the court declared:

> Philosophically it can be argued with some degree of logic that the provisions of I.C. 15-314 do discriminate against women on the basis of sex. *However, nature itself has established the distinction and this statute is not designed to discriminate, but is only designed to alleviate the problem of holding hearings by the court to determine*

eligibility to administer.... The legislature when it enacted this statute evidently concluded that in general men are better qualified to act as an administrator than are women. (Italics added.)

When Sally Reed appealed to the United States Supreme Court, the attorneys for Cecil Reed asserted in their brief presented to the highest court in the land:

The legislators in enacting the statute in question knew that men were as a rule more conversant with business affairs than were women. Appellant argues that the activities of women have changed, however, *one has but to look around and it is a matter of common knowledge, that women still are not engaged in politics, the professions, business or industry to the extent that men are....*
The Idaho Supreme Court observed there are differences in the sexes created by nature. Much of the criticism of appellant along such lines as classifying women with children and treating them as such may be a misinterpretation of the reasons. *We find in all species that nature protects the female and the offspring to propagate the species and not because the female is inferior. The pill and the conception of children in a laboratory and incubation in a test tube, if this occurs, and their rearing in nurseries and children's homes cannot get away from this prime necessity if the race is to be continued, and there will still remain a difference and necessity for a different treatment.* (Italics added.)

The language of sexism which imposes on the woman the label "wife and mother" has been used, and still is being used, to deny her the legal and political rights and duties enjoyed by men. No statutes exist which exempt or exclude husbands and fathers (as a class) from jury duty; the obligations and responsibilities of being a good husband and father have never been seriously used in any arguments against granting males the right to vote. The "wife and mother" label has circumscribed the woman's participation in the legal and political process, a circumscription which has not existed for husband and father.

Women as Infants

Legally and politically identifying women with children has been one means of infantilizing the woman, thus placing her in a dependent, subservient, and inferior position to men. The contradiction between legislators labeling her "potentate," "queen," and "dictator" and then identifying her with children and incompetents would seem so obvious as to be avoided. But there it is. Like children, women have been unable to make contracts; like children, women have been kept out of taverns; like children, women have been protected from obscene speech. If a class of adults are identified enough times with children, patterns of thinking about those adults are developed which infantilize them.

The statutes passed by legislators and the opinions of some judges have placed women and children into that class of persons who shall be protected from types of speech which men are allowed to hear. Like children, women must be protected from the vulgarities and obscenities of life and literature. North Dakota's legislature has passed legislation which reads: *"Any person who shall utter or speak any obscene or lascivious language or words in any public place or in the presence of females, or of children under ten years of age . . . is guilty of a misdemeanor."* (Italics added.)

New Jersey's Statutes Annotated includes legislation reading: *"Any person who, willfully and wantonly sends or conveys to any female an indecent, obscene or lascivious letter or communication is guilty of a misdemeanor."* Arizona's Revised Statutes also identifies women with children in attempts to protect the two groups from obscene language: *"A person who, in the presence or hearing of any woman or child, or in a public place, uses vulgar, abusive or obscene language, is guilty of a misdemeanor."* (Italics added.)

In effect, such statutes are saying that women are incapable of handling the rough and tumble language of everyday life. Like children, their ears should never hear the language men may speak, the powerful language of obscenity and abusiveness. Being innocent, chaste and pure, children and women run the risk of losing their innocence by hearing such language. While the woman as a chaste being and laws forbidding the slander of females are part of Maryland's Annotated Code, no similar legislation appears protecting the reputation of men's chastity. The Maryland Code reads: *"All words spoken falsely and maliciously touching the character or reputation for chastity of any woman, whether single or married, and tending to the injury thereof shall be deemed slander, and shall be treated as such in the several courts of law in this State."* (Italics added.)

The state code of Alabama provides that " . . . *any person who in the presence or hearing of any girl or woman, uses abusive, insulting, or obscene language* shall, on conviction, be fined not more than two hundred dollars, and may also be imprisoned in the county jail, or sentenced to hard labor for the county for not more than six months." (Italics added.) In *Jordan v. State*, the Court of Appeals of Alabama upheld in 1915 the conviction of one Mr. Jordan for uttering in front of his wife and mother-in-law the words "Yes, I pay for my liquor, and I will drink it when I damn please," the words being made in response to a remark made by his father-in-law, "You have been drinking again." In its opinion the Alabama court declared: "The evidence on the part of the state tended to show that this language was used by the defendant while intoxicated, in his own home, and in the immediate presence and hearing of the defendant's wife and mother-in-law, Mrs. Pitts. The intentional use of abusive, insulting, or obscene language in the presence or hearing of any girl or woman is a violation" of the Alabama statute. The court further stated that "if the language is intentionally used, it is immaterial that it was used in ordinary conversation, without intention that it should be heard by the girl or woman. The fact that the defendant was in his own house did not license him to use prohibited language, as the defendant's wife and mother-in-law were within the protection of the statute."

In 1948, the Supreme Court of Alabama decided in *Price v. McConnell* that the arrest of Gertrude Price was justified and she was not unlawfully arrested for stating, during an argument with her husband, in a cafe where women were present, "I'm going to Tuscaloosa and get me a damn job and you can take the baby." The high court of Alabama observed that "no complaint was made as to her conduct by the proprietress of the cafe or by anyone else present. It does not appear that any female heard her use the word 'damn.' But the evidence shows that women were present at the time the defendant [arresting police officer] claims she used that word in the cafe." Whether a girl or woman actually heard the word "damn" was not important, according to the court, for "to constitute a violation of such provision it is not necessary to show that a female heard the language used. It is the fact of presence, subject to insult if the language is heard, which is the essence of the offense."

When a California court upheld in 1969 the conviction of a young man in *People v. Cohen* for wearing in public a jacket, on the back of which were written the words "Fuck the Draft," it argued that the prohibition was needed, in part, to protect women and children:

> The gravamen of the defendant's offense was his selection of the public corridors of the county courthouse as the place *to parade before women and children who were involuntarily subjected to*

unprintable language. The expression used by the defendant to propagate his views is one of the most notorious four-letter words in the English language. Despite its ancient origins, it has yet to gain sufficient acceptance to appear in any standard dictionary. . . .

The defendant has not been subjected to prosecution for expressing his political views. His right to speak out against the draft and war is protected by the First Amendment. However, no one has the right to express his views by means of printing lewd and vulgar language which is likely to cause others to breach the peace *to protect women and children from such exposure*. (Italics added.)

Cohen appealed, and in 1971 the United States Supreme Court reversed the California court's decision; Justice John M. Harlan, writing for the majority in *Cohen v. California*, stated that this was not an obscenity case: "Whatever else may be necessary to give rise to the States' broader power to prohibit obscene expression, such expression must be, in some significant way, erotic. . . . It cannot plausibly be maintained that this vulgar allusion to the Selective Service System would conjure up such psychic stimulation in anyone likely to be confronted with Cohen's crudely defaced jacket." After asserting that "the state has no right to cleanse public debate to the point where it is grammatically palatable to the most squeamish among us," Justice Harlan said that "while the particular four-letter word being litigated here is perhaps more distasteful than most others of its genre, it is nevertheless often true that one man's vulgarity is another's lyric."

One of the dissenting Justices in *Cohen* was Chief Justice Warren Burger, who in another obscenity case spoke out against allowing speakers to use "foul mouthings" at meetings attended by men, women, and children. In *Rosenfeld v. New Jersey*, Chief Justice Burger, referring to a public meeting at which a speaker had used the term "motherfucker," declared in 1972 that "civilized people attending such a meeting with wives and children would not likely have an instantaneous, violent response, but it does not unduly tax the imagination to think that some justifiably outraged parent whose family were exposed to the foul mouthings of the speaker would 'meet him outside' and either alone or with others, resort to the nineteenth century's vigorous modes of dealing with such people." Having decided that women and children are to be protected from such language, the Chief Justice then suggests that the males might take it upon themselves to beat up the speaker, a violence which apparently would not take place if only men were present at the meeting. Like the California court in *Cohen*, the Chief

Justice of the United States Supreme Court expressed concern that the use of such "foul mouthings" would lead to breach of the peace by men who want to "protect women and children from such exposure" to "obscene" language.

The legal prohibition against using obscene and abusive speech in the presence of women and children is a further indication that women are not permitted to participate in this "man's world." The law allows strong language to be uttered by men in the presence of men, but prohibits it in the presence of women, the effect being to reinforce the stereotype of women as weak and fragile, like children.

Robin Lakoff, in *Language and Woman's Place*, deals with the social taboos against women using strong expletives to express themselves, and what Lakoff says about such social taboos explains also why women are prohibited from hearing "obscene" speech:

> Allowing men stronger means of expression than are open to women further reinforces men's position of strength in the real world: for surely we listen with more attention the more strongly and force-fully someone expresses opinions, and a speaker unable—for what-ever reason—to be forceful in stating his views is much less likely to be taken seriously. Abilities to use strong particles like "shit" and "hell" is, of course, only incidental to the inequity that exists rather than its cause. But once again, apparently accidental linguistic usage suggests that women are denied equality partially for linguistic reasons, and that an examination of language points up precisely an area in which inequality exists.

To be able to utter or to listen to obscene or abusive speech is often a release from frustrations and deprivations, as Ashley Montagu has suggested in *The Anatomy of Swearing*. A child is not allowed to swear in a frustrating situation; the child may cry. Montagu presents the following from a *Punch* cartoon to exemplify the point:

> Old Lady: Why are you crying, little boy?
> Little Boy: Because I bea'nt old enough to swear.

The child cannot participate in the adult, male adult, activity of swearing; the child cannot use vulgar language as a speaker and by law is to be protected from hearing obscene speech. Like the child, the adult woman has been socially prohibited from expressing herself in language which is allowed of men; like the child, the adult woman has been legally prohibited from hearing language which men are free to listen to. Like the child, the woman may cry. In a "man's world" participating in abusive and obscene talk, as speaker or listener, has been reserved for men.

Not only have women been placed in the same class as children in obscenity legislation and court opinions, but also in statutes and cases dealing with liquor control and contracts. Further, women have not only been placed in the same category with children, but also with the insane, slaves, and drunkards. The United States Court of Appeals, Fifth Circuit, deciding in *United States v. Yazell* in 1964 that married women are protected by coverture from personal liability upon a contract, declared: "This is a simple case of trying to hold a married woman liable on a contract which under the law of Texas she was incapable of making, and the claim is no more reasonable than to hold that a minor, or one of unsound mind, could be held liable on a contract despite his disability merely because the United States was a party to it." Like minors and people of unsound mind, women in Texas were incapable of making a contract.

Many turn-of-the-century court opinions placed women and children into the same class when it came to matters related to liquor consumption or entering a tavern. Representative of such infantilizing of women was the 1906 Kentucky Court of Appeals opinion in *Commonwealth v. Price* which declared: "*It shall be unlawful for any infant or female to go into or be in or drink intoxicating liquors in any saloon or place for sale of such liquors.* ...*" In 1902, a Colorado court upholding a conviction of a Denver saloon keeper who had admitted women into his wine room said in *Adams v. Cronin* that "the laws of many states prohibit the sale of intoxicating liquors to *Indians, minors, habitual drunkards and other classes of people, and in many of the Southern states before the Civil War sales to slaves and free Negroes were forbidden.*" (Italics added.)

This comparison of the status of women, children, and slaves was referred to by Gunnar Myrdal in his classic work *An American Dilemma*. Myrdal said in his now famous Appendix Five:

> In the earlier common law, women and children were placed under the jurisdiction of the paternal power. When a legal status had to be found for the imported Negro servants in the seventeenth century, the nearest and most natural analogy was the status of women and children. The ninth commandment—linking together women, servants, mules, and other property—could be invoked, as well as a great number of other passages of Holy Scripture. We do not intend to follow here the interesting developments of the

institution of slavery in America through the centuries, but merely
wish to point out the paternalistic idea which held the slave to be a
sort of family member and in some way—in spite of all differences—
placed them beside women and children under the power of the
paterfamilias.

Once the status of women was identified in legislation and court
opinions with that of children (and slaves and the insane), denying
the female the rights and duties expected by and from a male
became not only easier but apparently logical and legal. It was a
simple matter of definition, and the person who had the power to
define controlled the destiny of those being defined.

The Immorality of Women

While the woman has been and is portrayed as "mother and
wife," the "potentate" of the home, as an infant who needs to be
protected, we have the anomaly of the female also labeled the
seducer, the temptress who by legislative and judicial actions must
be controlled. When it was necessary to argue against granting her
the right to vote or to participate in jury duty, the males defined the
females as motherly, pure, and innocent. When it was necessary to
argue against permitting the female to participate in other domains of men's lives, the males defined her as immoral, unchaste,
and wicked.

The woman as the carrier of sin and evil was portrayed as such
especially in turn of the century court decisions dealing with
women as employees in taverns and the nonadmittance of women
and children to liquor establishments. In 1902, the Colorado
Supreme Court said in *Adams v. Cronin,* upholding a Denver
ordinance which prohibited women from patronizing "wine rooms":
"If a discrimination is made against women solely on account of
their sex, it would not be good; *but if it is because of the immorality
that would be likely to result if the regulation was not made, the
regulation would be sustained. That injury to public morality would
ensue if women were permitted without restrictions to frequent wine
rooms, there to be supplied with liquor, is so apparent to the average
person that argument to establish so plain a proposition is unnecessary.*" (Italics added.) Keeping the females out of the taverns
would apparently keep away immorality; the implication was that
with the women came the sin, a definition and perception of woman
with religious groundings.

The label of "immorality" was used in another 1902 decision
which upheld a Hoboken, New Jersey statute which prohibited
females from working in any "public place where intoxicating
liquor is sold." The Supreme Court of New Jersey said in *Mayor,
Etc. of City of Hoboken v. Goodman*: "Women may, constitutionally,
be barred from occupations that are subject to license.... The
supposed evil aimed at is the employment of women in connection
with a traffic likely to induce vice and immorality."

This portrayal of women as the bearers of sin prevailed for
decades after these decisions. In 1971, when the California statute
prohibiting women to work as bartenders was challenged, the
Attorney General of California argued that the statute was there to
protect women, since fewer women can be injured by drunken
customers if females are not permitted to work behind a bar; but he
also argued that the statute was intended to prevent improprieties
and immoral acts. In ruling the statute unconstitutional, the
California Supreme Court said in *Sail'er Inn, Inc. v. Kirby* that it
"in no way prevents the Legislature from dealing effectively with
the evils and dangers inherent in selling and serving alcoholic
beverages; it merely precludes resort to legislation against women
rather than against the particular evil sought to be curbed."

To the Attorney General's contention that women bartenders
would be an "unwholesome influence" on the public, the California
Supreme Court replied: "The objection appears to be based upon
notions of what is a 'ladylike' or proper pursuit for a woman in our
society rather than any ascertainable evil effects of permitting
women to labor behind those 'permanently affixed fixtures' known
as bars. Such notions cannot justify discrimination against women
in employment."

In asserting that sex is a suspect classification, the high court of
California declared:

> Sex, like race and lineage, is an immutable trait, a status into which
> the class members are locked by the accident of birth. What
> differentiates sex from nonsuspect statuses, such as intelligence or
> physical disability, and aligns it with the recognized suspect
> classifications is that the characteristic frequently bears no relation
> to ability to perform or contribute to society.... The result is that the
> whole class is relegated to an inferior legal status without regard to
> the capabilities or characteristics of its individual members....
> Where the relation between characteristic and the evil to be
> prevented is so tenuous, courts must look closely at classifications
> based on that characteristic lest outdated social stereotypes result in
> invidious law or practices.

Another characteristic which underlies all suspect classifications is the stigma of inferiority and second class citizenship associated with them.... Women, like Negroes, aliens, and the poor have historically labored under severe legal and social disabilities. Like black citizens, they were for many years denied the right to vote and, until recently, the right to serve on juries in many states. They are excluded from or discriminated against in employment and educational opportunities. Married women in particular have been treated as inferior persons in numerous laws related to property and independent business ownership and the right to make contracts.

The California Supreme Court, in its opinion, recognized the "protection" of women for what it really is, by stating: "Laws which disable women from full participation in the political, business and economic arenas are often characterized as 'protective' and beneficial. Those same laws applied to racial or ethnic minorities would readily be recognized as invidious and impermissible. The pedestal upon which women have been placed has all too often, upon closer inspection, been revealed as a cage."

Historically, language of sexism—the defining and labeling of all women as infantile, incompetent, immoral, mothers and wives—caged the females who, if treated as individuals, would have been free to demonstrate their intelligence and abilities. But they have also been trapped by the sexist language of the legislators and judges into whose hands has been placed the power to legally define women and their place in society.

The Woman as a Nonperson

The Mississippi Code, in its General Provisions, states that when the words "he" or "him" are used in the Code it includes both males and females: "The masculine to embrace the feminine. Words in the masculine gender shall embrace a female as well as a male, unless a contrary intention may be manifest." Illinois statutes provide that "words importing the masculine gender may be applied to females." As if it were not harmful enough to sanction the use of the generic "he" in nonlegal discourse, we have here (and in the statutes of other states) the institutionalizing of the language of sexism. The evil of using masculine pronouns to include women has been observed by people concerned about how language has been used to perpetuate sexism, including Lynne T. White, former president of Mills College:

> The grammar of English dictates that when a referent is either of
> indeterminate sex or both sexes, it shall be considered masculine.
> The penetration of this habit of language into the minds of little girls
> as they grow up to be women is more profound than most people,
> including most women, have recognized: it implies that personality
> is really a male attribute, and that women are human sub-
> species. . . . It would be a miracle if a girl-baby, learning to use the
> symbols of our tongue, could escape some wound to her self-respect;
> whereas a boy-baby's ego is bolstered by the pattern of our language.

What the legislators have done by legislating "he" to include
females is to institutionalize this concept of woman as a human
subspecies.

There have even been debates in the courts as to whether a
woman is a "person." In the case of *Minor v. Happersett*, the United
States Supreme Court, deciding in 1874 that it was constitutional
for Missouri to deny Mrs. Virginia Minor ("a native born, free,
white citizen of the United States, and of the State of Missouri, over
the age of twenty-one years, wishing to vote for electors for
President and Vice-President of the United States, and for a
representative in Congress, and other offices") the right to register
to vote, spent much time in its opinion trying to decide whether Mrs.
Minor was a "person." The high court granted that "women and
children" are "persons," for they are (among other things) "counted
in the enumeration upon which the apportionment is to be made."
The Court argued, however, that being a "person" under the
Fourteenth Amendment did not mean that women had the right to
vote, as men did. In deciding that the states could deny suffrage to
women, the Supreme Court declared in its final paragraph: "Being
unanimously of the opinion that the Constitution of the United
States does not confer the right of suffrage upon any one, and that
the constitutions and laws of the several States which commit that
important trust to men alone are not necessarily void, we affirm the
judgment."

In upholding the Virginia Supreme Court of Appeals' decision
that Belva Lockwood not be admitted to practice law in that
particular court even though she had been a member of the bar of
the United States Supreme Court and of the Supreme Court of the
District of Columbia, the highest court in the land in 1893 dealt with
Virginia's statute, which stated that "any person duly authorized
and practising as counsel or attorney at law in any State or
Territory of the United States, or in the District of Columbia, may

practise as such in the courts of this State." The Virginia court had decided that Mrs. Lockwood was not a "person" within the meaning of the statute, for males were the only "persons" intended to be included in that term. The United States Supreme Court concluded in *In re Lockwood* that "it was for the Supreme Court of Appeals to construe the statute of Virginia in question, and to determine whether the word 'person' as therein used is confined to males, and whether women are admitted to practise law in that Commonwealth." The result: Mrs. Lockwood was not a "person" and hence could not practise law before the Virginia court.

In 1931 the Supreme Judicial Court of Massachusetts, Suffolk, was faced with deciding whether a woman was a "person" as the term was used in the Massachusetts statute which read: "A person qualified to vote for representatives to the general courts shall be liable to serve as a juror." While the court agreed that in the general sense "person" did include women and that the word "by itself is an equivocal word," it finally decided in *Commonwealth v. Welosky* that "by the true construction of the statutes of this commonwealth, in the light of relevant constitutional provisions, women are not eligible to jury service and that the preparation of the jury lists from which the jury in the case at bar were drawn from men alone was right."

In addition to being designated "he" by legislators and labeled not a "person" by some courts, the invisibility and nonexistence of the woman has been compounded by her identity being integrated, upon marriage, with that of her husband. As Blackstone wrote: " ... the very being or legal existence of woman is suspended during the marriage.... " One manifestation of suspending that legal existence was and is the practice of the wife's giving up her maiden name and taking on the husband's surname. Forcing this name change has a detrimental effect on women, as Leo Kanowitz has pointed out in his *Women and the Law:* "The probable effects of this unilateral name change upon the relations between the sexes, though subtle in character, are profound. In a very real sense the loss of a woman's surname represents the destruction of an important part of her personality." Joyce Hertzler has also seen the implications of this name change: "A name carries with it certain evaluations made by the named one himself, as well as the evaluations of others regarding him. A change of name invariably means some change in these evaluations.... When a woman takes her husband's name upon marrying him, she undergoes certain transformations of ego, as well as leaving the circle of her original family and assuming the status of married woman, as her new name shows.

On various occasions, the courts have held that under certain circumstances the woman is required by law to use her married name, that she cannot use her maiden name even if she wanted to make that choice. In 1934 a New York District Court decided in *In re Kayaloff* that Anna Mersliakoff, a musician professionally known by her maiden name Anna Kayaloff, could not have her naturalization certificate issued to her in her maiden name, even though she feared "that possibly she will suffer financial loss should her naturalization certificate show her surname to be that of her husband. Also, a discrepancy between her musical union card and her naturalization certificate would thus come into existence." In deciding against her, Judge Knox argued:

> The union card should conform to the naturalization certificate rather than that the latter should yield to the union card. Further-more, as all are well aware, many professional women of note and standing, and who are married, are known in private life by the surname of their respective husbands. In the artistic circles in which such women move, they are known by their stage or professional names. It is my judgment that none of them has been damaged professionally by the fact that, upon marriage, she took the surname of her husband. I am not convinced that any loss will accrue to petitioner if she be denied a certificate in her maiden name.

The judge concluded that if she "wishes naturalization, the certificate must issue in the surname of her husband."

An Appellate Court of Illinois ruled in 1945 that a woman could not register to vote or vote under her maiden name. Antonia E. Rago, a member of the Illinois bar, who was listed under her maiden name in Gunthorp's legal directory of Chicago and in the Martindale-Hubbel *Law Directory*, who for more than six years had her own law office in Chicago under the name of Antonia E. Rago, married William MacFarland on February 12, 1944 and with his approval continued her practice of law under her maiden name. She wanted to remain registered as an elector and wanted to vote under her maiden name also, but the Board of Election Commissioners of Chicago ordered cancellation of her registration; she was told she would have to re-register under her married name.

The Appellate Court of Illinois in finding against Antonia E. Rago declared in *People v. Lipsky*:

Although petitioner places considerable reliance upon the additional stipulated facts showing that she had for some years practiced her profession under the name of Antonia E. Rago, that she had become commonly and widely known in the neighborhood as an attorney at law under that name as evidenced by a "bronze plaque or professional sign, about 18 inches square, fastened on the front house wall of her home" in Chicago, that she had under her maiden name taken an active part in the political activities of the neighborhood, had been admitted to practice in various courts and had certificates issued to her in that name, and that she would suffer substantial damage in respect to her professional reputation if she were not permitted to vote under her maiden name, in the view we take all these facts are immaterial and irrelevant to any of the issues in this cause and have no bearing whatever upon the duty of the plaintiff to register anew in accordance with the statute in order to preserve her right to vote as a registered and qualified elector in this state.

In September 1972, the Attorney General of Connecticut ruled that a married woman must use her husband's surname when she registers to vote. In 1972 the United States Supreme Court upheld the decision of a lower court which had found lawful Alabama's unwritten regulation requiring female driver's license applicants to use their husband's surname and Alabama's common law rule that the husband's surname is the wife's legal name.

Wendy Forbush had challenged the unwritten regulation, and as the United States District Court put it in *Forbush v. Wallace*: "The thrust of the complaint is that the refusal of the Department [of Public Safety] to issue plaintiff Forbush a driver's license in her maiden name because she is married is a denial of equal protection as guaranteed by the Fourteenth Amendment to the United States Constitution. Also under attack is Alabama's common law rule that the husband's surname is the wife's legal name.

In finding against Forbush, the lower court used a balancing test, balancing the state's interest in maintaining its rules regarding issuance of drivers' licenses and Forbush's interest in having her license issued in her maiden name:

In balancing the interest of the plaintiff and the members of plaintiff's class against the interest of the state, this Court concludes that the administrative inconvenience and cost of a change to the State of Alabama far outweigh the harm caused the plaintiff and the members of plaintiff's class. In balancing these interests, this Court notes that the State of Alabama has afforded a simple, inexpensive means by which any person, and this includes married women, can on application to a probate court change his or her name.

The court concluded that "the existing law of Alabama which requires a woman to assume her husband's surname upon marriage has a rational basis and seeks to control an area where the state has a legitimate interest." The United States Supreme Court agreed. Two hundred years after Blackstone, the married woman's identity through her name was still submerged into that of her husband's.

Conclusion

The woman's search for self-identity has been seriously hampered by a legal system which designates her a "he," debates whether she is a "person," and requires her in a variety of ways to depend on her husband's surname for recognition and identification. Like institutionalized racism, institutionalized sexism is difficult to root out, especially if the language of sexism is perpetuated by the judicial and legislative institutions in our society. While the woman may be able to deal with the day-to-day expressions of sexism, she will find more frustrations dealing with societal institutions which have pigeonholed her with labels and definitions relegating her to an inferior position, to a second class status. It is one thing to cope with the males in the office who call her "doll" or "toots" or "baby"; it is another thing to get rid of the stereotypes when the courts and legislatures of the land make them a part of their judicial opinions and legislation.

This breaking down of the idea that certain roles are too sissy or too mannish interests me a hell of a lot more than whether a writer uses "he" or "mankind" in a neutral sense.

Billy E. Barnes
writer

As a writer, I use my initials rather than my first name when I submit manuscripts to male editors. Unfortunately, the response is better.

J. (Jennie) Frye
teacher-writer

When I first heard the idea that language was sexist, I tended to feel that the notion was foolish. But after a while, it really dawns upon one that not only are [such expressions] possibly sexist by excluding half the population from the possibility of being, say, a fireperson, but they are not accurately descriptive.

Next the concept broadens, so that one realizes that even when a man addresses an adult female, or talks about her, he uses *girl* rather than *woman* because he actually doesn't accept an adult female as being on the same level as a male, adult or not. It would seem that the only possible result from the sexist speech pattern would be sexism in practice.

Jim Mack
editor

Virtually all *-man* combinations are dead metaphors and no one "sees" a man when the word *chairman* is said [any more] than one sees a forehead when one mentions the *brow* of a hill.

Gerald Trett
editor

To try to rewrite classic statements of the past will be futile, I think. On the other hand consciousness needs to be raised to prevent sexist language and thought in the future.

(name withheld)
editor

Sexism in the Language of Literature

H. Lee Gershuny

The sexist omissions and commissions of the English language, out of necessity, have been the cultural legacy of writers and poets. Their metaphors have echoed the stereotypes and archetypes of western mythology, where the natural world was created and personified by families of gods and goddesses and explored by demigod heroes, but not heroines. Women's roles as writers and heroines in literature were limited to their stereotyped roles as wives and mothers. Heroic figures may have had "a thousand faces," but those that revealed virtues, unfolded quests, and named the world all had the faces of men. By contrast, feminine "faces" and virtues were veiled by language that referred to woman indirectly, or implied her existence within "man."

Myth

Long afterward, Oedipus, old and blinded, walked the
roads.   He smelled a familiar smell.   It was
the Sphinx.   Oedipus said, "I want to ask one question.
Why didn't I recognize my mother?"   "You gave the
wrong answer," said the Sphinx.   "But that was what
made everything possible," said Oedipus.   . "No," she said.
"When I asked, What walks on four legs in the morning,
two at noon, and three in the evening, you answered,
Man.   You didn't say anything about woman."
"When you say Man," said Oedipus, "you include women
too. Everyone knows that."   She said, "That's what
you think."

—Muriel Rukeyser

In Rukeyser's Oedipus "Myth" revisited, the poet not only demonstrates the seriousness of the invisibility of the female gender in "man," but also suggests that language, myth, and literature have etched long-lasting images of male and female roles and have blinded human awareness to the existence of half the human race. In rendering women invisible, the English language has also made them nameless in literature and life. Yet naming, as well as being named, is at the root of creation. In life new beings are born from women's loins, but the father's surname names both male and female infants. The creators of literature, "authors, writers, and poets," are assumed to be male, in English, unless gender markers are added, as in "*woman* writer, and poet*ess*." In fact, the poet's power to conceive, create, name, and dominate is represented by male models who emulate the first Creator, referred to exclusively in masculine words—"God/He"—in Judeo-Christian literature.

The Genesis of "Man"

In Genesis 1 and 2, God, the Creator/Artist, names and divides the universe into heaven and earth, day and night, and land and sea. He also creates and names "man," who inherits His power to name other living creatures and have dominion over them. In Genesis 2, "Adam," the first man, not only names all the living creatures before woman is created, but also names her:

> And out of the ground the Lord formed every beast of the field, and every fowl of the air; and brought them unto Adam to see what he would call them: and whatsoever Adam called every living creature, that was the name thereof (Gen. 2:19).
> And Adam said, This is now bone of my bones, and flesh of my flesh: she shall be called Woman, because she was taken out of Man. (Gen. 2:23; King James Bible, with English revisions by Alexander Harkavy and Hebrew according to the Masoretic Text, Hebrew Publishing Co., New York, 1916. Hereinafter AV)

Woman is defined by man, but not given poetic powers to name their shared world. The naming power goes from God to "Adam"; Woman, not included in the English "Adam," names nothing. But "Man" is suddenly dignified with the proper name, "Adam," once God has endowed him with language-making powers. At this point, his dominion over other living creatures is symbolized in his own specific identity as "Adam." Woman is neither given the dignity of a proper name in Genesis 2, AV, nor the privilege of naming others.

At best, woman shares dominion of the earth with "man" only in the Genesis 1 version:

> And God blessed them, and God said unto them, Be fruitful, and multiply, and replenish the earth, and subdue it: and have dominion over the fish of the sea, and over the fowl of the air, and every living thing that moveth upon the earth (Gen. 1:28).

Genesis 2 not only partially contradicts the sequence of events leading up to the creation of man and woman in Genesis 1 and introduces the specific identification of man as "Adam," but also begins an interesting deviation from the Hebrew of the Masoretic Texts in Genesis 2. Although 'ādām is the Hebrew word for the genus "Man" in both Genesis 1 and 2, the English translation uses the word "man" as an equivalent for the Hebrew 'ādām only in Genesis 1, but in Genesis 2, the English "Adam" is suddenly used as a proper name. At that point, the Hebrew generic is no longer translated into the English generic—"man." In spite of the consistency of Hebrew semantics and morphology, the English translations are not consistent. The Hebrew generic, 'ādām, sometimes meant the English generic, "Man," and other times a specific man, mysteriously named "Adam." The ambiguity in English semantics not only suggests to the reader that "Man" in Genesis 1 is not the same as the specific "Adam" in Genesis 2, but also that an androgynous nature of humanity—that is the male/female duality implied in Genesis 1—is not the same nature as that in Genesis 2, since male and female creation is sequential in the latter as opposed to simultaneous in the former:

> And God said, Let us make man in our image, after our likeness: and let *them* have dominion over the fish of the sea, and over the fowl of the air, and over the cattle, and over all the earth, and over every creeping thing that creepeth upon the earth.
> So God created man in his own image, in the image of God created he him; male and female created he *them* (Gen. 1:26-27. Italics added).

In this context, "man" implies the English generic, with man and woman included, since it is the antecedent of "them." In Genesis 1, they are both made in God's image, at the same time, and both given dominion over other living creatures.

The English translation of Genesis 2 not only contradicts the androgynous nature of humanity implied in Genesis 1, but also anticipates the separate and subordinate position of woman narrated in the expulsion from Eden in Genesis 3. The Genesis 2 and 3 version, however, is the one promoted by the Judeo-Christian religious traditions as well as varied and rehearsed in English language literature. Although Phyllis Bird remarked in "Images of Women in the Old Testament," (In Ruether, *Religion and Sexism,* 1974):

> While the two creation accounts of Genesis differ markedly in language, style, date and traditions employed, their basic statements about woman are essentially the same: woman is along with man, the direct and intentional creation of God and the crown of his creation. Man and Woman were made for each other. Together they constitute humankind, which is in its full and essential nature bisexual (p. 72).

I think her interpretation is more applicable to the Hebrew versions and not the AV, where a distinction is made between "Man" in its generic sense and "man" in its specific and exclusive sense, as "Adam"!

In the *New English Bible* (1970. Hereinafter NEB), the word "man" is used throughout Genesis 1 and 2 and only becomes a specific "man," not yet "Adam," when woman is created from his rib. A note in the text refers to the parallel change in the Hebrew from '*ādām* to *ish*, the Hebrew for specific man. In this translation, man is not identified with the proper name "Adam" until God has pronounced judgment on both, and "man" has named his wife:

> To the woman he said:
> "I will increase your labour and your groaning, and in labour you shall bear children. You shall be eager for your husband, and he shall be your master."
> And to the man he said:
> "Because you have listened to your wife and have eaten from the tree which I forbade you, accursed shall be the ground on your account" (Gen. 3:16-17 NEB).
> The *man* called his wife Eve because she was the mother of all who live. The Lord God made tunics of skins for *Adam* and his wife and clothed them. (Gen. 3:20-21 NEB. Italics added).

As in the AV, "Man" achieves specific identity as "Adam" immediately after he has performed in the image of the masculine God, and named his wife, "Eve"—after God has already given him "dominion" and mastery over her! The changes from "Man" the generic to "Adam" the specific man appear only in English since the Hebrew remains 'ādām throughout Genesis 1-3.

This is not the only place the English translation is misleading. The gender of the Hebrew God, Ĕlōhîm, is not as definitive as English would have us believe. Although the Hebrew word Ĕlōhîm ends with the masculine plural morpheme im, it is translated as the masculine singular "God" in English. In the "Introduction" to the NEB, the Biblical scholars point out that Ĕlōhîm is one of the substitute names for Yahweh, the unspoken sacred name of the Hebrew God of the Old Testament. Nevertheless, the English translators in AV and NEB never note the distortion in the morphology of "God/He"—the English equivalent. The Hebrew, Ĕlōhîm, even as a euphemism, suggests a God of many parts or faces that may either be all masculine, or like the English pronouns they and we, may include both the masculine and feminine. Although Biblical exigesis is not our concern, the distortion of the English translations inherited from the King James Bible is!

Before God creates man in Genesis 1, the Hebrew as well as the English indicates the plurality of God's voice as "And God said, Let us make man . . . " (italics added) as well as the implicit plurality of the genus "Man" (Gen. 1:26-27). The Hebrew language of Genesis 1 suggests that from God, the many, were created both genders— male and female—at the same time. The English, however, suggests that from one masculine "God," who sometimes pluralizes Himself, male and female were created.

In Genesis 2, AV, on the other hand, not only does English morphology deviate from the Hebrew by maintaining the image of a masculine singular "God," but the narrative also deviates from the simultaneous creation of man and woman in Genesis 1 to a sequential one, where a specific man, "Adam," is the first human, and also the sole classifier and symbol-maker.

Secular Literature and the Creator as Male

In short, the ambiguity involved in the biblical story of human creation is partly due to the gender ambiguities inherent in English as the translating medium. The ambiguities of biblical literature in English were continued and developed in secular literature, so that the idea of poetic creation as both masculine and divine has been a consistent part of our literary heritage:

> ...By claiming for the poet the ability to utilize the creative imagination, Coleridge hoped to demonstrate that *the poet*, in effecting a reconciliation of opposite or discordant qualities, in fact *imitates the ongoing work of creation itself*. For Coleridge conceived that the whole universe, both in what he called its "eternal act of creation in the infinite I AM" and in its continuous repetition of that act in the process of synthesizing and recreation by individual minds, consists in the creative resolution of conflict and disparity (Giles B. Gunn, "Introduction," *Literature and Religion* 1971, p. 9. Italics added).

More recently, Northrop Frye expressed a similar understanding of poetic creation:

> ...the work of the imagination presents us with a vision not of the personal greatness of the poet, but of something personal and far greater: the vision of a decisive act of spiritual freedom, *the vision of the recreation of man* (Northrop Frye, *Anatomy of Criticism* [1957], p. 94. Italics added).

The effect has been to either trivialize women writers or render their creation of secular literature a taboo. For such behavior would violate their God-given assignment to procreate in pain rather than recreate themselves and return to Paradise in myth and metaphor. At best, the biblical literature called upon Woman to be a "wise woman" and an inspiration to her husband; the classical poet called upon female Muses for inspiration and direction, but not for poetic language. Even though women have been encouraged to become amateur writers and students of literature and the arts, it is traditionally expected that men will become the professionals. Women writers often adopted men's names or wrote anonymously, not only to gain a fair hearing as artists but also to protect themselves in traditional roles. Women writers who, like Aphra Behn, used their own names ran the risk of being criticized not for their writing but for behaving like the "bad woman." For a woman, to think and write creatively is to unsex herself; for a man, it is transcendence and apotheosis.

> From Sappho to myself, consider
> the fate of women.
> How unwomanly to discuss it!
>> —Carolyn Kizer, from "Pro Femina"

Anais Nin recalls in the first volume of her *Diary* that her struggles with herself as a writer were intricately entwined with her struggles as a woman. Yet her male mentors and friends invariably perceived the opposite and separated her womanness from the masculine creativity of the artist. In one dialogue with Otto Rank, her therapist and teacher, for example, she recorded:

> Then we talked about the realism of women, and Rank said that perhaps that was why women had never been great artists. They invented nothing. It was a man, not a woman, who invented the soul.
>
> I asked Rank whether the artists whose art was a false growth, an artificial excrescence, bearing no relation to their personal truth, insincere artists, were greater than sincere ones. Rank said this was a question which he had not yet answered for himself. "I may have to write a book for you, to answer it," he said.
>
> This statement gave me great pleasure. I said, "That would please me more than if I finished my own novel!"
>
> "There's the woman in you speaking," said Dr. Rank. "When the neurotic woman gets cured, she becomes a woman. When the neurotic man gets cured, he becomes an artist. Let us see whether the woman or the artist will win out. For the moment, you need to become a woman" (p. 291).

The belief that artistic creativity is exclusively masculine and the creativity of child-raising exclusively feminine is so deep that Nin spontaneously subordinated her novel to the work of Rank. In Rank's view, being an artist is antithetical to being a woman. As a healer of souls in the new religion of psychoanalysis, he perpetuated the sex roles inherited from Judeo-Christian stories of human creation. Not only is creation cast as masculine behavior but the struggle of the "neurotic man" to become an artist is made analogous to the biblical hero's struggle to gain dominion over the world as the artist recreating himself in original metaphors.

Metaphors of poetic creation often suggest this kind of spiritual and intellectual "fight" and "wrestling" that is more often personified by a male hero and demonstrated by the male writer. His artistic creation calls for the same kind of religious dedication that a "man" has to his God. Richard P. Blackmur, in discussing "Religious Poetry in the U.S." (*Literature and Religion*, 1971), compares the "Christian struggle" of European poets to join themselves to God with Jacob's "wrestling" dialogue with God:

> I would say rather that it is the great *wrestling* tradition which has inhabited the great majority of religious poets since the Council of Trent, ... The Reformation and the Counter-Reformation alike put upon us the compulsion to a wrestling ...: a wrestling with God, with the self, with conscience, and above all in our latter day with

> our behavior. Pascal stands as a natural monument of one form of
> this wrestling, Baudelaire as another, and Henry James and James
> Joyce as a kind of composite for our day (p. 158. Italics added).

The allusion to Jacob not only confirms the image of the male
artist, but also the poetic process as a serious "wrestling" match
between man, the artist-patriarch, and man, the god:

> And Jacob was left alone; and there wrestled a man with him
> until the breaking of the day.
> And when he saw that he prevailed not against him, he touched
> the hollow of his thigh; and the hollow of Jacob's thigh was out of
> joint, as he wrestled with him.
> And he said, Let me go, for the day breaketh. And he said, I will
> not let thee go, except thou bless me.
> And he said unto him. What is thy name? And he said, Jacob.
> And he said, Thy name shall be called no more Jacob, but Israel:
> for as a prince hast thou power with God and with men, and hast
> prevailed.
> And Jacob asked him, and said, Tell me, I pray thee, thy name.
> And he said, Wherefore is it that thou dost ask after my name? And
> he blessed him there.
> And Jacob called the name of the place Peniel: for I have seen
> God face to face, and my life is preserved (Gen. 32:25-31 AV).

In addition, we have here an echo of the Genesis 2 motif of the
poetic patriarch, whose name is of divine origin and who, in the
image of God, has "dominion" over the world he names. God,
however, has dominion over all, since He names His creatures but
remains the eternal mystery, unnamed by them.

The Greeks personified the divine spiritual power of poetic
lyricism in Orpheus, son of the god Apollo, who not only lulled the
dragon guarding the Golden Fleece to sleep, but also conquered the
Sirens with his songs and charmed Hades into releasing Eurydice,
his wife. Quite naturally, twentieth century male writers, film-
makers, and composers have seen in Orpheus an image of their own
potential and created contemporary variations on the original hero
and his journey. In the English language, we have derived the word
"orphic" to describe an artistic or philosophical statement re-
sembling the kind of music attributed to Orpheus. In myth and
metaphor, English letters has inherited an image of the writer as a
man with supernatural powers, who wrestles with and questions
God, names and divides the world according to his pleasure, and
subdues demons and death with the beauty and charm of his songs.

Woman as Writer: A Dilemma

The woman writer must violate a tradition of religious and literary names and metaphors to discover herself and her own songs. As part of the poetic process, she must also recreate herself into images that are drawn, on the one hand, from her own experience and, on the other, contradict the sex stereotypes she has inherited.

From the language of literature, the inheritance consists of the personification of the phenomenal world into gods and goddesses who duplicated the social stereotypes and biological roles of males and females. English and American literature, from the oral tradition of European mythology and biblical literature to the contemporary poet writing from inherited myths and metaphors, is replete with gender identification of the abstract and phenomenal world. I have space to discuss only a few selections from both extremes—the historically distant and psychologically deep past, the antecedents, and selections from the near present. I chose the following illustrations mainly because they demonstrate sexist tendencies in the language of literature and not as part of a general count of sexism in literature.

A description of Mother Earth, one of the parental antecedents, by the Greek poet Hesiod was translated as:

> Earth, the beautiful rose up,
> Broad bosomed, she that is the steadfast base
> Of all things....
> (Edith Hamilton, *Mythology*, 1942, p. 64).

Not only is the earth female, but her qualities are cast in terms of a woman's physical and sexual attributes. Although Father Heaven sired the children of Mother Earth, he does not give them the complete love and acceptance that Mother Earth does. In these early Greek myths of creation, mother is home with the children while father, objective and removed from mundane matters, rules heaven. Mother Earth has a big enough bosom to love all her children, regardless of their appearance.

In Old Testament literature, the qualities of the primordial Mother Earth are vested in the Jewish Mother, who, as heiress to God's judgment of Eve, "Mother of all living things," must define herself in terms of her sexual relationship to men and must respond

to the desires of her husband and master. Although she is bound by
the Mosaic Code with the rest of the community, she is addressed
only indirectly in its language. Phyllis Bird notes that:

> The majority of the laws, . . . address the community through its
> male members. Thus the key verbal form in the apodictic sentence is
> the second person masculine singular or plural [Hebrew]. That this
> usage was not meant simply as an inclusive form of address for
> bisexual reference is indicated by such formulations as the follow-
> ing:
>
> > Thou shalt not covet thy neighbor's wife . . . (Exod. 20:19).
> >
> > You shall not afflict any widow or orphan.
> > If you do . . . then your wives shall become
> > widows and your children fatherless (Exod. 22:22-24).
> >
> > You shall be men consecrated to me (Exod. 22:31).
> > > (Ruether, *Religion and Sexism*, p. 49).

In the tradition of biblical language and literature, woman is
usually invisible; when mentioned, she is the obedient wife and
daughter of Israel, the nurturing earth-mother of her children. She
achieves honor and dignity—"a woman of valor"—basically as a
wife and mother. After discussing the various roles of Old Testament women as daughters, mothers, wives, a judge, a prophetess, or
a Queen Mother, Bird points out that:

> The primary category to which all these women belong is that of
> wife. It is the comprehensive category that describes the destiny of
> every female in Israel. Yet the image of the wife is an elusive one. As
> wife alone she is all but invisible. . . . Wives figure most prominently
> in the patriarchal narratives, primarily because they are by their
> nature family stories, created and/or employed for the purpose of
> creating a history based upon a genealogical scheme. In these tales
> the wives are seen primarily, though not exclusively, as mothers,
> while daughters appear only as wives—accounting for external
> relations (*Religion and Sexism*, pp. 63-64).

A Jewish woman who did not want to be wife and mother was a
contradiction in terms; this dilemma still plagues identity crises of
modern American Jewish writers. Most notably, both Philip Roth
in *Portnoy's Complaint* and Erica Jong in *Fear of Flying* turned to
the new religion of psychoanalysis to resolve irreconcilable categories of self and other inherited from the traditions of Jewish
culture:

> Somewhere deep inside my head (with all those submerged memories of childhood) is some glorious image of the ideal woman, a kind of Jewish Griselda. She is Ruth and Esther and Jesus and Mary rolled into one. She always turns the other cheek. She is a vehicle, a vessel, with no needs or desires of her own. When her husband beats her, she understands him. When he is sick, she nurses him. When the children are sick, she nurses them. She cooks, keeps house, runs the store, keeps the books, listens to everyone's problems, visits the cemetery, weeds the graves, plants the garden, scrubs the floors, and sits quietly on the upper balcony of the synagogue while the men recite prayers about the inferiority of women. She is capable of absolutely everything except self-preservation. And secretly, I am always ashamed of myself for not being her. A good woman would have given over her life to the care and feeding of her husband's madness. I was not a good woman. I had too many other things to do (*Fear of Flying*, 1973, p. 210).

Isaac Bashevis Singer explored the extremes of irreconcilable sex-role categories in a modern story and play set in the Jewish ghetto of eighteenth century Poland, "Yentl, the Yeshiva Boy." After her father's death, his daughter, Yentl, was left alone.

> ... But Yentl didn't want to get married. Inside her, a voice repeated over and over: "No!" What becomes of a girl when the wedding's over? Right away she starts bearing and rearing. ... Yentl knew she wasn't cut out for a woman's life. She couldn't sew, she couldn't knit. She let the food burn and the milk boil over; her Sabbath pudding never turned out right, and her *challah* dough didn't rise. Yentl much preferred men's activities to women's. Her father Reb Todros ... studied Torah with his daughter as if she were a son. ... She had proved so apt a pupil that her father used to say:
> "Yentl—you have the soul of a man."
> "So why was I born a woman?"
> "Even heaven makes mistakes."
> (*An Isaac Bashevis Singer Reader*, 1971, pp. 135-36)

In effect, Yentl had to unsex herself, assume a masculine name and garb in order to study Hebrew scriptures with the male scholars at the yeshiva. A woman was not meant to question and interpret the "word of God." The philosopher-rabbi, like the poet-artist, was a man who "wrestled" with spiritual matters on high mountains and ladders, while his wife, mother of his children, took charge of mundane domestic rituals: cooking, feeding, sewing, and cleaning. The hierarchical separation of sex roles into higher and lower orders led easily into a moral order of good and bad people. Women, as the daughters of Eve, were "bad" when they seduced and diverted men from spiritual and artistic heights. They were "good" when they inspired men to climb. They had no responsibility for themselves, nor their own creative ambitions beyond child-bearing.

Sexual seductiveness is often linked, along with nurturance, in the personification of Mother Nature and Mother Earth and her numerous manifestations in literary allusions. In the following lines from Thomas Kinsella's poem, "Another September," Autumn, a sensual domestic, is mother of the sleeping, unspeaking woman-daughter, who, after love-making, nurtures lofty themes of Justice and Truth in the male poet:

> Domestic Autumn, like an animal
> Long used to handling by those countrymen,
> Rubs her kind hide against the bedroom wall
> Sensing a fragrant child come back again
> —Not this half-tolerated consciousness
> That plants its grammar in her yielding weather
> But that unspeaking daughter, growing less
> Familiar where we fell asleep together.
>
> Wakeful moth-wings blunder near a chair,
> Toss their light shell at the glass, and go
> To inhabit the living starlight. Stranded hair
> Stirs in the still linen. It is as though
> The black breathing that billows her sleep, her name,
> Drugged under judgment, waned and—bearing daggers
> And balances—down the lampless darkness they came,
> Moving like women: Justice, Truth, such figures.

Although Justice and Truth move "like women," they are shaped by the male imagination from the sexual love metaphors in the language describing the traditional relationship of woman to man—silent, domestic, sensual love partner, and bountiful, mysterious subjectivity. Woman is the moon to his Apollonian consciousness.

The "Brotherhood" of Intellect

Although Kinsella may have personified his own creative unconscious as a female lover-muse, other modern poets have frequently identified their subjective Self with male animals and projected their internal dialogues on to other male, instead of female, figures. William Meredith, "On Falling Asleep to Birdsong," writes,

In a tree at the edge of a clearing
A whippoorwill calls in the dark,
An American forest bird.
Lying in bed I hear him;

In Richard Eberhart's poem, "On a Squirrel Crossing the Road...," almost running over the squirrel inspires the poet to experience "all possible relationships between the small squirrel, myself as a slightly larger animal, and the immense idea of God" (Engle and Langland, eds., *Poet's Choice* [1966], p. 60). All possible relationships, however, are concerned with intellectual and intuitive knowledge of the other, yet each "other" participant in this knowledge is male:

On a Squirrel Crossing the Road in Autumn, in New England

It is what he does not know,
Crossing the road under the elm trees,
About the mechanism of my car,
About the Commonwealth of Massachusetts,
About Mozart, India, Arcturus,

That wins my praise. I engage
At once in whirling squirrel-praise.

He obeys the orders of nature
Without knowing them.
It is what he does not know
That makes him beautiful.
Such a knot of little purposeful nature!

I who can see him as he cannot see himself
Repose in the ignorance that is his blessing.

It is what man does not know of God
Composes the visible poem of the world.
                                    ...Just missed him!

The famous "Heavy Bear Who Goes With Me" of Delmore Schwartz's creative imagination is a male animal shadow of the poet. Again, the natural animal unconscious self duplicates the poet's gender as opposed to complementing it as female.

These few examples suggest that images of man's unconscious animal nature are not expressed as variations of the Mother Nature metaphor unless his relationship and connection with nature is seen as sexual and sensual. Intellectual knowledge of the other self tends to be personified, however, as an all-male dialogue! The personification of living creatures or neutral objects as female seems to have more to do with the poet's extending a metaphor of sensual, sexual interaction with those objects than their inherent female qualities. Needless to say, the poet has license to choose gender metaphors regardless of bias, but awareness of which gender and when and why it is chosen may make the poet more of a language maker than an offspring of language.

As inheritor of the language personifying the universe into traditional sex roles, Elizabeth Bishop, in her poem, "The Man-Moth," also describes *his* behavior in metaphors that are specifically of man (and not of the generic humanity) intellectually exploring the mysterious, passive feminine universe. Yet, the "man-moth" is a mask for the poet, whose language, in the process of imaginative probes, has either changed her mind to include woman in "man" or unsexed herself!

> Here, above
> cracks in the buildings are filled with battered moonlight.
> The whole shadow of Man is only as big as his hat.
> It lies at his feet like a circle for a doll to stand on,
> and he makes an inverted pin, the point magnetized to the moon.
> He does not see the moon; he observes only her vast properties,
> feeling the queer light on his hands, neither warm nor cold,
> of a temperature impossible to record in thermometers.
>
> But when the Man-Moth
> pays his rare, although occasional, visits to the surface,
> the moon looks rather different to him. He emerges
> from an opening under the edge of one of the sidewalks
> and nervously begins to scale the faces of the buildings.
> He thinks the moon is a small hole at the top of the sky,
> proving the sky quite useless for protection.
> He trembles, but must investigate as high as he can climb.

Although most of the natural world is not given specific gender identification in E. E. Cummings' poem eulogizing his father, "My father moved through dooms of love," the moon may represent the invisible, but implicitly present "mother"—

> my father moved through griefs of joy;
> praising a forehead called the moon
> singing desire into begin ...

Spring, however, is more definitely the female response to his father's orphic lyricism and, indirectly, the mother, observed by their children:

> My father moved through theys of we,
> singing each new leaf out of each tree
> (and every child was sure that spring
> danced when she heard my father sing)

In another Cummings poem, the female again is the invisible other—implicitly responding to the male's religious, intellectual, and poetical probes in sexual imagery:

> O sweet spontaneous
> earth how often have
> the
> doting
>
>   fingers of
> prurient philosophers pinched
> and
> poked
>
> thee
> , has the naughty thumb
> of science prodded
> thy
>
>   beauty   . how
> often have religions taken
> thee upon their scraggy knees
> squeezing and
>
> buffeting thee that thou mightest conceive
> gods
>   (but
> true
>
> to the incomparable
> couch of death thy
> rhythmic
> lover
>
>   thou answerest
>
> them only with
>
>   spring)

Just as Mother Earth may renew life in spring and bring forth ripe fruits, so does the same earth, personified as woman, take life in the role of the "femme fatale"; "La Belle Dame Sans Merci," silently and beautifully seductive, passively waits for man's embrace. Or like the "fond mother" of Henry Wadsworth Longfellow's poem, "Nature"... "takes away/ Our playthings one by one, and by the hand/ Leads us to rest so gently that we go..." As one might expect, Death was a male carriage driver in Emily Dickinson's poem, "Because I Could Not Stop for Death."

Even when human inventions and machines, as opposed to natural elements, are personified as female, they are usually described in imagery that suggests the male poet's sexual domination:

> she being Brand
>
> -new;and you
> know consequently a
> little stiff i was
> careful of her and(having
>
> thoroughly oiled the universal
> joint tested my gas felt of
> her radiator made sure her springs were O.
>
> K.)i went right to it flooded-the-carburetor cranked her
>
> up,slipped the
> clutch(and then somehow got into reverse she
> kicked what
> the hell)next
> minute i was back in neutral tried and
>
> again slo-wly;bare,ly nudg.   ing(my
>
> lev-er Right-
> oh and her gears being in
> A 1 shape passed
> from low through
> second-in-to-high like
> greasedlightning)just as we turned the corner of Divinity
>
> avenue i touched the accelerator and give
>
> her the juice,good

                              (it
        was the first ride and believe i we was
        happy to see how nice she acted right up to
        the last minute coming back down by the Public
        Gardens i slammed on
        the

        internalexpanding
        &
        externalcontracting
        brakes Bothatonce and

        brought allofher tremB
        -ling
        to a:dead.

        stand-
        ;Still)
                        —e. e. cummings

When the machine is male, however, he is either the image of the
Deists' God or a metaphor of man's energy and creativity:

        Air his fuel, will his engine, legs his wheels,
        Eyes the steer, ears the alert;
        He could not fly, but now he does—
                        —from Gregory Corso, "Man"

Science Fiction: Earthbound Stereotypes in Other Worlds

In science fiction, the literary genre that speaks most of cosmic
explorations, machines, alien races, and future humans, one might
hope to find new language, myths, and metaphors that transcend
present beliefs and stereotypes. In effect, science fiction, as a
synthesis of scientific inventiveness with the poetic creative imagination, combines the God/Man concerns of the Alpha of Genesis
with the Omega visions of the Apocalypse. In a sense, much of
science fiction is a literal recreation of man and his potential
destruction. Its connection to sexist language is obvious. Science
fiction has essentially not gone beyond Genesis 2 and 3 in a portrait
of humanity and of each sex.
    In her introduction to *Women of Wonder, Science Fiction Stories*

by Women about Women (1975), Pamela Sargent points out that women writers and female characters have been conspicuously absent in science fiction literature. When female characters do appear, however, they are either the stereotyped incompetent space-ship assistant or the voluptuous Mother Universe sex-object. Dr. Susan Calvin, Asimov's brilliant director of robotics in the science fiction classic, *I, Robot,* is portrayed as an asexual spinster, unsexed by her intellectual involvement with robots instead of people.

As for the gender of neutral, nonsexual machines and robots, we find that they sometimes echo the creation of Adam and Eve in the new myths of creation such as "For a Breath I Tarry," by Roger Zelazny, where Frost, a "primordial" computer consciousness, strives for rebirth as a man. In a modern variation of Genesis 2, the author begins his story—

> They called him Frost.
> Of all things created of Solcom, Frost was the finest, the mightiest, the most difficult to understand.
> This is why he bore a name, and why he was given dominion over half the Earth. . . .
> Yet there was something different about Frost, something which led Solcom to dignify him with a name and a personal pronoun. This, in itself, was an almost unheard of occurrence.

Although the Beta Machine governed the South Pole, the other half of the earth, while Frost governed the North Pole, it, like woman of Genesis 2, does not achieve human gender until after Frost/Man's birth and his awareness that—

> "Your Pole is cold," said Frost, "and I am lonely."
> "I have no hands," said Beta.
> "Would you like a couple?"
> "Yes, I would."
> "Then come to me in Bright Defile," he said, . . .

As with biblical literature, woman is second to and less than man; she responds to his need and call. The story concludes, "They called him Frost. They called her Beta." It is also significant that the first man of a new age originates in the North, the upper division of the earth, symbolizing consciousness and intellect, whereas Beta governed the lower division, a frequent symbol of sensuality and the unconscious in western literature.

Similarly in Alfred Bester's story, "Adam and No Eve," the last man returns to a cindered earth in chaos. After a preliminary exploration of the environment, the hero, Stephen Crane, an independent inventor-explorer who managed to escape the destruction of earth by chance, realizes at the end, "No more life. He, alone, was useless. He was Adam, but there was no Eve." The hope of rebirth exists, however, once Crane/Adam realizes that the Sea is actually Eve, the renewal of life:

> ... There could never be an end to life. Within his body, within the rotting tissues that were rocking gently in the sea was the source of ten million-million lives. . . .
>
> There need be no Adam—no Eve. Only the sea, the great mother of life was needed. The sea had called him back to her depths that presently life might emerge once more, and he was content.
>
> Quietly the waters rocked him. Quietly—Calmly—the mother of life rocked the last-born of the old cycle who would become the first-born of the new.

The visionary literature of science fiction tends to duplicate the myths and metaphors of the past—in creation stories and in gender roles.

In other science fiction, the gender of machines, if determined, is usually stereotyped in the role it plays. Hal, the male computer in *2001* by Arthur C. Clarke, for example, runs the spaceship and initiates an extraordinary revolution against the human operators. In "The Iron Chancellor," by Robert Silverberg, the old female robocook, "Jemima" is replaced by "Bismarck," named for *his* tyrannical control of Clyde, the robobutler, as well as the family that purchases him. In general, robots and computers are the personified male consciousness of their fathers, male science fiction writers as well as the sons of Frankenstein, the first man/machine/ monster created, ironically, by a woman—Mary Shelley.

In "Compassion Circuit," by John Wyndham, however, the Amazonian nurses of a sickly dependent wife are female robots. At first, George, the husband, perceives the robot that he bought for home care as "'Sleeping Beauty,' remarked George, reaching for the instruction book on *its* chest." (Italics added.) Nevertheless, Janet, the wife, names the robotnurse Hester. Once Hester becomes an attentive compassionate friend to Janet, she overcomes her initial "feminine" fear of machines and admires Hester's strength. Janet has an operation to transform her into a strong, cold robot-woman, which finally sends George tumbling in fear and horror down a flight of stairs to a life of crippling dependence on Janet. The significance of Hester and Janet as female robots created by a male writer is that the stereotyped female quality of compassion is personified as a cold programmed machine, whose major virtue is *her* "compassion circuit." Wyndham seems to suggest that programmed female "compassion" has its crippling effects on man, whereas female weakness and dependence are reliably sustaining to men. In addition, the story reminds us that culturally "programmed" stereotypes have been dangerously crippling human potential with machine-like application for centuries.

If the literature of the future maintains the past sex stereotypes, is there hope for new myths and metaphors in any literary genre? Partly in hope of finding an answer to my question, I read *Final Stage* (1974), a science fiction anthology of ultimate stories on universal themes, written expressly for this volume by the stellar writers. Harlan Ellison and Joanna Russ were asked to write on "future sex," which editors Edward L. Ferman and Barry N. Malzberg explained in a footnote as their decision to be fair in representing the theme so "that both sexes have a fair chance at it, and Ellison and Russ are certainly distinguished spokespersons."

In "An Old Fashioned Girl," the Russ story, male and female roles are simply reversed; the female narrator owns what the author calls in her "Afterword," a "Playboy Bunny with testicles" (p. 132). Fortunately, Russ is sensitive to the limits of role reversal when she confesses, "I wrote about a mechanical substitute for a man . . . , but I'd like to plead that the piece is part of a forthcoming novel in which there are lots of other kinds of sex" (p. 131).

In Ellison's story, "Catman," on the other hand, the author suggests a return to androgyny with a man's sexual intercourse with a computer. In a sensual fusion of metal and flesh, each partner shares in the sexuality of the other. Neil Leipzig's affair with the love machine is initially described by Ellison as:

> He spiraled upward into the machine—Lissajous pattern oscillo-scope sine and cosine waves from the x and y axes actually came together, pulsated in three dimensions and he teased himself the machine he the man with vernier knob stimulation—it came out green and the machine trembled, began to secrete testosterone, estrogen, progesterone . . .
>
> She, the machine, he, the machine, she, the man, he the machine . . . the man, he becoming she becoming machine (p. 164).

As a hero seducing a machine, however, he ultimately perceives it as female—a devouring goddess that becomes part mortal and transforms Neil, not into an androgyne, but into a man-machine:

> His pattern was a growing. The machine's was a throbbing. He passed the machine at a higher level every pulse. The machine grew frantic and drank more power. He tried to catch up, chasing the nymphomaniacal peaks as the machine beckoned him, teased him, taunted him, drew him on, then flashed away. He extended on metal limbs, the machine's soft flesh grew sunburned and dark and leather tough.
> Then he peaked out, it, she, peaked out, unable to draw more power from her source. They exchanged modes, as the point of destructive interference denied quantum mechanics and was reached: a millisecond of total sound and utter silence. Orgasm: metal became flesh, human became machine (pp. 165-66).

Although the language of religious and secular literature has perpetuated the cultural stereotypes of men and women, a search has begun for new words and metaphors as well as a revival of dormant ones to express the need for a male-female complement, instead of opposition and subordination. An exploration of the past with a sampling of "sexist" literature as well as voices of previously unheard and unseen women writers has been launched in the adoption of "Images of Women in Literature" courses in college English departments throughout the country. Course titles are sometimes interdisciplinary syntheses of women's literature in history or the image of women in literature and psychology, but reading lists usually include a representative sample of the great "women writers" from Austen to Plath, as well as male writers who made significant contributions, negative and positive, to shaping the image of women.

"Androgyny" is one of the more interesting metaphors to be revived from various quests for the new language. It has a long literary history, starting from the Genesis 1 narration discussed earlier, and its more graphic recording in Plato's *Symposium* as Aristophanes' image of humanity before they angered the gods, to Ursula K. LeGuin's science fiction novel *The Left Hand of Darkness* (1969). In this novel, a human male narrator is sent to a planet, where the inhabitants, Gethenians, are neuter except during "kemmer" when a Gethenian may become either male or female; they do not know which until kemmer. The implications of the "Gethenians" as a metaphor for an androgynous humanity are considered by the earthman:

Consider: there is no division of humanity into strong and weak
halves, protective/protected, dominant/submissive, owner/chattel,
active/passive. In fact the whole tendency to dualism that pervades
human thinking may be found to be lessened, or changed, on Winter.

The following must go into my finished Directives: When you
meet a Gethenian you cannot and must not do what a bisexual
naturally does, which is to cast him in the role of Man or Woman,
while adopting toward him a corresponding role dependent on your
expectations of the patterned or possible interactions between
persons of the same or the opposite sex....

... One is respected and judged only as a human being. It is an
appalling experience (pp. 93-94).

New Perspectives

"Women" poets, in dropping both the imitated male voice as well
as the self-conscious "turning-the-tables" role-reversal voice, are
recreating the language, metaphors, and myths of androgyny—

> ... Scorched within,
> I still burn as I swing,
> A pendulum kicking the night,
> An alarum at dawn, I deflect
> The passage of birds, ring down
> The bannering rain....
>
> —Carolyn Kizer, from "Hera, Hung from the Sky"

> I Am A
>
> Cosmonaut
> Cradled in dangers
> Orbiting a garden universe
> Snipping cosmos, probing Venus,
> Sighting summer's end blindly,
> Weightily weightless
> Spinning out of reach,
>   out
>   of
>   reach
> Signaling strangers.
>   —Lenore Marshall,
>   "I Am a Cosmonaut"

Neither Kizer nor Marshall has unsexed herself to write in images
that literally lift their central figures from the limits of "Mother
Earth." The birth of an androgynous semantics, as opposed to the

perpetuation of a sexist semantics, may be on its way. The man and woman who do not identify with the stereotypes are stepping into strange roles, using strange language unfamiliar to them and their milieu. We are each at the crossroads of liberating the "stranger" in ourselves:

The Stranger

Looking as I've looked before, straight down the heart
of the street to the river
walking the rivers of the avenues
feeling the shudder of the caves beneath the asphalt
watching the lights turn on in the towers
walking as I've walked before
like a man, like a woman, in the city
my visionary anger cleansing my sight
and the detailed perceptions of mercy
flowering from that anger

if I come into a room out of the sharp misty light
and hear them talking a dead language
if they ask me my identity
what can I say but
I am the androgyne
I am the living mind you fail to describe
in your dead language
the lost noun, the verb surviving
only in the infinitive
the letters of my name are written under the lids
of the newborn child
                                    —Adrienne Rich, 1972

I do feel women should retain their own identity. I am not Mrs. S. L. Root, Jr., I am Dr. M. Jean Greenlaw. I spent a long time becoming me and a few words don't change that process.

M. Jean Greenlaw
teacher

Until humans might evolve, or be altered by science, to become totally bisexual physically, capable of reproduction with or without a partner, differential designation is desirable. This applies to marital status and some form of identification with a current spouse as well as to sex, and is useful for the sake of convenience and clarity in communication via our language.

Earl Sherwan
editor

I have never been married, don't feel too badly damaged psychologically as a result and have almost reached the place where I resent being addressed as Ms. No doubt I'm swimming against the tide but I do believe that we are in grave danger of losing the benefit of the distinct sexual differences between men and women, primarily in the area of emotional reactions. I question the effectiveness of socking someone in the face with charges of sexism and then expecting him to be a willing supporter of our struggle for equal rights. Call me a Midwest reactionary, if you like!

(name withheld)
editor

Ms. fills a need, but its artificiality bothers me. Further, all the "M" titles are ridiculous in that they are unnecessary and somewhat archaic. They once filled a need in that they denoted a class between the titled aristocracy and the laboring class. I suspect computers will help to do them in—expense and lack of space.

George W. Hartung
teacher

Sexism in the Language of Marriage

Alleen Pace Nilsen

One of the few songs I remember from the halcyon era of the fifties starts out with the bold claim "Love and marriage go together like a horse and carriage!" I was a teenager then and I thought it was a wonderful song. But today in my more cynical adulthood, I might be tempted instead to think of a threesome consisting of love, marriage, and sexism. They are as intertwined as any social institutions that we have.

I must hasten to add that I am speaking of society in general, not necessarily of the one marriage and the one husband I know best. Because instead of quarreling in the public press with my husband, Don, I should be paying tribute to him. We were married while we were still undergraduates. It was before the days of the pill and we started our family right away. But even with the responsibilities of three children he unselfishly shared, and shared alike, while we worked and went to school to earn both our master's and our Ph.D. degrees.

This attitude didn't come easily. What the conscious mind intellectually recognizes as fair is not the same as what the subconscious mind emotionally accepts as appropriate. "Growing pains" accompany any significant social change, and when a couple sets up a true partnership marriage, they are probably going against the example set by their own parents, as well as the expectations of their friends and society at large. For example, when I at last received a regular faculty appointment at Arizona State University, where my husband had been teaching for two years, my father came to a celebration dinner with a package under his arm and a twinkle in his eyes. He had brought a present. It was a pair of pants for Don. They were handed over with the good humored explanation that since we were now equal, he just wanted to remind everyone who was "to wear the pants in the family."

This old cliche about *the pants in the family* is just one of hundreds of ways that the language reminds us of the different expectations we have for the man and for the woman in a marriage. Some of these attitudes are revealed through our everyday language, in the ways we divide various aspects of marriage into male and female domains.

Parenthood and family relations in general are in the domain of the woman. For example, *wife and mother* is a phrase more commonly heard than *husband and father*. And we have many family related metaphors based on feminine, but not masculine, words, e.g., *gold star mother; alma mater; granny knot; mother lode; mother superior; mother tongue; mother, daughter and sister languages; mother wit; piamater; mother of pearl; mother earth; mother of vinegar; mother nature;* and *maternal* or *motherly instincts*.

Word Pairings and Male Precedence

"Ladies first" goes the old saying, but except in the phrase *ladies and gentlemen* we seldom follow this advice. Instead we have such pairings as:

> Mr. and Mrs.
> he/she
> his and hers
> Sonny and Cher
> Jack and Jill
> Fibber McGee and Molly
> boys and girls
> George and Martha Washington
> men and women
> sons and daughters
> husbands and wives
> kings and queens
> brothers and sisters
> guys and dolls
> actors and actresses
> host and hostess

This kind of male-female pairing is so set in our minds that it becomes automatic. I recently read that someone chided the National Organization of Women because their charter started out with "We, men and women..." instead of "We, women and men...," which would have more accurately reflected their membership as well as their philosophy.

It is the general pattern in English for male words to come first. We make an exception only when something is so closely related to what we think of as the feminine domain that, without even realizing it, we switch over and break the pattern, putting the female first as in the following pairs, which all have to do with family relations and marriage.

> bride and groom
> mother and father
> mother and child
> aunt and uncle

Even these terms are sometimes interchanged so that the male comes first, and the phrase doesn't sound deviant except for *groom and bride*. We definitely think of a wedding as the bride's show, as evidenced by several language customs. It is the bride's parents who send out the announcements, and only recently have some people begun to name also the parents of the groom on the wedding announcement. The newspaper picture usually shows only the bride, and unless it's a celebrity couple the picture and accompanying story will appear on what is still called the *women's page* in many newspapers.

We went to a large wedding reception in a hotel the other night and the directory of events posted in the lobby read, "Cynthia Jenson Reception: Fiesta Room." I'm sure it was partly for the sake of efficiency that the sign maker didn't use the more complete "Cynthia Jenson and Robert Marshall Reception: Fiesta Room." During the couple's married life there will be hundreds of times when efficiency in listing their names is called for, but this announcement of the reception will probably be the last time Cynthia's name will be chosen over Robert's.

In nearly all semantic areas of English, nouns are considered basically masculine; if we need to specify that the referent is female, an extra word or an affix of some kind is attached. For example we have actor/actress, major/majorette, aviator/aviatrix, prince/princess, god/goddess, lawyer/woman lawyer, truck driver/lady truck driver. But when it comes to certain words related to marriage and sexual relations, the process is reversed. *Prostitute* is a female term, with *male prostitute* being the *unusual*. *Virgin* is another feminine term which must have a special context when it refers to a man. On the death of a spouse, the woman becomes a *widow*, the man, a *widower*. Women are more often given the title *divorcée*, while a man is simply described as "being divorced." At the beginning of a marriage the woman is the *bride* and the man is the *bridegroom*. As we have already seen, *bride* is a more important word than *groom*. This is further shown by the fact that it appears in several compounds (*bridal attendant, bridal wreath,* etc.) while *groom* in the sense of *bridegroom* is seldom used. Even the males' prenuptial party is called a *bachelor party* as compared to the female *bridal shower*. And a woman considers herself a bride for a whole year after the wedding, while a man considers himself a groom only on the day of the wedding.

"Married" as a Goal for Women Only

Men are married just as much as women, but marriage isn't the center of their lives. We never give little boys dress-up clothes in which to play groom, but we give little girls old lace curtains and white dresses so they can play bride. And we train little girls, but not little boys, to respond to the question, "What are you going to do when you grow up?" with some form of "I'm going to get married."

At prenuptial celebrations, men look backward while women look forward. It is as if each sex wants to emphasize and honor the state it considers ideal, hence men stress the single state and women stress the married. At a bridal shower, the entertainment consists of looking to the future through gifts which will enhance the comfort and the glamour of the new home. Games are played which revolve around daydreams predicting a romanticized future for the couple. At the bachelor party, the entertainment consists of looking to the past. It is one last fling with *the boys*, a nostalgic celebration in honor of *single blessedness* and freedom from the sex-related constraints usually thought to go along with marriage. The comments and the jokes made at both the bridal party and the bachelor party reflect our underlying attitude that marriage signifies success for a woman but defeat for a man. Perhaps this is one of the reasons society seems to ignore the marital status of men. Our consciousness of whether or not a woman is married is shown by our use of two titles, *Miss* and *Mrs.*, as contrasted to the all-purpose *Mr.*

In English a man's wife is jokingly referred to as his *ball and chain*. A similar metaphor exists in Spanish. The word for wife is *esposa*; the plural *esposas*, means handcuffs.

Compare the positive connotations of *bachelor* with the negative connotations of *spinster* or *old maid*. *Old maid* is the name of a children's card game in which the loser is ridiculed by being given this uncomplimentary title. It is also used metaphorically to mean the left-over kernels of corn that failed to pop. These are all negative concepts. *Bachelor* has such positive connotations that unmarried girls have tried to borrow them by labelling themselves *bachelor girls* or *bachelorettes*. We hear *bachelor* in such phrases as *bachelor pad* and *most eligible bachelor*. The connotations of the word are such that in Arizona the local sex newspaper is called *Bachelor Beat*. Judging from the advertisements, it isn't read by bachelors at all. Nevertheless the title conveys the idea of sexual freedom. We would never hear the term *most eligible spinster*, because beauty and youth are considered prime qualifications of a female's eligibility, and supposedly both are gone by the time a female is old enough to be called an *old maid* or a *spinster*; hence the words are mutually exclusive.

Playboy might be a synonym for *eligible bachelor*, though the qualities of a playboy are certainly not the same as those popularly ascribed to a "good" husband. Perhaps the reason a playboy is considered a *good catch* is that he supposedly has money and sophistication. It is as if we envy unmarried men because of the fullness of the life they lead with their extra freedom and extra money, while we pity unmarried women because we think they live only half a life. In an interesting bit of folk etymology, I heard of an *old maid* who specified in her will that she didn't want *Miss* written on her gravestone, because she hadn't missed as much as people thought she had.

It appears that society has certain expectations and that as long as behavior is fairly consistent with the expected, it goes unnoticed. For example, it is expected that every woman loves and serves her family, but such behavior is unusual in a man. We mark the unusual behavior with a word *family man*, but there's no such thing as a *family woman*. The same type of reasoning probably explains why we have the term *career woman* but not *career man*.

Wife as Property

It is ironic that although we consider marriage to be a desirable thing for a woman, we also look on it as making her the property of her husband. This is probably a leftover from the days when women could not get jobs, and so getting married was a cause for celebration, just as we celebrate when children who cannot take care of themselves are adopted by responsible adults. Because proprietary attitudes toward women go back into the dim reaches of history, it is not surprising that the language reflects this idea of ownership.

The most obvious example is the traditional wedding ceremony, in which the clergyman asks, "Who gives the bride away?" The father of the bride answers, "I do." If the father is not available, a male substitute is found, usually an older relative or friend of the family. After the father both literally and figuratively hands the bride over to the groom, the clergyman says,"I now pronounce you man and wife."

This part of the ceremony has irritated many women, because the two words *man* and *wife* do not seem parallel; *wife* is a relational term, but *man* isn't. Actually, in Middle English these were matching terms, because *wife* meant *woman*. And because a woman's role in life was then primarily in relationship to her husband, the word gradually took on its current meaning. We see it in its original sense of female or woman in the terms *midwife* and *housewife*. *Mid* is cognate with the Germanic *mit*, meaning *with*. The literal meaning of *midwife* is someone who is "with women." If the panelists on the television show "What's My Line" had understood this, they wouldn't have been so easily fooled the night a male midwife was a guest. A *housewife* is not—or at least isn't supposed to be—someone married to a house. Instead the word means something like "the woman of the house." Chaucer's *Wif of Bath* is about a woman of Bath, and the word *alewife* simply means a woman who sold ale, as a *fishwife* is a woman who sold fish. *Old wives' tales* are nothing more than the stories of old women.

The reason the wedding ceremony uses the phrase *man and wife* is that religion is a traditional and conservative force and its language appropriately lags behind the volatile, common language of the land; witness the use of Latin in the Catholic Church several hundred years after it became a "dead" language, and think how long Jewish religious leaders kept Hebrew alive. Even in "modern" churches the archaic *thee* and *thou* are common in prayers and the King James Version of the Bible is far more popular than the modern Standard Revised Version. But since *wife* now has a different meaning and most people feel there is no religious or sacred reason for maintaining the exact wording of the marriage ceremony, many clergymen have changed the wording to the more parallel *husband and wife*.

In all close relationships, we use what appears to be possessive structures when we say *my husband, my wife, my secretary, my boss, my boyfriend*, etc. But these terms are not really possessive so much as they are relational. They are probably deleted forms for such thoughts as "The man who is my husband," "The woman who is my secretary," etc. However we do find inconsistent usage among young people when a female talks about her *boyfriend*, but a male talks about his *girl* or his *woman*. It is interesting that, he, but rarely she, can delete *friend*. This deletion of *friend* takes away the relational meaning and makes it possessive. If a female talks about *my boy*, a listener is apt to think of a child, i.e., the female's offspring.

The term *wife-swapping* is another example of the attitude that the male owns the female. Feminists would prefer the term *swinging*, but as a disillusioned friend confided, "It doesn't matter what you call it, it's still the woman who gets screwed!" Practically everything we say about sex revolves around the attitude that it is the domain of the man. He *possesses* the woman. He makes a *sexual conquest* when he *deflowers* her by *taking away her virginity*, a set phrase that doesn't even allow her the dignity of giving it away.

Surname Customs and Women's Identity

One of the most far-reaching and troublesome effects of the male-ownership idea is evident in surnames. A woman's taking her husband's name relates to the idea that she is his property. I looked through a standard desk-size dictionary for ways we treat men and women differently and was surprised to find what appears to be an attitude on the part of editors that it is almost indecent to let a respectable woman's name march unaccompanied across the pages of a dictionary. A woman's name must somehow be escorted by a male's name, regardless of whether the male contributed to the woman's reason for being in the dictionary, or whether he, in his own right, was as famous as the woman. For example, Charlotte Brontë was identified as Mrs. Arthur B. Nicholls, Amelia Earhart was identified as Mrs. George Palmer Putnam, Helen Hayes was identified as Mrs. Charles MacArthur, Zona Gale was identified as

Mrs. William Llywelyn Breese, and Jenny Lind was identified as
Mme. Otto Goldschmidt. There were a few women such as tem-
perance leader Carry Nation and slave Harriet Tubman who were
listed without the benefit of a masculine escort, but most of the
women were identified as someone's wife. Of all the men, and there
were probably ten times as many men as women, only one was
identified as the "husband of . . . " And even this one example was
the rather unusual case of "Frederic Joliot-Curie (born Frederic
Joliot), 1900-1958; husband of Irene; French chemist; shared Nobel
prize . . . " Apparently when Irene and Frederic married they took
the hyphenated last name in honor of Irene's family.

This confusion indicates not so much the sexist attitude of the
dictionary editors, as the complexity of making "two into one."
Which *one* are they going to be? What name will the children have?
Surely the Joliot-Curie compromise couldn't work for more than a
generation. And what is an editor supposed to do with maiden
names, professional names, married names, etc.? The complexity of
the whole naming business may be a contributing factor to the
general absence of women in the historical record keeping of the
world.

Newspaper editors have a greater problem than dictionary
editors, because most of the people they write about are very much
alive and ready to object if they don't like the way their name was
written. Also when a new person pops into the news there probably
is no set pattern to be followed with regard to what version of her
name this particular woman prefers.

In 1971, I clipped out the Associated Press listing of the "best
dressed" because it illustrates the differences in the way we list
names. The men were listed as:

> Frederic Byers III of Pittsburgh and New York; Yul Brynner, actor
> of Tartar stock now living in Switzerland; Hernando Courtwright,
> Mexican-born hotelier of Los Angeles; John Galliher, American
> socialite of New York and London; Angus Ogilvy, British business-
> man married to Princess Alexandra of Kent; Armando Orsini, New
> York restaurant owner; Giorgio Payone, Roman public relations
> executive; Baron Alexis de Rede, Austrian-born Paris financier;
> Thomas Shevlin, Palm Beach socialite; Bobby Short, nightclub star
> born in Rockford, Ill.; Lord Snowdon, photographer, husband of
> Princess Margaret; and Sargent Shriver, Washington.

Notice that of these twelve men, the only two identified in relationship to their wives are Angus Ogilvy and Lord Snowdon, who in

true story-book fashion married real princesses. The list of women on the best dressed list started with Mrs. Harilaos Theodora-copulos, "American wife of the Greek ship owner," and then went on as follows:

> The Begum Aga Khan, British wife of the Moslem spiritual leader; Mme. Ahmed Benhima, wife of the Moroccan Ambassador to the United Nations; Diahann Carroll, American singer; Catherine Deneuve, French actress; Sophia Loren, Italian film star; Mrs. Denise Minnelli, Yugoslav residing in San Francisco; Mme. Georges Pompidou; Mrs. Richard Pistell, New York, former Marquesa Caroll de Portago; Mrs. Ronald Reagan, wife of the governor of California; Mrs. Samuel P. Reed, American socialite, daughter of Mrs. Charles Engelhard; and Mrs. Charles Revson, wife of the cosmetic magnate.

The five women given permanent status and elected to the Hall of Fame were:

> Mrs. William McCormick Blair Jr., Chicago-born wife of the former U.S. ambassador who now heads the Kennedy Center for the Performing Arts in Washington; Mrs. Alfred Bloomingdale of Los Angeles, wife of the founder of the Diner's Club; Mrs. Wyatt (Gloria Vanderbilt) Cooper of New York; Mrs. Kirk Douglas, Hollywood, born in Paris; and Mrs. Patrick Guinness, Lausanne, Switzerland and Paris.

Notice that only three of the seventeen women are identified in a way separate from their relationship to a man. These three are all in show business, but Gloria Vanderbilt's name was given in paren-theses in the middle of her husband's name, and it appears that Mrs. Denise Minnelli is using her married title along with her given name. Language purists object to this usage. Their feeling is that since *Mrs.* is an abbreviation for *Mistress* it must always be used with a man's name because someone cannot be the mistress of herself. But people who disagree point out that *Miss* is also a diminutive derived from *mistress*. If a woman must always use her husband's name with the title *Mrs.*, then when she marries she in effect loses not only her maiden name but also her given name.

Existing custom allows a woman no way to pass down either her family name or her given name. She cannot name her daughter Jennifer, Jr. or Stacy Ann II, nor can she handicap a child with her own last name. This idea is so far removed from the realm of possibility that people talk about illegitimate children as "children without names." Some pregnant girls marry for no other reason than to "provide a name for the baby." The feeling is very strong that before a person is really part of our society, he or she must demonstrate an affiliation with a father, by means of the surname.

Probably the most forceful way our present custom of naming affects the average woman is by making it doubly difficult for her to "make a name for herself." Obviously it is a distinct disadvantage to have to stop midway in life and begin all over. Few women are able to bring their name to the public's attention so that it will be recognized in all its alternate forms as is Jacqueline Bouvier, Jackie Kennedy, Mrs. John F. Kennedy, Jacqueline Onassis, and Mrs. Aristotle Onassis.

Women are beginning to defy the anonymity and the self-effacement imposed by cultural attitudes and the accompanying naming customs of marriage. Witness the tendency of many to resume their maiden names after divorce and the daring of a few in carrying their maiden names beyond the altar. How far these innovations may spread is hard to guess, but the fact that they are occurring reflects an awareness of a woman's identity as being continuous throughout life and belonging to her rather than to "the men in her life."

If changes are to occur in our language which will more accurately report truly definitive meanings for *male*, *female*, or *people*, they will have to be encouraged through and by members of the news media. Until the members of the news media begin to consciously avoid using linguistic sexism in their copy, it will be almost impossible to educate the general public.

Lucky Slate
editor

The first remarks I heard and the first articles I read displayed astonishing ignorance about other languages, the history of the English language, and the nature of social and linguistic change. Things improved. There has been some sensible commentary lately.

George W. Hartung
teacher

In my teaching I try to use nonsexist language whenever I can. It does feel strange to say "his or her," but I think that is part of breaking an old habit.... Beyond doing what we can with our individual speech, our energies are best spent pushing for nonsexist language in textbooks and other publications and in making people around us aware of the pervasive sexism in our culture.

Carolyn Allen
teacher

Rather than changing the form of words, I should think it would be more beneficial to encourage subtle changes in connotation, and the content of the information that the words convey. That a woman become chairman of the Rules Committee is more important than to change the title [for that job] to chairperson and continue to elect men to the position. Perhaps this is a matter of "change the custom and the language will change itself."

(name withheld)
editor

Sexism in Dictionaries and Texts: Omissions and Commissions

H. Lee Gershuny

In praise of the English language, Otto Jespersen, the noted Danish linguist, characterized it as "positively and expressly *masculine*, it is the language of a grown-up man and has very little childish or feminine about it." (Italics added.) Its logicality, openness to innovation, businesslike virility, energy and emotional restraint were qualities he regarded as both masculine and positive (*Growth and Structure of the English Language*, 1905).

The observations of a supposedly objective linguist, who described English itself in sexist terms, draws our attention not only to sexism in language, but also to the kinds of problems we face when we, the modern linguists and English instructors, discover how sexism operates in various fields of English discourse.

First, we have to deal with rigid verbal stereotypes of masculinity and femininity that are used not only to describe people and language, but also to judge and polarize the phenomenal world into superior/inferior and positive/negative. The inferior and negative poles tend to characterize the female stereotype, the superior and positive, the male.

The trouble with stereotypes is that they restrict behavior and understanding by constructing a static image of both sexes. Furthermore, assigning verbal qualities to each sex creates an illusion of biologically determined traits instead of suggesting their socio-cultural origins, or even an interplay of biology and environment. It is as though emotionality and passivity, usually assigned to the female stereotype, are qualities inherently absent in men. The passive man and the assertive woman are "unnatural" anomalies and are urged into psychotherapy to remedy behavior unbecoming the stereotype.

The verbal construct, then, governs a standard for self-image and self-evaluation which is introduced in the home and reinforced by educators and their resources—curricula and textbooks. In many instances, behavior is more affected by verbal qualities and admonitions; i.e., "men don't cry," and "girls don't fight," than a person's involvement in a particular social context. Fear of behaving in "unmanly" or "unfeminine" ways produces the "sex role stutterer," who is caught between the demands of a cultural expectation and the demands of self and reality.

The stereotypes also become rationalizations for socio-political hierarchies in which one sex is expected to direct and dominate the other because *his* traits are perceived as superior and "natural" to him; whereas, *her* "natural" traits, i.e., passivity, emotionality, domesticity, and dependence, are regarded as less desirable and inferior. When either sex behaves like the other, each is judged abnormal. But *he* may be insulted when called "effeminate" or a "sissy," whereas *she* may either be complimented that she "talks and thinks like a man" or be discouraged from stepping over the social-sexual boundaries.

The second problem suggested in Jespersen's observation is that esteemed authorities often make the greatest contribution to perpetuating cultural prejudices and personal biases. Because they are assumed to be objective and authoritative, they often have the greatest influence. This applies not only to individuals and institutions, but to almost anything in print.

Dictionaries: Perpetuators of Sexist Tradition

The Dictionary, one of the most popular authoritative documents and institutions of linguistic research, has echoed Jespersen's and the culture's biases in the guise of neutral descriptive linguistics. The Dictionary, whose word often settles legal disputes in court and semantic disputes in the classroom, is usually venerated with the same blind faith as the word of the Bible or God "Himself/Herself."

Some of the ways in which the English language and the dictionaries of the English language perpetuate cultural sexism are found in what Jespersen would have considered the virtues of the language: English semantics and morphology imply a male-dominated world; the female gender is invisible when impersonal and indefinite nouns and pronouns are used in ambiguous contexts:

A. Each doctor posted *his* office hours.
B. We need to be more concerned with problems of *man* and *his* universe.

Even though there are numerous women doctors, they remain symbolically invisible in Sentence A. In fact, to avoid misunderstanding we find it necessary to affix "woman" or "lady" to professions generally associated with males. To mean "woman" as well as man in Sentence B may depend more on the kind of problems referred to, but the clear implication is that the universe belongs to man to understand and master.

When the word "man" or "mankind" is used to refer to the entire human race, we are not sure that "womankind" is always meant to be included. This lack of an English pronoun that symbolically includes men and women has forced users of Standard English into uttering nonsensical statements, such as, "When we get abortion law repeal, everyone will be able to decide for *himself* whether or not to have an abortion," and "Man, like the other mammals, breast-feeds *his* young." Nor has American political history made it clear that "All men are created equal" was meant to include women.

All of this suggests that we need to pay attention to what is said as well as what is not said, for the female sex has been conspicuously invisible not only in the grammar and semantics of English, but also in its literature and the history of English discourse.

There is no gender ambiguity, however, when either "he" and its noun and pronoun variants or "she" and its variants appear in single illustrative sentences in the dictionary. I counted the number of sentences that contained either masculine or feminine nouns and pronouns and those that contained both, in the unabridged *Random House Dictionary of the English Language* (1966, hereinafter RHD). I found that in over two thousand sentences collected, those with masculine gender words outnumbered those using the feminine gender by about 3:1. In addition, masculine gender words appeared twice as often as feminine words.

The dictionary has thus unconsciously programmed the relative unimportance of the feminine gender in defining and being defined. The feminine is "the other" as de Beauvoir suggested, rather than the equal, at least in terms of linguistic visibility.

This invisibility would not be so serious, however, if it were only symbolic, but it reflects the real tendency to render women politically, economically, historically, and socially insignificant in

American culture. The woman conventionally stands hidden behind her boss or husband while he receives the glory and credit for
what is often a joint endeavor. Even though women constitute about
51 percent of the population, they are now identified as a "minority"
group in need of symbolic and real representation commensurate
with their actual numbers.

In a rigorous analysis of illustrative sentences in the *Random
House Dictionary* (1966), I found that stereotyped contexts are more
the rule than the exception for both genders. Males are stereotyped
about 65 percent and females about 75 percent of the times each
appear. Even though both appear in stereotyped contexts more
frequently than not, the data suggest that the feminine stereotype
may be the more rigid of the two. Although there may be more
unconventional roles available to women, in the illustrative sentences, women appear less frequently in such roles and in neutral
contexts. The examples tend to stereotype females.

In the sentences, females are most frequently associated with
domestic contexts—as mothers, wives, hostesses, launderers, cooks,
shoppers, gardeners, and servants; next in frequency are occupations and behavior associated with the world of fashion and
glamor. Emotional situations are the third most frequent context in
which females appear in the sentences; contexts of illness and
weakness come next. An occasional sentence makes reference to a
specific profession such as teacher, receptionist, artist, editor,
secretary, and singer. Taken collectively, the sentences present a
culturally stereotyped definition of the female.

A few examples indicate how the above roles are linked with the
feminine gender. The words being illustrated are italicized.

1.   *Tears* rushed to her eyes.

2.   The new bride was in *tears* over her unsuccessful dinner.

3.   She enjoys *tearing* down her friends, when they aren't around.

4.   She burst into tears upon hearing of his death but it was only a
     grandstand play.

5.   She gave us *overdone* steak.

6.   Her constant complaining just sticks in my *craw*.

7.   She always wears a *crazy* hat.

8.   She never has the sense to hold her *tongue* at the right time.

9.   My mother-in-law is no *bargain*.

10. She *romanticized* her role as an editor.

If given half a chance, I am sure we could all create sentences that illustrate the particular meanings of the words defined in the dictionary without denigrating the female sex, within the negative connotation of the stereotype!

Notice that when "she" finally has the role of "editor" in Sentence 10, she treats it "romantically" rather than professionally. Although sentences 1-3 illustrate different meanings for the same word, the feminine gender is used with each. Surely there are contexts in which *tears* can be associated with either children, parents (neutral) or males.

The big surprise came, however, when I discovered which stereotyped role was most frequently associated with the male gender. The masculine gender associated with "delinquent" or "bad guy" appears twice as many times as in contexts identifying the male with business and money:

11.   He's hitting the bottle pretty *hard*.

12.   He was *hauled* before the judge.

13.   He is *good* for nothing.

14.   He *gambled* all his hard-earned money away in one night.

15.   His crimes against humanity were most *unnatural*.

It would appear that the editors, mainly men, have not only reinforced the standard male and female stereotypes, but in emphasizing the "bad guy" image have unintentionally expressed their own identification with the rebel in society and the underdog who resists strict moral codes. From a perception of his own powerlessness, the rebel or outcast opposes the social forces that would shape him. To conceive of the "bad guy" in the first place is to suggest his "victimization" at the hands of authorities he perceives as more powerful than he. If we acknowledge that this is a male-dominated society, why would the major male trait be portrayed as resisting that world? There are several possible explanations: the "bad guy," whether he is cast as convict or alcoholic, may be expressing opposition to the power that dominated a part of his early life. Ironically, this "power" is female, operating in the socially stereotyped role of mother and teacher.

Patricia Cayo Sexton stated in her book, *The Feminized Male* (1969), that men "are often victims, in school and home, of the female's repressed antagonism and legitimate resentment of male privileges" (p. 24). Although Sexton demonstrates the vicious social cycle victimizing both sexes, she emphasizes the male's rebellion not only against female dominance but also against unrealistic he-man roles established by the males who control schools but do not teach in them, and who control political and economic affairs but judge domestic affairs and child raising as inferior and "emasculated" social roles.

Thus, the two major images of the male and female presented in the RHD demonstrate the social doublethink operating in sex stereotypes. The male-dominated culture defines women as inferior and assigns them to low-status domestic roles. By accepting the female stereotype, however, women dominate the training and education of young males, who, in turn, either rebel or express fear of women's early domination and "power." When males perpetuate an image of female inferiority, however, the woman becomes less frightening to them, as do blacks to whites who insist on their inferiority. And so the cycle goes.

The second most frequent male stereotype in the dictionary sentences casts males in roles related to business and investments. The male gender is also linked, in a sentence or two, to specific occupations such as journalist, doctor, warden, publisher, minister, genius, architect, and captain. Assertiveness, strength, dominance, rationality, independence, and courage are some of the stereotypically male qualities illustrated in the sentences:

16.   He refused to let anyone *get* ahead of him in business.

17.   He *got* ahead by sheer determination.

18.   His hands *clenched* as he faced his enemy.

19.   He is *unequaled* as an architect.

20.   Nothing in the painting escaped his *microscopic* study.

21.   He must *seize* on a solution, however risky!

22.   He *packs* a better punch than any heavyweight in years.

23.   He has a *strong* voice.

When *both* masculine and feminine gender appear in the same sentence, however, the situations represented are most often marriage and family life; next come unspecified social settings. In these sentences, the male gender appears in the stereotypically feminine world of home and family only when the feminine gender is represented, but it is perhaps symbolic that females do not appear in the stereotyped world of the male, even in social relationship to him. Men appear in the home as husbands, but women do not appear as partners in the business world. This lack of interchangeability of roles, on the symbolic level, tends to fix behavioral possibilities according to static concepts and images. In the following illustrative sentences, the female role is one of dependence and submission in relation to the dominant male:

24. He is the *pivot* of her life.
25. She left her native land on her husband's *account*.
26. He really *hypnotizes* the women; they believe anything he tells them.
27. He *gave* her his arm when they crossed the street.
28. She depends *on* her father for money.
29. Abandoned by her lover, she *pined* away.
30. Her father never allowed them to *talk* back.
31. He was his mother's sole *support*.
32. She *trembled* at his voice.
33. She sat near the telephone waiting for his *call*.

Such sentences reinforce the kind of stereotyped relationship between the sexes that encourages men to dominate women and women to express their resistance and rebellion by attempting to dominate and control their husbands and/or sons. The following sentences, in effect, reinforce a male-female rivalry in what are already stereotyped roles. In some cases an implicit hostility between the sexes is suggested:

34. He is always *sarcastic* about her appearance.
35. He *dipped* her pigtails into the inkwell.
36. She was *boiling* when he arrived late.
37. He *chafed* at her constant interruptions.
38. He wouldn't even give her the *time of day*.
39. Women with shrill voices get on his *nerves*.
40. He *exposed* the secret she had confided to him.
41. He is suspected of having *done* away with his first wife.
42. You could see him *turn* off as she kept up her chatter.
43. It was only too apparent that his mother rules the *roost*.
44. She promptly *turned* him in to the police.
45. She made a *monkey* out of him in front of all his friends.

46. She's *death* on his friends from the office.

47. She loves to *bait* him about his male vanity.

48. He lets his wife lead him by the *nose.*

49. He couldn't see that she was leading him up the *garden* path because he might be useful.

50. He'll get *hell* from his wife for working so late again.

51. He once did her a good *turn.* She repaid it with a bad *turn.*

52. If she starts *nagging* at her husband, I'm going home.

53. Her disdainful look crushed the *confidence* of the brash young man.

The female assertiveness expressed as dominance over males in Sentences 43-53 may impress most readers as more objectionable than the male dominance or hostility toward the female expressed in Sentences 34-42. The last group seem extreme, whereas the earlier group seem like the cultural norm. Not only is sex role defined and stereotyped, but female expressions of ambition, intellect, aggression, assertion, and independence are also cast as negative behavior, trivialized or omitted entirely from the dictionary and textbooks.

Texts Teach More Than Subject Matter

Textbooks purporting to teach the specifics of an academic discipline have concomitantly taught secondary information—sex roles and social values. Researchers have conducted both formal and informal investigations of a wide variety of textbooks, from elementary school readers to professional scholarly journals, to ferret out the sexism in word and image. One of the more extensive formal studies was conducted by Lenore J. Weitzman and Diane Rizzo over a period of three years on the "latent content of the most widely used textbook series in the United States in each of five subject areas: science, arithmetic, reading, spelling, and social studies" ("Sex Bias in Textbooks," *Today's Education,* January/ February 1975). They obtained data on the sex, age, racial distribution, and activities of the textbook characters by grade level and subject area. They discovered, for example, stories about boys predominated in every grade.

In science texts, only boys are told they can explore the moon. In math problems, the masculine gender is stereotypically assigned to earning money; the female, to dividing pies and baking cakes. According to Weitzman and Rizzo, "despite the Equal Pay Act of 1963, we found math problems in which girls were paid less than boys for the same work" ("Sex Bias in Textbooks," p. 52). These researchers also found in readers and spellers "a surprising amount of antagonism and hostility toward females. In the spelling series, female characters are yelled at and pushed around. In the reading series, they are shown as stupid and clumsy three times as frequently as males" (p. 52). According to the published studies of textbooks, language that suggests cooperation and partnership between males and females is practically nonexistent.

As a member of the Woodward School "Sex-Role Committee" in Brooklyn from 1970-72, Barbara Grizzuti Harrison recorded in *Unlearning the Lie: Sexism in School* (1973) informal observations of how texts, teachers, children, curriculum, and parents all learn and teach the lessons of sex role stereotyping only too well. Women's roles in shaping American history are not only absent from the stereotypically masculine worlds of science and politics, but also in conventional roles as wives and mothers. Although students are told that the early colonist had to manufacture many of the things that *his* family needed, they are not told that many of the colonists carrying on this manufacturing were women. The intrepid pioneers are men, and women, if mentioned, are included with the list of children, bags, and cattle accompanying the "pioneers."

> They read that man climbed out of the trees to hunt, and that he also made pots. There is little in what they read that reminds them that the 'man' who made pots was a woman. History is literally taught in terms of man's development, and in the very structure of the language teachers use is inherent the idea of man's superiority over women—the use of the word mankind, for example, when what is meant is humanity, and the automatic use of a male pronoun (*Unlearning the Lie*, p. 20).

The collective research of Carol London, Brett Vuolo, and Adrienne Yurick, members of the same Sex-Roles Committee, noted that the contributions of such women as Phyllis Wheatley and Anne Bradstreet, America's first professional poets; Maria Mitchell, astronomer; Sarah Bagley and Mary Harris Jones, leaders in the labor unions; and Prudence Crandall and Myrtilla Miner, the first to set up schools for black girls, are a few of the more obvious omissions from the history texts they examined—

> ... texts that we all might have encountered in high school and college—as well as books published within the last ten years. We have found that women just don't seem to be part of American history. Here are a few examples: Henry Steele Commager's *Documents of American History* (1962), a compilation of 665 documents, includes four by or about women. *A Documentary History of the American People* (Craven, Johnson and Dunn, 1951), a Columbia University text, contains 238 documents—three by or about women! *The Oxford History of the American People*, by Samuel Eliot Morrison (1965) sums up the role of women in colonial times in four lines! Mr. Morrison also sees fit to place his two lines covering the nineteenth Amendment under the heading, "Bootlegging and Other Sports." Nevins and Commager's *Pocket History of the United States* (subtitled "The Story of a Free People") contains four sentences about women. (*Unlearning the Lie*, p. 95).

Similar omissions were discovered in texts from almost every academic discipline represented on a faculty committee for "Women's International Year 1975-76" chaired by Dr. Doris Fitzgerald at Manhattan Community College, CUNY. In the Data Processing Department, for example, Professor Daniel Rosich reported that in one text, Ivan Flores' *Operating System for Multiprogramming with a Variable Number of Tasks* (1973), the author refers to a program that has "locks and keys" to memory blocks exclusively, but inconsistently, with masculine gender pronouns. The program and its metaphorical elements are gender-neutral in English and in the professional programmer's jargon, yet this particular author personified key program commands as masculine: GETMAIN (a program command) is the antecedent for "He called Cpurge to create space in the region" (p. 180).

Even in courses in the secretarial sciences, a career usually assigned to women, textbook explanations and examples exclude the feminine gender a disproportionate number of times. Professors Anna Porter and Donna Santo reported that out of a total of 231 letters used in *Developing Shorthand Skills* (1967), 20 percent are addressed to women, whereas 80 percent are addressed to men. The students, mostly female, type from an exercise book, *College Typewriting*, that refers only to the masculine gender as seeking a job in the business world, developing *his* skills and improving *his* appearance. Instructions to the student-typist begin: "Men who know how a skill is acquired do not deny the vital need for rapid finger action.... An expert typist will, for example, read copy very carefully. His eyes will follow the lines at an even rate" (Lesson 135). The typist, as female, is invisible even though a "she" and not a "he" is probably typing the copy meant to encourage her to emulate the visible male expert in the text! Nor are women represented in other careers referred to in secretarial science texts.

In *Gregg Shorthand for Colleges*, (2nd ed., Vol. I), a letter addressed "Dear Sir:" opens with "The policeman, the fireman, the physician—all provide protection for you in their own special, efficient fashions. But do you have a man to protect your financial needs?" (Lesson 9). Not only does "man" in the first sentence preclude "Sir's" conceiving of a woman as a financial expert, but the context also implies that police*man*, fire*man* and physician are the other men engaged in other kinds of protection. The letter emphasizes the need for a particular financial expert by repeating several times that the "National Finance man" is the one to trust.

In other letters, there are always "businessmen and salesmen" but never "businesswomen or saleswomen." The gender of professors, bosses, manufacturers, college graduates, journalists, company presidents, and bankers is identified as masculine from the pronominal reference "he" or greetings such as "Dear Mr. Banker." The only time "she or her" appears is when the antecedent is "secretary." Instead of implying either gender, in each context, the grammatical generic "he" actually establishes the masculine gender for all roles except secretary, since "she" is exclusively reserved for that role. In the *Handbook for the Legal Secretary*, as well, the lawyers are pictured and referred to as men and the judges are given men's names, whereas the legal secretary is always female.

Dr. Doris Fitzgerald reported that the required text for a sequence of four accounting courses, *Accounting Principles* (1973) contains only two references in its 868 pages to women as owners of a business—one is a "telephone answering service" and another is a laundromat. Although 50 percent of the students enrolled in accounting courses at Manhattan Community College are female, they are symbolically invisible in their own textbooks.

My own informal examination of a representative sample of college English handbooks and rhetoric texts published after 1972 indicated that English language texts are far ahead of other disciplines in "de-sexing" illustrative sentences and prose passages.

A serious attempt to include significant writing by women in a Freshman English rhetoric text was indicated by Arthur M. Eastman *et al.*, editors of *The Norton Reader: An Anthology of Prose*, in their 1973 Preface: "For their tireless efforts in bringing to this Third Edition more selections by and about women, the editors gratefully acknowledge the assistance of Dr. Joan E. Hartman of

Staten Island Community College and Dr. Carol Ohmann of Wesleyan University" (p. xiv).

In Hulon Willis's *Brief Handbook of English* (1975), masculine and feminine gender appear approximately the same number of times in illustrative material. When Mother is mentioned so is Dad, when husbands so are wives, and when girls appear so do boys in unstereotyped contexts. In fact, the author seems to use neutral and plural nouns and pronouns whenever possible. I observed a similar balance of male and female representation among the numerous model writers cited in Hans P. Guth's *Words and Ideas: A Handbook for College Writing* (1975). In a handbook written by a woman and a man, Suzanne E. and Roderick A. Jacobs, *The College Writer's Handbook* (1973), the student writer is alternately referred to as "he" and "she."

Even if the dictionary and textbook editors were to deliberately balance the representation and use of male and female words in definitions and illustrative and informative statements, it would be useless and even damaging to both sexes if contexts continued to promote rigid sex stereotypes and a superior/inferior relationship between men and women. Besides having relatively low social and economic status, the stereotyped female roles and professions are usually described as having unattractive, negative qualities. The stereotyped librarian, for example, was described by A. P. Sable in "The Sexuality of the Library Profession":

> She's a she, wears a long, unfashionable dress down to her calves, sits at a desk in view of all library users with a crabbed, tightly pursed look upon her face. Bespectacled, hair pulled back behind her ears, she is unfailingly and eternally middle aged, unmarried and most uncommunicative. She exists to put a damper on all spontaneity, silencing the exuberance of the young with a harsh look or hiss of air . . . an ultimately pitiable figure with no outside interest (*Wilson Library Bulletin*, April 1969).

In *Gregg Shorthand for Colleges*, the image of the female secretary is implied not only through model letters but through admonitions and advice to the student, whose skills, voice, and appearance are meant to be an asset to her male boss. At one point, she is warned:

> Many women talk in a high register which grates on the ears—and they talk too fast! With a little study and practice, it is possible for anyone to correct those bad habits. . . . (2nd ed. Vol. I, p. 18).

On the same page "The Secretary's Creed" not only summarizes professional attitudes and responsibilities but also confirms female subservience to the male, since there is no ambiguity as to the sexes of the boss and "his" secretary:

> I will be alert so that my boss need tell me only once what he desires.
>
> I will be loyal to my boss and will not gossip about his business activities even with close personal friends....
>
> I will study the business so that I may be able to relieve my boss of all possible details (p. 11).

With some justification, Prof. Marie Heinz of the Department of Secretarial Sciences at Manhattan Community College, pointed out that this creed "gives a list of things a secretary should do including learning her boss' job so that the poor boy doesn't overwork himself. I think it would at least be fair play to have 'A Boss' Creed' that might include being considerate of his secretary. It reminds me of all the articles in publications that tell how a woman should take care of her man. You never see an article on how a man should take care of his woman."

Lesson 36 then attempts to reinforce the relationship between "you and your boss" which, in effect, is between any "her and him":

> A businessman wants his secretary around when he needs her. He doesn't want her to be chatting with another secretary on another part of the floor, spending time in the powder room, or making personal telephone calls.

The dependency of "girls" on men as well as the secretary's tendency to simple-mindedness and gossip is implied in this and subsequent directives:

> ... no businessman wants an office gossip opening his mail, answering his telephone, and meeting his callers....
>
> A businessman wants a girl who can make simple decisions, one who won't run to him for answers to routine questions.

The secretary is not only warned against behaving like the typical dependent, irresponsible, gossipy girl, but she is also encouraged to remain calm and polite when everything goes wrong, take challenging tasks, and "deal with the unexpected without losing her poise." If the authors had considered the possibility of either male secretaries or female lawyers and businesswomen, I wonder whether the instructions for personality and character development would have remained as consistent with the sex stereotypes.

When addressed or referred to in business letters in these secretarial science texts, females often appear in stereotyped roles. A sample letter addressed "Dear Co-ed:" is not concerned with books or college, but with selling her shoes. Other letters addressed to women invite them to join a sewing class, learn a language, suggest a "man" for a job, or buy furniture on sale. On the other hand, masculine gender in the letters is associated with managers, foremen, department heads, organization heads, lawyers, doctors, and a railroad president.

Besides sex-role stereotyping, my informal survey uncovered patterns in the kinds of proper names used for men and women in secretarial science texts. On ten random pages in *Gregg Shorthand for Colleges, Vol. I*, I found twice as many men's names as women's. Although women's married names appeared with their own female first names, as in "Mrs. Pauline Hopkins" and "Mrs. Edith Booth," last names for both men and women were often male names, as in "Paul Morris, Mrs. Keith, Mrs. A. C. Paul, and Mr. Alexander." Men's names also appeared with middle initials, as in Fred C. Harper and James C. O'Brien, whereas women's names did not. It is my conjecture that use of a middle initial is associated with power and prestige; there is a primitive element of power and mystery in not revealing the full name, as in Franklin D. Roosevelt, Harry S. Truman, John F. Kennedy, and Richard M. Nixon. My own experience in using my first name initial, "H.," indicates that most people are convinced that the gender ambiguity of "Lee" is resolved as masculine, once the initial "H." is attached. After all, I've been told, what woman would call herself "H. Lee"? The irony is that if I were to use my full first name, they would still be convinced that my name was that of a male!

Although all names in the sample from *Gregg Shorthand for Colleges* were ethnically neutral, i.e., typical of Anglo-Saxon Americans, like Page, Drew, Smith, Abbott, Booth, and Hastings, some names had specific denotative and connotative meanings in English. The strongest name for a woman was "Mrs. Law," but it was offset by "Mrs. Strange." Except for "Howard Short and Tom Small," in general, men's names tended to connote and denote strength and power: Mann, Lyons, Strong, King, Frank, Yale, Young, Alexander, and Powers.

Again, the English handbooks I examined generally steered away from stereotyping either sex. In Lloyd A. Flanagan's *Approaches to Exposition: What, How and Why* (1974), I found a few stereotyped contexts: Dr. Bragg, the judge, writer, gambler and tiger all received masculine referents, whereas the nurse was identified as "she." On the other hand, in more contexts stereotypes were resisted, both genders were represented in the same illustration, or the situation described was gender-neutral.

> Water skiing provides a girl with the opportunity to develop herself physically. When she skis, she uses almost all of her muscles (p. 91).

> Men would not listen to their leaders; children would not obey their fathers; and many women went their own way not paying attention to anyone (p. 104).

> Mary is tall; her brother Mike is short (p. 154).

> John more nearly resembles his mother than his father (p. 154).

> The men struggled and wept, while the women shook their heads in wonderment (p. 218).

In addition, two of the three model essays in this volume were written by female students. In one context, the feminine gender is used for a business executive, but that executive's behavior is stereotyped as the good housekeeper, making a comfortable home away from home at the plant:

> (1) Following the death of the company's president, another executive took over the business of running the company. (2) From that time on, the employees' working conditions began to improve. (3) First, she provided a clean and nicely decorated lunchroom. (4) Shortly after that she engaged a catering service to supply delicious hot cafeteria food for all shifts (p. 123).

When texts depict women in conventionally male roles and professions, a woman's work is often trivialized or described as dependent on that of others. In one textbook, the caption under an illustration of a woman scientist read: "The Project the young woman is working on is not her own idea. She was assigned to work on it. And she has been using her scientific knowledge to help develop a useful, safe drug which her company can then produce and sell. As an employee working on someone else's idea, she is typical of thousands of scientists working in industry today" (Marjorie B. U'Ren, "The Image of Women in Textbooks," *Women in Sexist Society*, 1971, p. 324).

In a collection of papers titled *Semantic Syntax* (1974), the "Notes on the Contributors" describe George Lakoff as "Professor of Linguistics at the University of California at Berkeley," whereas Robin Lakoff, whose article is *not* coauthored, is nevertheless described as "George Lakoff's wife, and *also* a Professor of Linguistics at Berkeley." (Italics added.) According to the entry, Ms. Lakoff's marital status is of primary importance, but her professional stature is secondary and trivialized as "also a Professor."

Recent Efforts toward Reform

In the last few years, some publishing companies have taken deliberate steps to avoid sexism in the language of their works and raise the consciousness of their editors and authors. Scott, Foresman & Co., for example, issued "Guidelines for Improving the Image of Women in Textbooks" (1972), and McGraw-Hill issued "Guidelines for Equal Treatment of the Sexes in McGraw-Hill Book Co. Publications" (1974). The *American Heritage School Dictionary*, produced by a McGraw-Hill subsidiary, was also the first dictionary to include "Ms." among its word entries.

In reviewing recent manuscripts for college English texts submitted to one New York publisher, I noticed that, although no official company policy had been set for "equal treatment of the sexes," the authors themselves seemed to be making a conscious effort to use male and female pronouns and nouns equally and to create lively, original, unstereotyped contexts for both genders in illustrative sentences.

What is required, however, is a new standard of "good" English in dictionaries and textbooks that is not antithetical to descriptive linguistics. That any language can be used to reflect cultural prejudices, or that biases against certain groups exist in the society goes without saying. The major dictionary and textbook publishers, however, may begin to realize that it is not necessary to stereotype and/or denigrate males and females in order to illustrate meaning and usage or develop professional skills. Plural and neuter pronouns already exist in English, so that neither gender need be identified in illustrative sentences, directions, narrations, and other rhetorical modes employed by textbook writers. By continuing to omit the feminine and use English gender in stereotyped ways, educators are running the risk of restricting human possibilities rather than widening them.

I do not think that changes in linguistic sexism can be mandated. However, it seems that often "grammarians" are the last to accept any change in word usage and language patterns. . . . As a teacher, I feel that a significant impact on the area of linguistic sexism can be made by discussing the subject with young people. As youth becomes aware, I think that guidelines for publishers, policy statements, etc. might become unnecessary.

Our society is "youth oriented" now and we individuals who work closely with the English language and youth should realize the potential we have to initiate change.

Judy Mohr
teacher

I do not believe change can be mandated, but it certainly can be taught on the grade school level. Speech patterns could possibly be changed in a generation or so this way.

Jim Mack
editor

A problem I've come across lately is a seeming fear by textbook publishers of having, e.g., any women who cook or any doctors who are males. . . . How sexist is a husband who never cooks or a wife who never repairs plumbing? I've got no simple answers, of course, but I find publishers who work with a formula to be somewhat amusing, although probably not dangerous.

Bruce Cronnel
educational researcher and
developer

When we wrote the "Framework in Reading for the Elementary and Secondary Schools of California" in 1972-73, the entire booklet had not a "he" or a "she" in it! It wasn't easy, but it can be done. We wanted to avoid the non-conscious reference to the students having trouble learning to read as "he," the teacher as "she," and the school administrator as "he"—so we left them out entirely. This booklet was adopted by the State Board of Education in 1973 and is now state policy.

Alpha Quincy
school principal

Sexism in Children's Books and Elementary Classroom Materials

Alleen Pace Nilsen

Probably not a day goes by in which some bit of sexism is not practiced through speech, action, or attitude in every elementary school in the country. It may be nothing more than a gesture, a look, a lift of the voice, or a pat on the shoulder. Or it may be something as blatant as a game that excludes girls, division of school bus into seats for girls and seats for boys, restriction of boys from certain classes and of girls from other classes, or definition of different sets of career expectations for girls and boys. This sexism is not fostered exclusively by adults. Children are surprisingly conservative in sticking to what they have learned as appropriate sex roles and in applying pressure to conform on their peers.

A discussion of all aspects of sexism in elementary education would fill several books, so this chapter will be limited to sexism as it appears on the printed pages of materials read by children of elementary school age. The reason for focusing on the printed page is twofold. First, it is the most visible kind of sexism and the easiest to document, because it is in solid black and white. It can be turned to again and again for checking and reanalysis. Second, the printed page holds a special place in our culture. Print, in most minds, suggests veracity. We as a culture respect what we read. Even adults who have been educated in critical thinking sometimes experience, as a reflex, the notion that if a statement appears in public print, it must be true. Children with their limited experience, are more apt than adults to put their trust in the printed page. Much of what we do in school is based on building children's trust in books. This is all to the good; how would children learn from their reading if they did not trust the material? But while we are teaching children to put their faith in what they read at school, we are obligated to make sure that school reading material is deserving of that trust.

Children's Books—a Male-Oriented Medium

The first place children meet sexism on the printed page is in their primers and in the books they select from the library. In the years between 1950 and 1970, these books were overwhelmingly oriented towards boys. When George W. Norvell did his study, *The Reading Interests of Young People* (D.C. Heath, 1950), one of his conclusions was that boys preferred to read about boys while girls would read about either boys or girls. According to the study, this preference for reading about males began to manifest itself in the fourth and fifth grades and continued unabated until adulthood.

Publishers, with sales in mind, took the findings to heart and searched for more stories about boys. In 1964, the instructor of a class in writing for children told us students that it was unwise to write about girls, because doing so would automatically cut our sales potential in half. Scott O'Dell's 1961 prize-winning historical novel, about a young Indian girl accidentally left on the *Island of the Blue Dolphins* when her tribe moved away, was initially rejected by an editor, who asked O'Dell to change his main character to a boy.

This publishing preference for boys continued into the seventies. A survey I made of 80 picture books that won the Caldecott Medal or were runners-up between 1950 and 1970 showed a steady decline in the number of females portrayed in what are generally considered our highest quality books for preschool and early elementary grades. Between 1951 and 1955, females made up 46 percent of the characters depicted in these books; between 1956 and 1960, 41 percent; between 1961 and 1965, 35 percent; and between 1966 and 1970, females made up only 26 percent of the characters (*College English*, May 1971).

What has been the effect of these years of increasing male orientation in children's books? One result was that the bias became so obvious that people all over the country began to notice, make studies, and come independently to similar conclusions. One of the first to publish such findings was a group called Women on Words and Images. They studied the 134 books from 14 major publishers used as reading texts in three suburban New Jersey communities. In their booklet, *Dick and Jane as Victims: Sex Stereotyping in Children's Readers*, they reported that five boys were pictured for every two girls; six men were written about in biographies for every one woman; four male folk or fantasy characters were depicted for every one female. Analyzing the content of the stories, they found that clever girls appeared only 33 times, compared to 131 clever boys. In nearly all of the stories, females played a supportive, appreciative role while males were showing their strength, bravery, and leadership skills.

Another result of the male orientation of children's books is hypothetical but likely. Everyone was led to expect all the good stories to be about boys. Recent researchers have pushed the age where sex affects the choice of reading material down from the middle grades to the lower grades. Typical of the statements found in teacher training textbooks is this one from *Reading and the Elementary School Child: Theory and Practice for Teachers* by Robert M. Wilson and Maryanne Hall (Van Nostrand Reinhold Company, 1972):

> As early as first grade, there are some differences in interests between boys and girls, but these differences become much more evident as children move through the elementary grades. Girls tend to read more widely than boys and will read stories with masculine main characters, while boys in the intermediate grades tend to reject books they label "girls' books." When choosing books to read to the whole class, therefore, a teacher must consider sex preferences (pp. 222-23).

It is this kind of statement which makes me wonder whether by concentrating on "boy books" we have trained a progressively younger group of boys to expect and want their sex to dominate in whatever they read. Sylvia-Lee Tibbetts explored this thought in an article, "Sex Differences in Children's Reading Preferences," in *The Reading Teacher* (December 1974, pp. 279-81).

From the very beginning of their lives, when dresses with scratchy ruffles are put on female babies and ribbon bows are taped to their bald heads, little girls are trained to be malleable and to acquiesce. The fact that they will read about boys as well as girls may be related to their overall cooperativeness (whether inherent or culturally implanted) and to their tendency to read more of everything. This doesn't mean that they don't have preferences.

As part of my doctoral dissertation, I had a matched sampling of boys and girls help me select pictures they thought would be good to illustrate a proposed book. The boys showed a preference for pictures of males; the girls, for pictures of females. Of the total number of pictures chosen, the girls selected 62 more pictures of females than of males, while the boys selected 59 more pictures of males than females. With more than a dozen sets of pictures from which to choose, only twice did the selections go against this trend. An apparent explanation for this divergence is that the subject matter was of more interest to one sex than the other. A picture of a man holding a baby (both were apparently males) got more girls' votes, probably because the girls were attracted to the picture of the baby. And a picture of a young girl fishing got more boys' votes, no doubt because the boys were attracted to the sport.

This indicates that it may be an oversimplification to classify children's reading preferences on the basis of sex only. The activity of the characters is probably of equal or greater importance, which leads to another question: Could the books about boys be preferred because they are more exciting to both sexes? The cultural limitations we have placed on girls make it unlikely that stories about "dainty little girls" will have the same appeal as stories about "rough and tumble" boys. Yet we are not willing to relinquish the stereotyped role for girls in books. This year in one of our local schools, Rosa Guy's book *The Friends* was taken off the library shelves by a principal who felt that one of its leading girl characters "talked and acted in a way that we wouldn't want our girls to imitate."

Boys do read honest stories about females who are doing interesting things. They like *Harriet the Spy, Charlotte's Web,* and *Island of the Blue Dolphins.* Older boys like *The Diary of Anne Frank* and *To Kill a Mockingbird.* They reject books which glorify the feminine role, i.e., those that teach girls to be little ladies. The same older boys reject romances, no doubt because the male characters are so false. A counterpart of this sub-literature, the men's magazine, projects an image of the playgirl which girls reject as equally unreal. It seems that what is being rejected is dishonesty.

Texts and Teaching Materials— Subtle and Unsubtle Stereotypes

We do not look for falseness or dishonesty in many of the school books we give to children. Nobody thinks to call readers, spellers, and math books sub-literatures. Yet the ways they picture the sexes are frequently unreal. For example, several different groups examining school texts found that illustrations usually picture boys as physically larger than girls. This is contrary to real life, in which the later-maturing boys are frequently smaller than girls of the same age. The stereotype originates in the adult point of view.

Dishonest stereotyping has also resulted from adults' mind-set that all authors are males. Historically, most great writers have been men, and today, the majority of adult books are by male authors. But most people do not realize that children's books are more often written by women.

To find out what children think about sex as related to particular jobs, I gave a set of 12 sentences to my research sample group of 50 boys and 50 girls. The children were to add tag questions (either *Wasn't he?* or *Wasn't she?*) at the end of the sentences. These children grouped most career roles either at the male or at the female end of a continuum. Nurse, teacher, dancer, and secretary were given between 99 and 86 percent "feminine" answers. Doctor, plumber, farmer, truck driver, and boss were given between 99 and 92 percent "male" answers. The children made less definite assumptions about cook, clerk, and author.

One sentence, "The author was writing a book. . ." received 79 *he's* and 21 *she's*. It caused more consternation than any other statement: eleven children out of 100 first indicated one pronoun, then changed their minds and chose the other. Six changed *he* to *she*; five changed from *she* to *he*. Out of 12 sentences, this was also the one that elicited the most spontaneous comments. For example, several children said, in effect, "This one's hard because it could be either." A fifth-grade girl who was especially well read remarked, "It sounds like a 'wasn't he' but I think 'wasn't she's' make better stories." Perhaps the confusion the children felt is the same that prompted adults to invent the term *authoress* to identify women writers.

The supposition that all writers are men has led to a practice which perpetuates that falsehood. When women write they often adopt masculine-sounding pen names or use initials. They probably began doing this in hopes of receiving a better initial reading by prospective publishers. However, writers such as S. E. Hinton (Susan Elizabeth) have openly said that their publishers encouraged them to use a masculine-sounding name because young readers would be more apt to select their books and would have more faith in the authenticity of the material—particularly if it were about sports, conflict, or adventure.

To continue to give the impression that women do not think about and cannot write about such subjects is in direct conflict with the facts. It promotes a false perception of the world. The excitement, adventure, and conflict that appear in books written by the following authors must be a part of the female psyche—because these writers are all women: D. N. Ahnstrom, E. M. Almedingen, H. F. Brinsmead, Nicholas Charles, John Clarke, Paige Dixon, J. A. Evans, C. H. Frick, Wilson Gage, S. E. Hinton, E. L. Konigsburg, R. R. Knudson, Lawrence, A. M. Lightner, Julian May, E. Nesbit, Ellsworth Newcombe, Andre Norton, K. M. Peyton, Henry Handel Richardson, R. H. Shimer, and P. L. Travers.

We perpetuate another false image by allowing girls to be portrayed as passive while boys are shown as active. This again reflects traditional adult expectations about sex roles. In real life, little girls are just as active as little boys.

Lenore Weitzman studied the spelling texts officially adopted throughout California during the 1960s and found that consonants were represented as boys while vowels were represented as girls. Unfortunately this metaphor was adopted by a group of teachers who wanted to write an exciting and entertaining set of prereading and early reading materials. These people created the Alpha Time and Alpha One reading programs. The 1969 edition, still in use in some schools, features the Huggables, plastic blow-up toys representing each letter. Boys are the consonants and girls, the vowels.

After pupils have learned all the consonants and taken part in many "fun" activities centered around each letter, the vowels are introduced. First comes Little Miss A, who goes "A'choo, A'choo" all the time. According to the musical record that accompanies the program, when she first appears at a gathering of all the boy letters, this is what ensues:

> "No, no," they cried, "it can't be true!
> Not with so much work to do.
> Can that be a girl we see?
> We didn't know it would be a she!"
> Some of the boys just sulked and pouted,
> But others were very angry and shouted,
> "A girl! A girl! Oh, go away;
> A girl's no good for work or play."
> (Alpha One, p. 281)

At last the boys let Little Miss A stay, but she is lonely and "She cried and cried until the boys promised to meet her sister." Her sister Little Miss E, who is so weak she must exercise all the time, comes in with tears in her eyes. She is the picture of begging helplessness as she says, "Maybe I'm not very strong, but please, oh please, let me belong" (p. 281).

The stereotype that girls have health problems is overworked in this series as shown by the sneezing Little Miss A and the weak Little Miss E, who are followed by Little Miss I, who itches all the time and Little Miss O, whose "throat hurt so that off to the doctor she had to go." Little Miss Y is a dainty and delicate creature who must hide behind her umbrella all the time because "I'm terribly afraid, you see, the sun is really after me!" (pp. 282, 283). The consonant boy characters have entirely different personalities. They play the dominant leadership roles quite literally putting the girls in their places. Compare the sampling of lines spoken by the boy consonants (on the left) to those spoken by the girl vowels (on the right):

Boy Consonant Lines	Girl Vowel Lines

It looks like we are stuck again;
We much prefer to work with men.
You don't look like very much;
You'd probably break at the
  slightest touch.
	Boys, why must you make fun of
	  me?
	Is it only because I am a she?

Girls, girls, why don't you smile? Can't you be happy for just a while?	Now, now, Mr. Q. depend on me, In all your words I'll always be; When I'm with Q, I make no sound;

The girls are really getting out of
  hand.
I think I'll hit them with a rubber
  band.
	Boo hoo, boo hoo, boo hoo, boo hoo.
	We don't like what you want to do.
	One sound is hard, as well you
	  knew;
	How will we ever remember two?

Vowels, I see tears on every face.
Enough of this! You'll flood the
  place!
	And when our sounds are short and
	  weak
	You must make it safe for us to
	  speak.

Miss O, no complaining, don't you
  dare!
Here I come. Beware! Beware!
	Protection is what our short sounds
	  need;
	The boys should protect us - is that
	  agreed?

Little Miss A, now that I stand next to you, Tell me what you'll have to do.	Oh please, Mr. R, don't change me. I don't learn too easily!

(Alpha One, pp. 274, 275, 281, ff.)

After protests from various chapters of the National Organization for Women and from feminist educators in general, the program was somewhat revised so that in 1974 a different version was available in which, according to the publishers, a spirit of cooperation takes the place of domination and/or ostracism. The manipulation, whining and crying are gone, as well as "Little" in the titles of the vowels. But it is impossible to remove the sexist attitudes from the series, because its whole point is to stress differences between vowels and consonants and the way they "behave." Although it's true that vowels and consonants behave quite differently, little boys and little girls have similar needs and desires. The creators of the Alpha programs, like the stepsisters in the old version of "Cinderella," had to cut off a few toes to make things fit.

I discussed the problem with a graduate class of reading instructors, who suggested this alternative: The consonants should be children of both sexes with varied personalities, playing together. The vowels could then be robots or computerized dolls which would be manipulated by the real people.

A graduate student in reading at Arizona State University, Susan Jenkins, investigated the psychological effect of the Alpha One program on children. She went to three comparable classes of first graders. One class had used the original Alpha One program throughout kindergarten and the first seven months of first grade. The second class had used the program in kindergarten and intermittently throughout the first seven months of first grade. The third class had used other more traditional reading material throughout their schooling. In individual interviews, Jenkins had the children identify certain activities such as crying, playing tricks on others, being mean, building things, worrying about their clothes, being sick, being stupid, and figuring out solutions, as either male or female. There was a direct correlation in the three classes between the length of exposure to the Alpha One program and the degree to which the children identified the activities as belonging in the male and female domains as stereotyped in the Alpha One reading program. There was a statistically significant difference between the class that had not seen the Alpha One program and the one that had used it exclusively.

Perhaps the results would have been different if the children had been using the revised version. And certainly there are enough variables affecting all groups of children that more studies need to be made before conclusions are drawn. But it does appear that just as feminists fear, children do learn the psychological and sociological values from the content of their reading programs.

Between 60 and 80 percent of the time spent in elementary school is devoted to teaching reading and related skills. Because language arts materials receive so much attention, it is especially important that they be free from bias. But until people in the feminist movement began pointing out inequities, reading texts were openly and purposely made to appeal to boys. One of the points Rudolf Flesch made in the 1950s in *Why Johnny Can't Read* was that school was a feminine place and that little boys felt confined and intimidated. To compensate for the "feminine orientation" in schools, we created new and exciting supplemental readers. Dick and Jane, Jack and Janet, Alice and Jerry, and Tom and Betty, who played together in the beginning readers, were pushed aside to make room for easy-to-read books with all-male casts including Cowboy Sam, Sailor Jack, and Dan Frontier. The feeling was that since it seemed harder for boys than girls to learn to read, we should do all we could to make the materials appealing to boys.

A factor that contributed to this boy-orientation of school materials was the Soviet launching of Sputnik, which set off an education explosion slanted toward science and math. In 1961, Congress passed the National Defense Education Act, which allotted federal funds to school libraries specifically for the purchase of science books. These were not texts but enrichment materials, and publishers scrambled to get books on the market that would qualify for purchase under this act. Many of the books were historical accounts of scientific discoveries, and, because men have made most of the discoveries, these were books about men. Other books outlined experiments for children to perform.

Partly because in English we refer to unknown persons as *he*, and perhaps because adults envisioned bright young men helping us overtake the Russians, nearly all of the artists' drawings for these books depicted boys. When girls were shown, they were in the background appreciatively watching the clever boys, who turned knobs or poured fluids from one test tube to another. Taken collectively, the view of sex roles created by these books was appallingly prejudiced. The inescapable conclusion is that society's prime concern, at that still-recent date, was for the education of boys, and that girls were second-class citizens, welcome to come along and get what they could.

A vivid illustration of this attitude was an article that appeared in *Instructor* magazine a few years ago. It told about a public school that had experimented with all-boy classes in kindergarten. It described this innovation in glowing terms, telling about the interesting activities and the warm relationship existing between the men teachers and the boys. Pictures showed them rough-housing together. If the school had all-male kindergartens it must also have had all-female kindergartens; but not one word was said about the desirability or effect of having only girls in a class.

Animal Characters—Human Stereotypes Extended

Another set of materials that grew out of this period were the easy-to-read books that Dr. Seuss and his fellow craftsmen created about fantasy creatures and/or personified animals. It was thought that children could identify with these characters regardless of race, creed, color, or sex. But the matter of sex was not so simple because of the problem of English gender, or perhaps human psychology. It appears that unless we have evidence to prove that an animal is female, we use the masculine pronoun, whether or not we make a conscious decision that the animal is male. When an author uses a masculine pronoun to refer to an animal, an artist is committed to follow suit and make the illustration "masculine." Both children and adults would think the artist had made a mistake if he or she drew a feminine-looking animal, for example one with an apron, when the author had referred to the character with a masculine pronoun. As a result, practically all the animals in books for young children are males, including Albert the Albatross, Zeke the Raccoon, Julius the Gorilla, Harry the Dirty Dog, Little Bear, Chester the Horse, and Sam the Firefly.

In books of this type, the only well-rounded female character I can think of is Frances, the badger in a series by Lillian and Russell Hoban. Other females, besides those playing mother roles, were introduced by authors who needed someone in the plot with a personality trait popularly ascribed to females. Examples are *Old Rosie, The Horse Nobody Understood* (Moore), the foolish little red hen in *The Rain Puddle* (Holl) and the silly goose *Petunia* in a series of books by Roger Duvoisin. Female animals are depicted as lonely, like the hippopotamus in *Lonely Veronica* (Duvoisin); or they are fashion conscious like *Miss Harriet Hippopotamus and the Most Wonderful* (Moore) and the shrew in *Shrewbettina's Birthday* (Goodall). That shrew had to be protected by others, as did the camel in *The Camel Who Took a Walk* (Tworkov) and the hen in *Rosie's Walk* (Hutchins).

I wondered whether authors of children's books were somehow to blame for treating all humanized animals as if they were males unless proven otherwise. To find out whether this was an artificial usage taught to children in school, I made a study of pronouns children use as they talk about animals. I took 16 pictures of eight animals (two of each animal in different poses so the children would have to be specific in their descriptions) from moderately popular children's books. The animals were not clothed, nor were they involved in activities specifically thought of as related to one sex or the other. I had both prints and slides made. A matched sampling of 50 boys and 50 girls, ages four through 12, participated. One child was shown a projected slide while the other child, who could not see the slide, had all the photographs spread in front of him or her. The child looking at the slide was to describe the picture well enough that the child with the photographs could select the correct one.

The children thought that they were being timed to see how efficiently they could make these match-ups. What was really being recorded were the pronouns they were using. In all the conversations, these 100 children used a total of 3,020 pronouns. Only 17 of these pronouns were feminine. The others were almost equally divided between masculine and neuter pronouns: 1,542 masculine and 1,461 neuter. There was some indication that the children used neuter pronouns when they had an inkling that the animal was not male. For example, in talking about two pictures of a cat (cats are often thought of as feminine) the children used nearly 60 percent neuter pronouns, and for this animal, more than half of the 17 feminine pronouns were used. One picture showed a donkey with a fat stomach, and three children said, "It's pregnant," as if they recognized that "He's pregnant" would be deviant, but just didn't feel natural about saying "She's pregnant." Younger children had basically the same usages as the older children.

Just what these statistics prove is hard to determine, except that they do show that it doesn't occur to people to use feminine pronouns as either general all-inclusive terms or as terms for unknown entities. Perhaps one thing that can be gained from the experiment is the realization that it will require a conscious effort on the part of writers of children's fantasy books to include females in other than stereotyped roles.

Making the Break with "What Comes Naturally"

Most of the stereotyping which today appears so blatant was not purposely planned. It developed because people were doing "what came naturally." They were taking the easy path, and if we wish to reverse the trend, then at least for the next few years we are going to have to take the more difficult path.

The easy path for teachers is to continue to use the same old readers with all the male-oriented stories. The difficult path is going to the library or a bookstore and bringing in for class use many of the new books that present refreshing images of girls who are assertive and boys who are gentle, mothers who have good jobs and fathers who help around the house, and both males and females who feel free to express themselves and to develop whatever talents and qualities they desire regardless of stereotyping. If we bring to class the best in children's literature, the really honest and true-to-life stories, then we will not have to worry so much about false stereotypes or the exclusion of girls from the story.

In the text material designed for remedial reading classes, where the stories center around such "male interests" as motorcycles, hot rods, drag racing, and sports, there is a strong "macho" feeling inherent in context and vocabulary. A professor of reading at Arizona State University observed that perhaps the materials used in remedial programs work against, rather than for, the intended cure, because they continue to build up the very attitudes that were at least partially responsible for landing the student in the clinic in the first place. A majority of the students who come to reading clinics belong to families with a strong feeling of machismo which translates into "Reading is for sissies and girls—men have more important things to do." A similar attitude makes many boys resist learning to write and spell.

Besides influencing text writers to create macho content in remedial readers, the idea that boys and not girls have trouble with reading leads to a kind of sexist segregation in the classes. A director of a children's remedial reading laboratory told me that teachers are much more hesitant to send a girl than a boy for special help. When a girl is finally referred to the reading clinic, her entering scores will be much lower than average because the teacher has held out, not wanting to send a "sweet little girl" into that tough world of all-boy reading classes.

In teaching language usage, the easy path is to teach children the rule that *everyone* should be followed by *his*. The difficult path is to teach them how complex the problem of grammatical gender is, how it does not correlate perfectly with sex, and how they must sometimes choose whether they want to be correct in relation to grammar rules or in relation to meaning.

The easy path is to ignore the ambiguity in *man* and related words. Teaching children that words change meanings and cannot always be interpreted literally is more difficult. We talk about the *person*ality of our dog; we *dress* in pants, and we do *silk* screening without using silk. *Black*boards are seldom black; *silver*ware usually isn't silver, and *station* wagons seldom pick people up at stations. Last fall the airline employees struck under the *Railroad Employees Act*, a grown man was *kid*napped, and most of us *butter*ed our bread with margarine.

Although words do change their meanings, there is no excuse for us to be sloppy as writers, illustrators, editors, teachers, or critics. When we use a word like *man* in the generic sense, we are obligated to follow through with the same meaning and make sure that illustrations show that meaning. This has not been done in the past. Illustrators have taken the easy path and have drawn what first came into their heads, and this was usually men.

At two libraries, I checked each children's book that had a generic *man* word in the title, then counted the number of males and females to see if the artist had really expressed the all-inclusive meaning. Books with generic titles for the youngest children were those about prehistoric people. These are written for children in primary grades and could be a useful tool for teaching the all-inclusive meaning of either *man, caveman,* or *prehistoric man.* No doubt there were as many prehistoric females as males. But in the five books I found (*The First Men* by May, *How Man Began* by Bateman, *Looking at Man's Past* by Stilwell, *The Making of Man* by Cornwall, and *Prehistoric Man and the Primates* by Scheele), there were 267 pictures of males compared to 33 of females.

Perhaps the language was an influence, with the word *man* triggering the artists to think of males. And since there are no prehistoric people for artists to look at while painting, they must rely on their imaginations and on the stereotypes in their own minds, which probably consist of males doing the exciting things like hunting and building fires and running and leaping while the females stayed in the caves and prepared food and tended the babies. Another reason it was easier to draw males than females relates to our reluctance to show nudity in children's books. It is easier for an artist to cover up male genitalia than female.

My study yielded nine other books which used *men* or *fathers* in a generic sense. They were *The Color of Man* by Cohen, *Every Man Heart Lay Down* by Graham, *Man and His Tools* by Burns, *Man and Insects* by Newman, *Man and Magic* by Appel, *Man and Mastiff* by Kay, *Man in Space to the Moon* by Branley, *Manned Space Flight* by Faget, and *Meet the Pilgrim Fathers* by Payne. Males still outnumbered the females in these books, but the ratio was only about three to one, 310 males compared to 96 females. The only book approximating equal representation was *The Color of Man*, which pictured 47 males, 47 females, eight people whose sex was undistinguishable, 10 male groups, one female group, and 29 mixed-sex groups. It is significant that this book was illustrated not with drawings but with photographs. This is another example of the difference between the world that really exists, i.e., in photographs, and the world that we as adults perceive and present to children, i.e., in imaginative drawings.

Gender Rules in English—Challenges for the Girl Child

One reason I feel we must teach children about gender is that it is a fairly sophisticated system that disagrees with the system of natural gender which children learn early in life. This goes both for lexical items incorporating some marker of masculine and for the pronoun system. I made a study to see what pronouns children use in their natural speech about other children; it yielded fairly conclusive evidence that children's pronoun usage does not match the adult system or the system used in printed school materials. I began the study because, of all the differences in language between men and women, it stands to reason that the area of gender would be one in which we might expect to find major differences in interpretation and usage, due to the close correlation in English between physical sex and grammatical gender.

A common distinction which linguists make when they talk about the grammatical rules a speaker uses in everyday language is that between rules children learn naturally and early in their lives and rules they learn formally, either in school or through some other kind of overt instruction. In talking about these rules, William Labov explained that most linguistic rules are "automatic, deepseated patterns of behavior which are not consciously recognized and are never violated." (*The Study of Nonstandard English*,

1969, p. 29). He called these Type I rules. As an example he gave the contraction of *is* to *'s* when *that is* becomes *that's*. He went on to say that Type I rules are "hard to detect simply because they are never violated and one never thinks about them at all."

Type II rules are "The kinds of rules which are taught in school." When a Type II rule is violated, the mistake is noticed and, if made in school, is usually corrected by the teacher. As examples of Type II rules he gave the censuring of *ain't* and the censuring of double negatives. There is no clear-cut dividing line between Type I and Type II rules. As Labov has shown with speakers of nonstandard English, what is a Type I rule for some speakers may be a Type II rule for others. This depends on the circumstances surrounding the speaker during the first few years of learning to talk.

The hypothesis that I tried to test, based on the concept of Type I and Type II rules, is that when learning to speak, young boys and young girls have sufficiently different experiences in relation to both lexical and grammatical markers of gender that the standard English rule of using a masculine marker in a generic sense comes close to being a Type I (naturally developed) rule for boys, but a Type II (formally taught) rule for girls. If this is indeed the case, it would be at least a partial explanation for the different ways male and female speakers and writers respond to the adoption of such terms as *chairperson*.

It is reasonable to conjecture that because of the egocentricity which psychologists describe as a normal developmental stage of all young children, a boy who is accustomed to hearing such words as *he*, *him*, and *his* used in relationship to himself will feel a closer affinity to these terms than will a young girl who has instead developed an emotional response to *she*, *her* and *hers*. Next to a child's name and perhaps the word *baby*, these pronouns are among the most consistent terms a baby hears in reference to himself or herself. Although they are not said directly to the baby, such colloquial sentences as the following are frequently said in the homes of babies and have the common feature of resulting in some positive action related to the baby:

1. Get the baby—will you dear—*he's* crying.
2. Susie, hand *her her* rattle.
3. Look how strong *he's* getting!
4. Here's *her* bib.
5. *She's* darling, isn't *she*?

Sentences like these are spoken around babies much more often than they are around either adults or children, because not expecting an answer from the baby, people sometimes feel more comfortable talking about, rather than to, a baby. Nevertheless they sometimes say sentences similar to numbers 3 and 5 directly to a baby, with particular emphasis on the pronouns.

A young boy who is accustomed to hearing himself and his possessions referred to with masculine pronouns has excellent readiness for acquiring the standard formal rules guiding the treatment of gender in English. As he expands his world to include progressively larger circles of environment and acquaintances, he simply expands the number of things referred to with masculine pronouns. It's a very natural process for him to learn that every creature not obviously female is treated as masculine. This parallels the young boy's actual experience with real life and the pronouns he has heard, which because of his sex have been predominantly masculine. He has no reason to question the naturalness of the standard rule. It fits directly into his Type I grammar. The only unusual requirement is that at some stage in his development he learn to include females in the body of referents. At what age or stage of linguistic development and to what extent this happens has not been studied. And since throughout childhood the use of this "fuller" interpretation of masculine gender is mainly a matter of reception rather than production, there is little overt signalling to tell whether or not the boy has reached this level.

Neither do we know precisely when and if a girl has reached this level of linguistic maturity. But an important point for appreciating the rationale behind the present study is the fact that girls travel towards an understanding of this fuller concept of gender—that is, the existence of a masculine gender denoting both male and female—by a different route.

A young girl becomes accustomed to hearing herself and things related to her referred to with feminine pronouns. Contributing to this is the fact that in the colloquial kind of spoken English commonly used with children, gender follows a "natural" rather than "grammatical" form. It would be fairly safe to assume that during the very early years of a girl's life she probably has equal, if not greater, experience with feminine pronouns than with masculine ones. But when she begins to expand her environment, unlike the boy, she does not simply enlarge her set of referents for the pronouns she is already accustomed to. Instead, she has to change her expectations and become accustomed to new pronouns.

If it is true that males and females respond differently to standard rules concerning English gender, then there should be some evidence of this difference during the period of language acquisition and learning. To look for this difference, I used a matched sampling of 50 boys and 50 girls—10 each from nursery school, first, third, fifth, and seventh grades. In individual oral sessions the children were given 12 sentences to which they were to add tag questions. Four of these sentences described activities considered masculine by popular stereotyping. Four more described activities popularly considered feminine. The four sentences most relevant to the matter at hand depicted activities which probably would be as culturally appropriate for a male as for a female. These sentences were:

> The child was eating lunch...
> The child was watching TV...
> The child was talking...
> The child was wearing new shoes...

In the sentences which contained the masculine stereotypes (the child was building a robot, was fighting, was winning the race, and was tough), the majority of children regardless of sex or age responded with "Wasn't he?". In the feminine sentences (was pretty, was baby-sitting, was crying, and was sitting by the swings), a majority of children regardless of sex or age responded with "Wasn't she?", showing that even at an early age, children have acquired the culturally implanted stereotyping of what is appropriate for boys and for girls. To the neutral sentences, girls had a tendency to respond with "Wasn't she?" while boys tended to respond with "Wasn't he?" This was particularly evident in the nursery school group in which 28 out of the 40 pronouns used by boys were *he* and 27 out of the 40 pronouns used by girls were *she*. In the four sentences, the 50 boys used a total of 116 masculine pronouns and 84 feminine. The 50 girls used 120 feminine pronouns and 80 masculine. If they had divided the pronouns randomly between masculine and feminine, they would have used 100 of each.

At first glance it would seem there is nothing very remarkable about the fact that when talking about neutral subjects, girls tend to use feminine pronouns and boys tend to use masculine pronouns.

In my particular sampling, the ratio was approximately three pronouns that correlated with the sex of the speaker to every two that referred to people of the opposite sex. But when this is considered in conjunction with the fact that the language of school, i.e., the printed language of adults, uses masculine pronouns in a ratio estimated at between three-to-one and five-to-one, then we see that the stage is set for the kind of difference that Labov talks about when he explains Type I (naturally learned) and Type II (school learned) rules. When boys grow up, they continue to use pronouns in approximately the same ratio they used as children, but it is just the opposite for girls. Their adult speech is expected to be an inverse picture of their naturally developed childhood speech.

From the foregoing discussion it appears that we have a Type I and a Type II rule difference; but a major component is missing: the instruction in school which is needed to help children make the transition between their naturally learned language and the language of standard formal English. Neither men nor women have really made the transition. Although most men are perfectly content with the system of grammatical gender as it now stands, numerous studies and examples from usage show that they have not really learned to mentally include women when they use generic terms. Part of the evidence in support of this contention is the present state of confusion, with writers wavering back and forth between generic and literal interpretations, even within the same paragraph. Women, as shown by recent protests from the feminist movement, feel very uncomfortable about the whole system of gender. As this study indicated, the mental transition from a Type I rule about gender to a Type II rule about gender is much greater for them. When men interpret generic pronouns and other lexical items literally instead of generically, they are not disturbed by any psychological response within themselves. It probably doesn't even occur to them that someone is being excluded. But when women interpret generic terms as meaning "males only," they are psychologically jarred and offended because they feel left out.

Deciding what to do about sexism in children's reading is no easy matter. But in several areas the way seems clear and steps are being taken to correct inequities. Publishers have responded surprisingly fast to requests for more balance in their old, male-oriented catalogues. New career books featuring women and men working side by side in a variety of professions are rolling off the presses, along with biographies of successful and interesting women. Within a recent six-week period, the Children's Literature Preview Center at Arizona State University received copies of eighteen biographies of women, all written for the elementary school level. The focus in fiction has also changed. In 1973, the year after the first big wave of feminist criticism of the male orientation of children's literature, the Caldecott Medal for the best picture book of the year went to *The Funny Little Woman* by Arlene Mosel (Dutton, 1972), and the Newbery Medal for the best piece of fiction went to *Julie of the Wolves* by Jean George (Harper & Row, 1972). Contrary to what might have been expected, both of these books are enjoyed by boys as well as girls.

Another bright spot on the horizon is that colleges of education throughout the country have become very much aware of the problem, and few new teachers graduate without at least having heard about the issue. Unfortunately, because of adverse economic conditions, many of these new graduates are not getting jobs as teachers and fewer new books are finding their way into schools. Most textbooks still reflect the old sexist biases, because it takes several years to put a text series together. The textbooks now on the market were started before the feminist movement drew attention to inequities. And even when nonsexist textbooks become available, schools will not have the money to immediately discard all the old books and buy new ones. This means that school librarians and classroom teachers will have an added burden over the next few years. It will be up to them to spot inequities in the printed materials they are using, talk these over with students, and search out supplementary materials which can serve as a counterbalance.

I admire your attempts to purge American English of sexist words and expressions.... I confess that words which introduce sex where I think the quality being described does not need this modification ("poetess") have always bothered me.... I wish you godspeed if you think the fight is worth fighting. My personal, skeptical, view is that it has about as much chance of acceptance as Shaw's phonetic (fonetic?) spelling or Esperanto.

Hamilton Carson
editor

Yes, I think guidelines for publication are important and necessary.... At least it is a beginning. *Fifteen* publishers made voluntary changes in their textbooks after sexist material was pointed out to them before the California adoption. Some were minor changes—but it's one step.

Alpha Quincy
school principal

Our editorial policy at Coast (determined jointly by myself and our managing editor, who is a woman) is more concerned with clarity and a certain purity in the use of the language than it is with the rather laughable and probably hopeless attempts (and meaningless ones, at that) to rid English of all sex-determined language—what we call "McGraw-Hillism" around here.

Colman Andrews
editor

Since all linguistic change must come slowly, I am sure that changes in the language pertaining to sexism will also take time. I remember my own reactions have regularly followed a pattern. At first, I resist the change. I think—"how silly to insist on saying 'chairperson' instead of 'chairman,' but I now consider the term 'chairperson' completely acceptable. Probably in a year or two, I shall be offended if anyone speaks of me as a 'chairman.'"

(name withheld)
teacher, administrator

Appendix: Guidelines for Nonsexist Use of Language in NCTE Publications

The longer we worked on this book, the more aware we became of the diversity of opinion about both the advisability and the feasibility of language guidelines. Certainly it would seem that if there is any group who is going to get together and agree on a concerted plan of action, it should be the English teachers. But on the other hand, if there is any group who ought to realize the complications, it likewise should be the English teachers.

However, by 1975 this was an issue that as professionals we could no longer ignore. Not only were we getting questions from students and fellow faculty members, but at social gatherings in a refreshing change from the days when grammar teachers were avoided as if they had halitosis, we were actually being sought out to either settle disputes or to add fuel to the fire as people argued about the feminist movement and its relationship to the English language. And so it was an expected action when the membership passed the resolution asking that guidelines be written to help NCTE members, writers, and editors avoid using sexist language. The authors of the guidelines had input from a great many members, plus they had the advantage of being able to study the guidelines of several major publishers. We are happy to devote the last section of this book to these guidelines, not because they are necessarily the last word in the continuing debate over sexism in English, but because they are a big step in increasing general understanding and in leading us to recognize sexist attitudes that underlie sexist language.

—Alleen Pace Nilsen

At the 1974 NCTE Convention members adopted a resolution calling for the preparation of guidelines for NCTE publications and correspondence to help insure the use of nonsexist language. We sought

reactions and suggestions from members of the Committee on the Role
and Image of Women in the Council and the Profession, from editors of
Council journals, from professional staff members at NCTE. Copies
of the guidelines went in the fall to all members of the Board of
Directors. At the 1975 Convention the Board of Directors adopted a
formal policy statement which read in part: "The National Council of
Teachers of English should encourage the use of nonsexist language,
particularly through its publications and periodicals."

The Directors did not vote on the guidelines themselves. Had they done
so, it would require a later action of the Directors to add to or modify
the guidelines. They are reproduced here to guide all interested
Council members in implementing the policy adopted by the Directors.

—Robert F. Hogan
NCTE Executive Secretary

Introduction

"Sexism" may be defined as words or actions that arbitrarily assign roles or
characteristics to people on the basis of sex. Originally used to refer to practices that
discriminated against women, the term now includes any usage that unfairly
delimits the aspirations or attributes of either sex. Neither men nor women can
reach their full potential when men are conditioned to be only aggressive, analytical,
and active and women are conditioned to be only submissive, emotional, and passive.
The man who cannot cry and the woman who cannot command are equally victims of
their socialization.

Language plays a central role in socialization, for it helps teach children the roles
that are expected of them. Through language, children conceptualize their ideas and
feelings about themselves and their world. Thought and action are reflected in
words, and words in turn condition how a person thinks and acts. Eliminating sexist
language will not eliminate sexist conduct, but as the language is liberated from
sexist usages and assumptions, women and men will begin to share more equal,
active, caring roles.

Recognizing these problems, members of the National Council of Teachers of
English passed a resolution at their 1974 convention directing the Council to create
guidelines ensuring the use of nonsexist language in NCTE publications and
correspondence. Although directed specifically to NCTE editors, authors, and staff,
the guidelines will also benefit members at large. Whether teaching in the classroom,
assigning texts, determining curriculum, or serving on national committees, NCTE
members directly and indirectly influence the socialization of children. They help
shape the language patterns and usage of students and thus have potential for
promoting language that opens rather than closes possibilities to women and men.

These guidelines are not comprehensive. They identify sexist usages that plague
communication and discuss specific problems that NCTE encounters in its role as an
educational publisher. The guidelines do not offer a new dogmatism. Detailed and
vigorous arguments continue over many of these language patterns. These debates

have not been resolved; rather, an attempt has been made to identify usages that concerned men and women find objectionable and to propose alternatives.

General Problems

Omission of Women

1. Although man in its original sense carried the dual meaning of adult human and adult male, its meaning has come to be so closely identified with adult male that the generic use of man and other words with masculine markers should be avoided whenever possible.

Examples	Alternatives
mankind	humanity, human beings, people
man's achievements	human achievements
the best man for the job	the best person for the job, the best man or woman for the job
man-made	synthetic, manufactured, crafted, machine-made
the common man	the average person, ordinary people

2. The use of man in occupational terms when persons holding the jobs could be either female or male should be avoided. English is such a rich language that alternatives to the much maligned _____-person (as in congressperson) can almost always be found (representative).

Examples	Alternatives
chairman	coordinator (of a committee or department), moderator (of a meeting), presiding officer, head, chair
businessman, fireman, mailman	business executive or manager, fire fighter, mail carrier

In the interest of parallel treatment, job titles for women and men should be the same.

Examples	Alternatives
steward and stewardess	flight attendant
policeman and policewoman	police officer

3. Because English has no generic singular—or common-sex—pronoun, we have used he, his, and him in such expressions as "the student...he." When we constantly personify "the judge," "the critic," "the executive," "the author," etc., as male by using the pronoun he, we are subtly conditioning ourselves against the idea of a female judge, critic, executive, or author. There are several

alternative approaches for ending the exclusion of women that results from the pervasive use of the masculine pronouns.

a. Recast into the plural.

Example	Alternative
Give each student his paper as soon as he is finished.	Give students their papers as soon as they are finished.

b. Reword to eliminate unnecessary gender problems.

Example	Alternative
The average student is worried about his grades.	The average student is worried about grades.

c. Replace the masculine pronoun with one, you, or (sparingly) he or she, as appropriate.

Example	Alternative
If the student was satisfied with his performance on the pretest, he took the posttest.	A student who was satisfied with her or his performance on the pretest took the posttest.

d. Alternate male and female examples and expressions.

Example	Alternative
Let each student participate. Has he had a chance to talk? Could he feel left out?	Let each student participate. Has she had a chance to talk? Could he feel left out?

4. Using the masculine pronouns to refer to an indefinite pronoun (everybody, everyone, anybody, anyone) also has the effect of excluding women. In all but strictly formal usage, plural pronouns have become acceptable substitutes for the masculine singular.

Example	Alternative
Anyone who wants to go to the game should bring his money tomorrow.	Anyone who wants to go to the game should bring their money tomorrow.

5. Certain phrases inadvertently exclude women by assuming that all readers are men.

Example	Alternative
NCTE convention-goers and their wives are invited . . .	NCTE convention-goers and their spouses are invited . . .

Demeaning Women

1. Men and women should be treated in a parallel manner, whether the description involves jobs, appearance, marital status, or titles.

Examples	Alternatives
lady lawyer	lawyer
Running for Student Council president are Bill Smith, a straight-A sophomore, and Kathie Ryan, a pert junior.	Running for Student Council president are Bill Smith, a straight-A sophomore, and newspaper editor Kathie Ryan, a junior.
Senator Percy and Mrs. Chisholm	Charles Percy and Shirley Chisholm or Mr. Percy and Mrs. Chisholm or Senator Percy and Representative Chisholm

2. Terms or adjectives which patronize or trivialize women or girls should be avoided, as should sexist suffixes and adjectives dependent on stereotyped masculine or feminine markers.

Examples	Alternatives
gal Friday	assistant
I'll have my girl do it.	I'll have my secretary do it.
career girl	professional woman, name the woman's profession, e.g., attorney Ellen Smith
ladies	women (unless used with gentlemen)
libber	feminist
coed	student
authoress, poetess	author, poet
man-sized job	big or enormous job
old wives' tale	superstitious belief, story, or idea

Sex-Role Stereotyping

1. Women should be shown as participating equally with men; they should not be omitted or treated as subordinate to men. Thus generic terms such as doctor or nurse should be assumed to include both men and women; "male nurse" and "woman doctor" should be avoided.

Examples	Alternatives
Writers become so involved in their work that they neglect their wives and children.	Writers become so involved in their work that they neglect their families.

Sally's husband lets her teach part-time.	Sally teaches part-time.

2. Jobs, roles, or personal characteristics should not be stereotyped by sex.

Examples	Alternatives
the elementary teacher ... she	elementary teachers ... they
the principal ... he	principals ... they
Have your Mother send cookies for the field trip.	Have your parents send cookies for the field trip.
Write a paragraph about what you expect to do when you are old enough to have Mr. or Mrs. before your name.	Write a paragraph about what you expect to do when you grow up.
(spelling exercise) While lunch was <u>delayed</u>, the ladies chattered about <u>last night's</u> meeting.	While lunch was <u>delayed</u>, the women talked about <u>last night's</u> meeting.

Sample Revised Passages
Many of the general problems just discussed overlap in practice. Substantial revisions are sometimes necessary:

Example	Alternative
O'Connors to Head PTA	O'Connors to Head PTA

Jackson High School PTA members elected officers for the 1975-76 school year Wednesday night at the school cafeteria.	Jackson High School PTA members elected officers for the 1975-76 school year Wednesday night at the school cafeteria.
Dr. and Mrs. James O'Connor were elected co-presidents from a slate of three couples. Dr. O'Connor, a neurosurgeon on the staff of Howard Hospital, has served for two years on the PTA Budget and Finance Committee. Mrs. O'Connor has been active on the Health and Safety Committee.	James and Marilyn O'Connor were elected co-presidents from a slate of three couples. James O'Connor, a neurosurgeon on the staff of Howard Hospital, has served for two years on the PTA Budget and Finance Committee, and Marilyn O'Connor, president of the League of Women Voters, has been active on the PTA Health and Safety Committee for three years.
Elected as co-vice-presidents were Mr. and Mrs. Tom Severns; secretary, Mrs. John Travers; and treasurer, Mrs. Edward Johnson. Committee chairmen were also selected. Each chairman will be briefed on his responsibilities at a special meeting on June 3. The revised budget	Elected as co-vice-presidents were Jane and Tom Severns; secretary Ann Travers; and treasurer, Susan Johnson. Committee coordinators were also selected and will be briefed on their responsibilities at a special meeting on June 3. The revised budget will be presented at that meeting. Dick Wade, principal of Jackson High

will be presented at that meeting.

Principal Dick Wade announced that Mrs. Elizabeth Sullivan had been chosen Teacher of the Year by the Junior Women's League. She was nominated in a letter written by ten of her students. Each student discussed how she had influenced him.

Mrs. Sullivan, an English teacher at Jackson for ten years, is the wife of Joseph Sullivan, a partner in the law firm of Parker, Sullivan and Jordon, and the mother of two Jackson students.

Smartly attired in a blue tweed suit, Mrs. Sullivan briefly addressed the group, expressing her gratitude at receiving the award.

School, announced that Elizabeth Sullivan, an English teacher at Jackson for ten years, had been chosen Teacher of the Year by the Junior Women's League. She was nominated in a letter written by ten of her students. Each of the students discussed how they had been influenced by her.

Sullivan briefly addressed the group, expressing her pleasure at receiving the award.

Specific Problems

The under-representation of female writers and scholars in many fields has been variously attributed to systematic neglect of women or to the broader social conditions which have discouraged women from pursuing professional careers. This neglect of women has no relation to their competence; research shows people rate a work more highly when it is attributed to a male author than when it is attributed to a female author. Quality need not be sacrificed in urging that an honest attempt be made to represent female as well as male writers and scholars.

Books or Collections of Articles Discussing Professional Issues

1. Authors of monographs and editors of collections should use and encourage the use of nonsexist language. Readers will be aware that language cannot be altered when articles are reprinted from another publication.

2. Sexist language in a direct quotation cannot be altered, but other alternatives should be considered.

   a. Avoid the quotation altogether if it is not really necessary.

   b. Paraphrase the quotation, giving the original author credit for the idea.

   c. If the quotation is fairly short, recast as an indirect quotation, eliminating the sexist language.

Example	Alternative
Among the questions asked by the	Among the questions asked by the school

school representatives were several about curriculum areas, including the following question: "Considering the ideal college graduate, what degree of knowledge would you prefer him to have in the following curricular areas for an executive position:...?"

representatives were several about curriculum areas, including a question asking what degree of knowledge the ideal college graduate should have in the following curricular areas to obtain an executive position:...

Booklists

1. A committee choosing items for a booklist should seek books that emphasize the equality of men and women and show them in nontraditional as well as traditional roles. Children's favorites may contain sexist elements; these books may be included provided the annotations reflect awareness of the sexist elements.

Example	Alternative
More than anything, sixteen-year-old Sandy wants to date Joe Collins, captain of the tennis team. Sandy's interest in pets now seems childish and her friends boring. The schemes she contrives to attract Joe's attention make for delightful reading.	More than anything, sixteen-year-old Sandy Draper wants to date Joe Collins, captain of the tennis team. A determined Sandy gives up her interest in pets and neglects her friends as she tries to attract a shy Joe. Readers can decide for themselves whether Sandy's actions are realistic.

If this is impractical, the introduction or preface should explain why some of the books were chosen despite their sexist elements. The committee should encourage teachers to review books for classroom use; if the books reflect sexist attitudes, teachers should discuss these attitudes and the changing roles of women and men.

When selecting picture books, the committee should also be careful that the illustrations show males and females actively participating in a variety of situations at home, work, and play.

2. Careful consideration should be given to the organization of booklists. Books should not be categorized by traditional male and female interests. Special efforts should be made to include books that portray males and females in nontraditional roles.

3. All annotations in the booklist should be cast in nonsexist language.

Examples	Alternatives
Through the discovery of new cave paintings in southern France, the author reconstructs the life of prehistoric man and shows him as a person remarkably similar in feelings and emotions to man today.	Through the discovery of new cave paintings in southern France, the author reconstructs the life of prehistoric men and women and shows them as people remarkably similar in feelings and emotions to people today.

Forceful analysis of the black's image of himself and the present state of the black revolution.

Forceful analysis of the black's self-image and the present state of the black revolution.

Amy is certain that she is going to be a nurse when she grows up, but a sudden case of tonsillitis and her subsequent encounter with a lady doctor change her mind.

Amy is certain that she is going to be a nurse when she grows up, but when a sudden case of tonsillitis leads to her encounter with Dr. Jane Gilmore, Amy changes her mind.

Teaching Units

Giving careful thought to the topic of a unit, its organization, and the examples and questions to be used will help prevent sexist treatment. For example,

Fiction and poetry units should include materials by and about both women and men. If an obviously sexist piece is included, the discussion questions should bring out this fact.

A unit on classics should be accompanied by questions that promote discussion of the treatment of women and why their image differs from that of men.

Activities should not be segregated by sex; e.g., girls may build stage sets, boys may sew costumes.

Units on usage and spelling should include examples that promote nontraditional views of male and female roles.

Examples	Alternatives
Jill carefully stitched the hem in her new dress.	Jill balanced carefully as she reached for the next branch of the old tree.
Eddie quietly crept up the back stairs.	Eddie quietly cradled the sick kitten.
After passing the exam, the steel mill made Tom an apprentice rigger. (misplaced modifier)	After graduating from college, Macpherson and Associates hired Nancy as an apprentice architect. (misplaced modifier)

Research

1. Careful consideration should be given to the methodology and content of research to ensure that it carries no sexist implications. (This does not deny the legitimacy of research designed, for example, to study sex differences in the performance of certain skills. Researchers are encouraged to consult the American Psychological Association *Guidelines for Nonsexist Use of Language* listed in the bibliography.)

2. The sample population should be carefully defined. If both males and females are included, references to individual subjects in the report of the research should not assume that they are male only.

3. The examples used for case studies should be balanced in numbers of male and female subjects if both sexes were involved in the study.

Reference Books (Bibliographies, Indexes, Style Manuals, Teacher's Guides)
Reference books can be implicitly sexist through their organization and content—what is left out can be as telling as what is included. If the subject has been studied primarily by men, a special attempt should be made to discover whether women have also made significant contributions.

Journal Articles
1. Articles which contain sexist language but are otherwise acceptable for publication should be returned to the author with a letter of explanation, perhaps encouraging the author to rewrite the article and suggesting that she or he consult these *Guidelines*. Alternately, the editor may choose to edit such articles to eliminate sexist language.

2. Instructions to prospective authors in the front matter of the journal should include a notice to the effect that

> In keeping with the *Guidelines for Nonsexist Use of Language in NCTE Publications*, the editor reserves the right to edit all articles which contain sexist language.

Conclusion

Important as language is, improving it is to little purpose if underlying assumptions and traditional omissions continue. The Committee on the Role and Image of Women in the Council and the Profession works to ensure equal treatment of women and girls as students, teachers, administrators, and Council staff. If women never enter the author's world, it little avails a journal or book editor to scrupulously eliminate "man . . . he" references. However, when authors or editors do find it necessary to use selections that contain sexist language or sexist attitudes, the attitudes should be discussed in the introduction, in a headnote, or in some other appropriate place.

The dramatic changes in language now taking place pose a special challenge to NCTE members and staff. Whether the members work as teachers, authors, or editors, they not only help shape students' language patterns but are also viewed by the public as custodians of what is "correct" in the language. The very newness of these changes in our language offers English teachers a unique opportunity. Under their guidance, eliminating sexism can bring new vitality to the English language.

References

Authors and editors who would like to see further examples of sexist language and suggestions for how to cope with them should refer to these publications, sources of many items in the NCTE *Guidelines*.

Guidelines for Creating Positive Sexual and Racial Images in Educational Materials. New York: Macmillan Publishing Company, 1975. (Available from the publisher, 866 Third Avenue, New York, New York 10022.)

Guidelines for Equal Treatment of the Sexes. New York: McGraw-Hill Book Company, 1972. (Available from the publisher, 1221 Avenue of the Americas, New York, New York 10020. Reprinted in *Elementary English* 52 (May 1975): 725-733.)

Guidelines for Improving the Image of Women in Textbooks. Glenview, Ill.: Scott, Foresman and Company, 1972. (Available from the publisher, 1900 East Lake Avenue, Glenview, Illinois 60025.)

Guidelines for Nonsexist Use of Language. Prepared by the American Psychological Association Task Force on Issues of Sexual Bias in Graduate Education. *American Psychologist* (June 1975): 682-684.

Guidelines for the Development of Elementary and Secondary Instructional Materials. New York: Holt, Rinehart and Winston School Department, 1975. (Available from the publisher, 383 Madison Avenue, New York, New York 10017.)

"'He' Is Not 'She.'" Los Angeles, Calif.: Westside Women's Committee. (Available from the publisher, P.O. Box 24020, Village Station, Los Angeles, California 90024.)

Additional copies of the *Guidelines* are available from NCTE, 1111 Kenyon Road, Urbana, Illinois 61801 (1-15 copies free; more than 15, 6¢ each prepaid). Ask for Stock No. 19719.

Bibliography of Sources Cited*

Ace, Goodman. "Top of My Head" column: "The If-ful Thinker," *Saturday Review*, May 3, 1975.

Adams v. Cronin, 69 P. 590 (1902).

Albee, Edward. Interview in *The New Yorker*, June 3, 1974.

Alpha One and *Alpha Time* Reading Programs. Plainview, N.Y.: New Dimensions in Education, 1969.

American Heritage School Dictionary. Boston: Houghton Mifflin Company, 1972.

"An Airline's Ad Encounters Some Turbulence." *Life*, October 29, 1971.

Anchor Embroidery. *100 Embroidery Stitches*. New York: Charles Scribner's Sons, 1971.

Andelin, Helen B. *Fascinating Womanhood*. New York: Bantam Books, Inc., 1975.

Anderson, Pat B. "Still Fighting Prejudice: Women in the Law." *Los Angeles Times*, September 14, 1975.

An Intelligent Woman's Guide to Dirty Words, Vol. 1. Loop Center YWCA, (37 S. Wabash, Chicago), 1973.

Appel, Benjamin. *Man and Magic*. New York: Random House, Inc., 1966.

Asimov, Isaac. *I, Robot*. New York: Doubleday & Company, Inc., 1963.

Baker, Russell. Columns in the *New York Times* and affiliated newspapers. August 26, 1972 and March 4, 1973.

Baldridge, H. David. *Shark Attack*. New York: Berkley Publishing Corporation, 1975.

Bateman, Walter L. *How Man Began*. Westchester, Ill.: Benefic Press, 1966.

Bayer, Ann. "A Women's Lib Exposé of Male Villainy," *Life*, August 7, 1970.

Berg, Stephen and Mezey, Robert. *The New Naked Poetry*. Indianapolis: The Bobbs-Merrill Co., Inc., 1976.

Bester, Alfred. "Adam and No Eve." In *Beyond Control*. Edited by Robert Silverberg. New York: Dell Publishing Co., 1972.

Birk, Newman B. and Birk, Genevieve B. *Understanding and Using English*. Indianapolis: Odyssey Press Publishers, 1951.

Blackstone, William. *Commentaries on the Laws of England*. Book I, Chapter 15. Oceana, 1966.

Bradwell v. Illinois, 83 U.S. 130 (1872).

Branley, Franklin M. *Man in Space to the Moon*. New York: Thomas Y. Crowell Company, 1970.

Burns, William A. *Man and His Tools*. New York: McGraw-Hill Book Company, 1956.

*In some cases, the editions of the works listed in this bibliography are the ones most readily available when this book went to press. Thus sources cited here may not correspond in every case to page references used by the authors.

California v. Cohen, 81 Cal. Rptr. 503 (1969).

Caprio, Frank. *Female Homosexuality*. Secaucus, N.J.: Citadel Press, 1967.

"The Carpenter," *The Cook and the Carpenter*. Plainfield, Vermont: Daughters, Inc., 1973.

Ciardi, John. "Manner of Speaking" column: "Creative, Uh, Writing," *Saturday Review*, May 3, 1975.

City of Hoboken v. Goodman, 51 A. 1092 (1902).

Clarke, Arthur C. *2001*. Norton, 1968.

Cohen, Robert. *The Color of Man*. New York: Random House, Inc., 1968.

Cohen v. California. 403 U.S. 15 (1971).

Commonwealth v. Price, 94 S.W. 32 (1906).

Commonwealth v. Welosky, 177 N.E. 656 (1931).

Congressional Record, 49th Cong., 2d Sess. (1887).

Congressional Record, 63rd Cong., 3d Sess. (1915).

Cornwall, Ian Wolfian. *The Making of Man*. New York: David McKay Co., Inc., 1960.

Crichton, Michael. *The Terminal Man*. New York: Alfred A. Knopf, Inc., 1972.

Cummings, E. E. *100 Selected Poems* by E. E. Cummings. New York: Grove Press, Inc., 1959.

de Beauvoir, Simone. *The Second Sex*. New York: Alfred A. Knopf, Inc., 1953.

_____. Introduction to *La Batarde*, by Violette Leduc. New York: Farrar, Straus & Giroux, Inc., 1965.

DeKosenko v. Brandt, 313 N.Y.S. 2d 827 (1970).

Dick and Jane as Victims. Women on Words and Images, P.O. Box 2163, Princeton, N.J. 08540, 1972.

Dodson, Fitzhugh. *How to Parent*. Plainview, N.Y.: Nash Publishing Corporation, 1970.

Duvoisin, Roger. *Lonely Veronica*. New York: Alfred A. Knopf, Inc., 1963.

_____. *Petunia*. New York: Alfred A. Knopf, Inc., 1950.

Eastman, Arthur M. et al. *The Norton Reader: An Anthology of Prose*. New York: W. W. Norton & Company, Inc., 1973.

Eble, Connie C. "If Ladies Weren't Present, I'd Tell You What I Really Think." Paper read before the South Atlantic Modern Language Association, November 4, 1972.

Ellison, Harlan. "Catman." In *Final Stage*. Edited by Edward L. Ferman and Malzberg, Barry N. New York: Penguin Books, Inc., 1975.

Engle, Paul and Langland, Joseph. *Poet's Choice*. New York: Dell Publishing Co., Inc., 1966.

English, Horace B. and English, Ava Champney. *A Comprehensive Dictionary of Psychological and Psychoanalytical Terms*. Longmans, 1958.

Faget, Max. *Manned Space Flight*. New York: Holt, Rinehart and Winston, 1965.

Ferman, Edward L. and Malzberg, Barry N. *Final Stage*. New York: Penguin Books, Inc., 1975.

Flanagan, Lloyd A. *Approaches to Exposition: What, How and Why*. Cambridge, Mass.: Winthrop Publishers, Inc., 1974.

Flesch, Rudolf. *Why Johnny Can't Read*. New York: Harper & Row, Publishers, 1955.

Flores, Ivan. *Operating System for Multi-Programming with a Variable Number of Tasks (OSMVT)*. Boston: Allyn & Bacon, Inc., 1973.

Forbush v. Wallace, 341 F. Supp. 217 (1970).

Friedan, Betty. *The Feminine Mystique*. New York: W. W. Norton & Company, Inc., 1963.

Frontiero v. Richardson, 411 U.S. 677 (1973).

Frye, Northrop. *Anatomy of Criticism*. Princeton, N. J.: Princeton University Press, 1957.

George, Jean. *Julie of the Wolves*. New York: Harper & Row, Publishers, 1972.

Gilman, Richard. "Where Did It All Go Wrong?" *Life*, August 13, 1971.

Goffman, Erving. *Encounters: Two Studies in the Sociology of Interaction*. Indianapolis: The Bobbs Merrill Co., Inc., 1961.

_____.*Relations in Public*. New York: Basic Books, Inc., Publishers, 1971.

Goodall, John S. *Shrewbettina's Birthday*. New York: Harcourt Brace Jovanovich, Inc., 1971.

Gold, Herbert. "Review of *The Glory of the Jewish Defense League* by Meir Kahane," *New York Times Book Review*, June 8, 1975.

Goldstein, Richard. "S & M: The Dark Side of Gay Liberation," *Village Voice*, July 7, 1975.

Gornick, Vivian. "Feminist Writers, Hanging Ourselves on a Party Line?" *Ms.*, July 1975.

Graham, Alma. "The Making of a Nonsexist Dictionary," *Etc.: A Review of General Semantics* 31, No. 1 (1974).

Graham, Lorenz. *Every Man Heart Lay Down*. New York: Thomas Y. Crowell Company, Inc., 1970.

Greer, Germaine. *The Female Eunuch*. New York: McGraw-Hill Book Company, 1971.

"Guidelines for Equal Treatment of the Sexes." New York: McGraw-Hill Book Company, 1974.

"Guidelines for Improving the Image of Women in Textbooks." Glenview, Ill.: Scott, Foresman & Co., 1972.

Gunn, Giles B. *Literature and Religion*. New York: Harper & Row, Publishers, 1971.

Guth, Hans P. *Words and Ideas: A Handbook for College Writing*. Belmont, Calif.: Wadsworth Publishing Co., Inc., 1975.

Guy, Rosa. *The Friends*. New York: Holt, Rinehart and Winston, 1973.

Hage, Dorothy. "There's Glory for You," *Aphra*, 3:3, Summer 1972.

Hamilton, Edith. *Mythology*. Boston: Little, Brown and Company, 1942.

"Hard-Talking Lobbyist." *New York Times*, March 6, 1972.

Harrison, Barbara Grizzuti. *Unlearning the Lie: Sexism in School*. New York: Liveright, 1973.

Heinlein, Robert A. *Glory Road*. New York: Berkley Publishing Corporation, 1970.

Hoagland, Edward. "Survival of the Newt," *New York Times Magazine*. July 27, 1975.

Hoban, Russell. *Bread and Jam for Frances*. New York: Harper & Row, 1964.

Holl, Adelaide. *The Rain Puddle*. New York: Lothrop, Lee & Shepard Company, 1965.

Hoppe, Arthur. "It Beats Listening to Speeches, Anyhow," *Nashville Banner*, September 19, 1975.

Hoyt v. Florida, 368 U.S. 57 (1961).

Hoyt v. State, 119 So. 2d 691 (1959).

Hutchins, Pat. *Rosie's Walk*. New York: Macmillan, Inc., 1967.

In re Kayaloff. 9 F. Supp. 176 (1934).

In re Lockwood, 154 U.S. 116 (1894).

The Interpreter's Dictionary of the Bible. Nashville, Tenn.: Abingdon Press, 1962.

Jacobs, Suzanne E. and Jacobs, Roderick A. *The College Writer's Handbook*. New York: John Wiley & Sons, Inc., 1973.

James, Muriel and Jongewald, Dorothy. *Born to Win*. Reading, Mass.: Addison-Wesley Publishing Co., Inc., 1973.

Jespersen, Otto. *Language: Its Nature Development and Origin*. New York: W. W. Norton & Company, Inc., 1964 (Henry Holt and Company, Inc., 1922).

——————. *Growth and Structure of the English Language*. New York: The Free Press, 1968. (First edition, 1905; First American edition, Macmillan, 1948).

Job Title Revisions to Eliminate Sex- and Age-Referent Language from the Dictionary of Occupational Titles Third Edition. Washington, D.C.: U.S. Department of Labor, 1975.

Johnston, John and Knapp, Charles. "Sex Discrimination by Law: A Study in Judicial Perspective." *New York University Law Review*, 46 (October 1971).

Jong, Erica. *Fear of Flying*. New York: Holt, Rinehart and Winston, 1973.

Kanfer, Stefan. "Sispeak: A Misguided Attempt to Change Herstory," *Time*, October 23, 1973.

Kanowitz, Leo. *Women and the Law*. Albuquerque: University of New Mexico Press, 1969.

Kay, Helen. *Man and Mastiff: The Story of the St. Bernard Dog through History*. Macmillan, Inc., 1967.

Kelly, Eileen. "Alpha One Reconsidered." *New York State NOW*, 1, No. 4 (1974).

Key, Mary Ritchie. "Linguistic Behavior of Male and Female." *Linguistics* 88 (August 15, 1972).

_____.*Male/Female Language: With a Comprehensive Bibliography*. Metuchen, N.J.: Scarecrow Press, 1975.

King James Bible with English revisions by Alexander Harkavy and Hebrew according to the Masoretic Text. New York: Hebrew Publishing Co., 1916.

"Kissing 'the Girls' Goodbye: A Discussion of Guidelines for Journalists." *Columbia Journalism Review*, May/June 1975.

Kizer, Carolyn. "Pro Femina." In *No More Masks: An Anthology of Poems by Women*. Edited by Florence Howe and Ellen Bass. New York: Anchor Press, Doubleday & Co., Inc., 1973.

Kowalski, Gene. *How to Eat Cheap but Good*. New York: Popular Library, 1974.

Kramer, Cheris. "Wishy-Washy Mommy Talk," *Psychology Today*, June 1974.

Labov, William. *The Study of Nonstandard English*. Urbana, Ill.: National Council of Teachers of English, 1969.

Lakoff, Robin. *Language and Woman's Place*. New York: Harper & Row, Publishers, 1975.

_____."You Are What You Say," *Ms.*, July 1974.

Lawrence, Barbara. "Dirty Words *Can* Harm You." *Redbook*, May 1974.

Leech, Geoffrey N. *Towards a Semantic Description of English*. Bloomington, Ind.: Indiana University Press, 1969.

LeGuin, Ursula K. *The Dispossessed*. New York: Harper & Row, Publishers, 1974.

_____.*Left Hand of Darkness*. New York: Ace Books, 1974.

Leslie, Louis A. *Gregg Shorthand for Colleges*, Vol. I. New York: McGraw-Hill Book Company, 1973.

Leslie, Louis A. and Coffin, Kenneth B. *Handbook for the Legal Secretary*. New York: McGraw-Hill Book Company, 1968.

Lessenberry, D. D., et al. *College Typewriting*. Cincinnati: South-Western Publishing Company, 1969.

"The Liberated Lady Has a Dirty Mouth." *Psychology Today*, August 1972.

Luce, Clare Boothe. "*A Doll's House*, 1970." *Life*, October 16, 1970.

Lyons, John. *Introduction to Theoretical Linguistics*. New York: Cambridge University Press, 1969.

Madow, Leo. *Anger*. New York: Charles Scribner's Sons, 1974.

Malko, George. "How to Get Interviewed by Dick Cavett—in Several Tricky Lessons." *Saturday Review*, June 24, 1972.

Marshall, Lenore. *Latest Will*. New York: W. W. Norton & Company, 1969.

May, Julian. *The First Men*. New York: Holiday House, Inc., 1968.

McClintock, Jack. "Blades with Class," *Esquire*, July 1975.

McCormack, Patricia. "Women's Lib Adds Church to List," United Press International wire service story, January 25, 1971.

McDowell, Margaret B. "The New Rhetoric of Woman Power," *The Midwest Quarterly*, 12:2, Winter 1971.

Merle, Robert. *Malevil*. New York: Warner Books, Inc., 1975.

Miller, Casey and Swift, Kate. "One Small Step for Genkind," *New York Times Magazine*, April 16, 1972.

—————. *Words and Women: New Language in New Times*. New York: Anchor Press, Doubleday & Company, 1976.

Miller, Merle. "From Madcap to Dowager." *Saturday Review*, May 3, 1975.

Minor v. Happersett, 88 U.S. 162 (1874).

Montagu, Ashley. *The Anatomy of Swearing*. New York: Macmillan, Inc., 1967.

Moore, Lilian. *Old Rosie, the Horse Nobody Understood*. New York: Random House, Inc., 1952.

Moore, Nancy. *Miss Harriet Hippopotamus and the Most Wonderful*. New York: Vanguard Press, Inc., 1963.

Morris, William and Morris, Mary, eds. *Harper Dictionary of Contemporary Usage*. New York: Harper & Row, Publishers, 1975.

Mosel, Arlene. *The Funny Little Woman*. New York: E. P. Dutton & Co., Inc., 1972.

Myrdal, Gunnar. *An American Dilemma*. New York: Harper & Row, Publishers, 1944.

New English Bible. New York: Oxford University Press, Inc., 1970.

Newman, L. H. *Man and Insects*. New York: Natural History Press, Doubleday & Company, Inc., distributor, 1966.

Newton, Huey and Blake, Herman. *Revolutionary Suicide*. New York: Harcourt Brace Jovanovich, Inc., 1973.

Nierenberg, Gerald I. and Calero, Henry H. *How to Read a Person Like a Book*. New York: Hawthorn Books, Inc., 1971.

Nilsen, Alleen Pace. "Women in Children's Literature." *College English*, May 1971.

Nin, Anais. *Diary*. Vol. 1. New York: Harcourt Brace Jovanovich, 1974.

Niswonger, C. Rollin and Fess, Philip E. *Accounting Principles*. Cincinnati: South-Western Publishing Company, 1973.

O'Dell, Scott. *Island of the Blue Dolphins*. Boston: Houghton Mifflin Company, 1961.

Oxford English Dictionary. New York: Oxford University Press, Inc.

Payne, Elizabeth. *Meet the Pilgrim Fathers*. New York: Random House, Inc., 1966.

People v. Lipsky, 63 N.E. 2d 642 (1945).

Price v. McConnell, 36 So. 2d 80 (1948).

Random House Dictionary of the English Language. New York: Random House, Inc., 1966.

Reed v. Reed, 465 P. 2d 635 (1970).

Reed v. Reed, 404 U.S. 71 (1971).

Renault, Mary. The *Middle Mist*. New York: Popular Library, 1975.

Rich, Adrienne. *Diving into the Wreck, Poems 1971-1972*. New York: W. W. Norton Company, 1973.

Rosenfeld v. New Jersey, 408 U.S. 901 (1972).

Roth, Philip. *Portnoy's Complaint*. New York: Random House, Inc., 1969.

Ruether, Rosemary R. *Religion and Sexism*. New York: Simon and Schuster, Inc., 1974.

Sable, A. P. "The Sexuality of the Library Profession," *Wilson Library Bulletin*, April 1969.

Sachs, Jacqueline, Lieberman, Philip, and Erickson, Donna. "Anatomical and Cultural Determinants of Male and Female Speech," *Language Attitudes: Current Trends and Prospects* by Roger W. Shuy and Ralph W. Fasold. Washington, D.C.: Georgetown University Press, 1973.

Sail'er Inn, Inc. v. Kirby, 95 Cal. Rptr. 329 (1971).

Sargent, Pamela. *Women of Wonder, Science Fiction Stories by Women about Women*. New York: Random House, Inc., 1975.

Scheele, William Earl. *Prehistoric Man and the Primates*. New York: World Publishing Company, 1957.

Schneider, Joseph W., and Hacker, Sally L. "Sex Role Imagery and Use of the Generic Man," *American Sociologist*, February 1973.

Schulz, Muriel R. "How Serious is Sex Bias in Language?" *College Composition and Communication*, May 1975.

Sedler, Robert. "The Legal Dimensions of Women's Liberation: An Overview." *Indiana Law Journal*, 47 (Spring 1972).

Seuren, Pieter A., ed. *Semantic Syntax*. New York: Oxford University Press, Inc., 1974.

Sexism in Textbooks Committee of Women at Scott, Foresman. "Guidelines for Improving the Image of Women in Textbooks." Glenview, Ill.: Scott, Foresman and Company, 1972.

Sexton, Patricia Cayo. *The Feminized Male*. New York: Random House, Inc., 1969.

Sherr, Lynn. "*Miss, Mrs.*, or *Ms.*?: Neuter Title for Women," Associated Press wire service story, Spring 1971.

Showers, Paul. "Signals from the Butterfly," *New York Times Magazine*, July 27, 1975.

Shuy, Roger W. and Fasold, Ralph W. *Language Attitudes: Current Trends and Prospects*. Washington, D.C.: Georgetown University Press, 1973.

Silverberg, Robert. "The Iron Chancellor." In *Beyond Control*. Edited by Robert Silverberg. New York: Dell Publishing Co., Inc., 1972.

Singer, Isaac Bashevis. *An Isaac Bashevis Singer Reader*. New York: Farrar, Straus, & Giroux, Inc., 1971.

Sissman, L. E. "Plastic English," *The Atlantic*, October 1972.

Skinner, B. F. *Beyond Freedom and Dignity*. New York: Bantam Books, Inc., 1972.

Sohn, David. "Viewpoint: A Talk with Henry Maloney," *English Journal*, February 1976.

Stanley, Julia P. "The Semantic Features of the Machismo Ethic in English." Paper read before the South Atlantic Modern Language Association, November 4, 1972.

State v. Hall, 187 So. 2d 861 (1966).

Staton, Mary. *From the Legend of Biel*. New York: Ace Books, 1975.

Stilwell, Hart. *Looking at Man's Past*. Austin, Tex.: Steck-Vaughn Company, 1965.

Taylor, John G. *Black Holes: the End of the Universe?* New York: Random House, Inc., 1974.

Thorne, Barrie and Henley, Nancy, eds. *Language and Sex*. Rowley, Mass.: Newbury House, Publishers, Inc., 1975.

Tworkov, Jack. *The Camel Who Took a Walk*. New York: E. P. Dutton & Co., Inc., 1951.

United States v. Yazell, 334 F. 2d 454 (1964).

United States v. Yazell, 382 U.S. 341 (1966).

U'ren, Marjorie B. "The Image of Woman in Textbooks." In *Woman in Sexist Society*. New York: New American Library, 1972.

Valentine, Dan. *American Essays*, #1. Salt Lake City: Publishers Press, 1966.

Valparaiso University Law Review. Symposium Issue, 1971.

Von Frisch, Karl and Von Frisch, Otto. *Animal Architecture*. New York: Harcourt Brace Jovanovich, Inc., 1974.

Webster's New World Dictionary of the American Language. New York: World Publishing Company, 1964.

Weitzman, Lenore J. and Rizzo, Diane. "Sex Bias in Textbooks." *Today's Education*, January/February 1975.

Willis, Hulon. *A Brief Handbook of English*. New York: Harcourt Brace Jovanovich, Inc., 1975.

Windeyer, W. J. V. *Lectures on Legal History*. 2d ed. Sydney, Australia: The Law Book Company of Australasia, 1949.

Wright, Boyd. "Person the Lifeboats! The Language is Sinking." *Columbia Journalism Review*, May/June 1975.

Wyndham, John. "Compassion Circuit." In *Spectrum 4*. Edited by Kingsley Amis and Robert Conquest. New York: Berkley Publishing Corp., 1965.

Zelazny, Roger. "For a Breath I Tarry." in *Alpha*. Edited by Robert Silverberg. New York: Ballantine Books, 1970.

About the Authors

Alleen Pace Nilsen first noticed linguistic sexism while reading children's books. In 1973, she did her Ph.D. dissertation at the University of Iowa on the topic, "The Effect of Grammatical Gender on the Equal Treatment of Males and Females in Children's Literature." Her more recent work has been supported in part by a faculty research grant from Arizona State University, where she teaches children's and adolescent literature in the College of Education.

She is the editor of the *ALAN Newsletter* for the Assembly on Literature for Adolescents of NCTE and is "Books for Young Adults" review editor of *English Journal*. With her husband, Don L. F. Nilsen, she is coauthor of *Semantic Theory: A Linguistic Perspective* and *Pronunciation Contrasts in English*. She is a member of the NCTE Committee on the Role and Image of Women in the Council and the Profession.

Haig Bosmajian, after receiving his Ph.D. from Stanford University in 1960, taught at the University of Connecticut and the University of Idaho; he is now a professor in the Department of Speech at the University of Washington. His interests in rhetoric, language, and freedom of speech have led to the publication of several books on these subjects: *The Language of Oppression, This Great Argument: The Rights of Women* (coeditor), *The Principles and Practice of Freedom of Speech, The Rhetoric of the Civil Rights Movement* (coeditor), and others. His articles include "The Abrogation of the Suffragists' First Amendment Rights," "The Language of Sexism," "Chief Justice Warren Burger and Freedom of Speech," "The Language of White Racism," "Freedom of Speech and the Heckler," "The Sources and Nature of Adolf Hitler's Techniques of Persuasion," and others.

Courses he teaches at the University of Washington include The Rhetoric of Social and Political Movements, Speech in a Free Society, Obscenity and Freedom of Expression, and Public Speech. He has been a member of the Speech Communication Association's Freedom of Speech Commission and now serves on the NCTE Committee on Public Doublespeak.

H. Lee Gershuny writes, "My interest in language began with my first high school research on propaganda techniques and continued when I learned Hebrew while exploring an alternative life style on a kibbutz in Israel. In the process, I not only learned Hebrew, but also rediscovered English!"

After a year at the Hebrew University of Jerusalem, Gershuny completed a B.A. (1962) and M.A. (1966) at City College of New York; she continued her research in the English language with a study of "The Role of Syntax (Active and Passive Voice) in Understanding a Numbering Concept." On an NDEA fellowship at Yeshiva University (Summer 1963) she continued her study of Hebrew.

"I became interested in sexism in English after a chance glance at a page in the *Random House Dictionary*," Gershuny comments. This launched the research for her doctoral dissertation, *Sexist Semantics in the Dictionary*, which was awarded a Kenyon Prize from the International Society for General Semantics (1973). Related articles appeared in *ETC: A Review of General Semantics* (1974) and *College English*, the Public Doublespeak Column (April 1975). In 1975, she was appointed to the NCTE Committee on Public Doublespeak.

At present, she is an assistant professor of English at Borough of Manhattan Community College/City University of New York, where she teaches courses in The Image of Women in English and American Literature, and in freshman composition. She is developing interdisciplinary programs in computers, language, and literature with Professor Daniel Rosich of the Data Processing Department.

Julia P. Stanley has recently moved to the University of Nebraska-Lincoln, where she is an assistant professor. She previously taught at the University of South Dakota (1976) and the University of Georgia (1968-1974). She has her B.A. from the City College of the City University of New York (1966) and her Ph.D. from the University of Texas at Austin (1971). Her major areas of research are stylistics, sociolinguistics, and language use, and she has published articles in *Linguistics*, *Foundations of Language*, *College Composition and Communication*, *College English*, and *Bucknell Review*.

Stanley, who was recently described by a colleague as "bright but fierce," is a member of the NCTE Committee on Public Doublespeak and the editorial board of *Linguistics and the Real World*.

0575057289

05750289

Southern Methodist Univ.   br
396S4
Sexism and language /

3 2177 00914 1845

DATE DUE

WITHDRAWN